SHE
THE WORLD'S MOST BEAUTIFUL WOR...
BEFORE SHE WAS EVEN A WOMAN.

By 26 she was twice divorced, once widowed,
the loneliest woman in the world,
wondering what could possibly lie ahead.

Two Oscars, seven marriages and a sea of headlines later
she is still the consummate star,
beginning again at 50, fresh from her
triumphant Broadway debut in "The Little Foxes."

ELIZABETH TAYLOR, undaunted, undimmed, the
fabulous beauty who continues to break all
the rules...

ELIZABETH TAYLOR: HER LIFE, HER LOVES, HER FUTURE

by Ruth Waterbury
with Gene Arcerci

BANTAM BOOKS
TORONTO · NEW YORK · LONDON · SYDNEY

ELIZABETH TAYLOR:
HER LIFE, HER LOVES, HER FUTURE
A *Bantam Book* / *published by arrangement with*
E. P. Dutton Inc.

Grateful acknowledgment is made to The Ladies' Home Journal
*for permission to reprint material from "Elizabeth, My
Daughter," by Sara Sothern Taylor, which appeared in the
February, March and April, 1954, issues of the magazine,
Copyright © 1954 by the Curtis Publishing Company.*

Bantam edition / July 1982

ISBN 0-553-22613-4

Published simultaneously in the United States and Canada

ACKNOWLEDGMENTS

I owe thanks to many Hollywood residents for assistance on this book—and particularly to Mrs. Francis Taylor, Elizabeth's mother. Elizabeth also read the galleys herself and made useful comments on the final chapter, as noted in the introduction.

The MGM publicity staff was particularly helpful, digging into their memories and the studio files for anecdotes about the young Elizabeth Taylor, whom most of them have known since her little-girl arrival on the Metro lot.

Pandro Berman, Elizabeth's first major producer, gave me hours as well as the benefit of his wit and wisdom. Helen Rose, the very chic fashion designer and Elizabeth's long-time friend, talked, she says, more openly than she ever had before.

I talked to many directors but especially to two very great ones, who had a dominant influence on Elizabeth's career. George Stevens first directed her when she was little more than a giggling child and turned her into an artist. Richard Brooks has directed her several times, but especially during the desperate time right after she became Mike Todd's widow. I am most grateful to them for the insight they gave me into her character.

Finally, and deeply, I thank two very great friends, Constance Palmer Littlefield and Constance MacCormack, for the monumental job of research they did for me.

RUTH WATERBURY

I would like to thank Cathy Camhy for giving me the opportunity to work on this book; William Holland and Dan Scott for all their help, and the *San Francisco Chronicle* for allowing me to use their files.

GENE ARCERI

INTRODUCTION

When I started to write this book, I had no idea what a prolonged and sometimes frantic adventure it would be. I worked on it for nearly three years and delivered the original manuscript to my publishers late in the winter of 1962. Then I flew off to Egypt to interview two new stars named Peter O'Toole and Omar Sharif. It was there that I received a worried call: the Burton-Taylor story had broken in Rome. What was I going to do about the ending of my book, which carefully proved that Eddie Fisher was the one true love of Miss Taylor's life?

I said I guessed we'd just have to wait, as the rest of the world waited. Finally, in the spring of 1963, the end seemed clear enough to put down on paper. Publication was announced for June, whereupon a request came from London, where the Taylors and Burton were living, for galley proofs. They were sent at once by my publishers. Weeks passed.

On August 7, 1963, the phone rang in my house in Hollywood and Richard Hanley, Elizabeth Taylor's secretary and an old friend, said: "I think it would be smart for you to come over here and discuss your book. There are some small points at issue, but with you here in person, I'm pretty sure it can be straightened out. Could you come immediately?"

I was startled, and the timing couldn't have been worse. I had magazine assignments, and I was due to work in Louella Parsons' office for a month, a stint I do every summer. I had to get a passport in two days, pack, get travelers' checks and all the rest—and fly over the Pole to London and back within a week.

But I went, and with high hopes. I thought I could correct any errors that Elizabeth or her mother had found within three days.

I never saw Elizabeth, and saw Sara Taylor, who was

charming, for only a few minutes. I had no opportunity to discuss these corrections with anyone. My phone calls were not answered. Dick Hanley, after one cordial lunch, seemed to be avoiding me. Presently, after nearly three days in the Dorchester Hotel, luxurious but not a home away from home, I took stock of the situation and decided I must return to America. After all, I had other things to do.

A few weeks later my publishers had a letter from Elizabeth's lawyers. They said the Taylors objected to certain passages in my book, but that perhaps if I were to go to London to talk the matter over, it could all be adjusted.

My publishers wrote back, pointing out that I had been on that merry-go-round already.

Presently we got the galleys back. Mrs. Taylor had made some changes, and so had Elizabeth. They were generally minor and quite understandable, and we made them. Now it's clear, for instance, that it was Francis Taylor, and not Sara, who cooked the scrumptious hot dogs at the picnic at which Elizabeth met Glenn Davis. That and a few other important mistakes have been straightened out, and the lawyers have corrected my style here and there.

So here, after nearly five years, is my book. I have wanted to tell not only a true and significant story of this most beautiful and controversial woman of our time but also something of the anatomy of stardom—the talent, beauty, temperament, and intelligence it takes to reach it, and the resistance to pressures necessary to stay there.

CHAPTER ONE

Poverty has produced some very persuasive personalities, particularly in the Hollywood scheme of things.

Ava Gardner grew up a barefoot girl in the dust of a village called Grabtown, North Carolina. Mickey Rooney was hidden for the first months of his life in dressing-table drawers while his mother kicked up her heels in a traveling burlesque show's chorus line.

Marilyn Monroe was never sure of her parentage and never as a little girl had a permanent home, though she worked as a child in many "homes" in Los Angeles.

Sophia Loren at least knew her father, even if he was not married to her mother.

The list of such backgrounds is endless in Hollywood.

Elizabeth Taylor is a golden exception. She was born with a Georgian silver spoon in her porridge, an Aubusson rug under her feet, and a double set of lashes around her violet eyes.

Her parents, Francis and Sara Taylor, with their three-year-old son, Howard, lived in a most correct British manner with a house called "Heathwood" in the fashionable Hampstead section of London and a country house down in Kent named "Little Swallows."

The Taylors were not British, however. They were American. In Kansas, Sara and Francis Taylor had been American middle class, neither rich nor poor, but well educated and comfortable. In London, however, they had become smart, in touch with two worlds, the peerage on one hand and the bohemian set on the other.

This new status had come about not only because they were handsome, charming, and intelligent but also because Francis Taylor ran an excellent art gallery. He represented in England and on the Continent his uncle, Howard Young, who was an important New York art dealer. If one had to be "in trade," it was delightful to be in the art world, and the ambitious Taylors took advantage of it.

The eight-and-a-half-pound baby girl named Elizabeth for both her grandmothers and Rosemond for her aunt, Mabel Rosemond Young, was born to these superior parents on February 27, 1932. She was a sorry sight. She did not open her eyes for ten days. Her head, ears, arms, and back were covered with black fuzz. However, the obstetrician assured the Taylors that she was perfectly healthy and would probably improve. It was a meek debut for a baby who was to become celebrated for her beauty.

But her birth was a very happy event. Sara and Francis were romantic aesthetes, in love with life and one another. While it was not apparent to outsiders, Sara was a strong personality. Born Sarah Warmbrodt, she had been adventurous enough in her teens to rename herself Sara Sothern and to desert Kansas City and invade Broadway.

Sara was intelligent. She was pretty. Sara had talent. So she was noticed by Broadway producers and presently she was enjoying a small career as a leading lady. One play in which she appeared, *The Fool*, not only took her all over the United States but even to London for a run. Nevertheless when her school crush, handsome Francis Taylor, finally mustered up nerve enough to propose to her, she gave up the theater and became his wife.

It is a curious thing about women who give up careers for marriage. The career drive seems to disappear in them, but actually it merely goes underground, only to manifest itself later in some other form. Certainly this was true of Sara Taylor. Her drive lay dormant for nearly a dozen years. Then it manifested itself with startling repercussions in its effect upon her daughter's life.

As for Francis Taylor, he was, as a young man, as blond as Sara was dark. They were and continued to be a truly compatible pair, with much the same frame of reference for all things.

When they first married, it was fortunate that Francis could make an excellent living traveling from Paris to Berlin, from Rome to Switzerland, from Spain to Ireland, and any other locale where he might find pictures to be purchased or sold. Francis had already been in the art business for eleven years and had made such trips with his uncle. They had a

2

gallery at 35 Old Bond Street, called the Howard Young Galleries.

Until their first child was on the way, the Taylors usually lived in deluxe hotels, meeting the rich and idle—those who considered themselves the best people. At the prospect of starting a family, however, Sara began to want a solid establishment. They decided on London as their main base and purchased their first home, "Heathwood." They also began looking about for a country place, since as affluent Londoners they could not be expected to spend weekends in town.

Their first-born, quite properly, was a son, and they promptly named him for his influential New York uncle. "When he was born, baby Howard looked like a Botticelli angel, he really did," said Sara Taylor. "He had a mass of yellow curls all over his head. His eyes were large and very blue. He was strong and vivacious always. He never was the slightest bit of trouble, and he began cutting his teeth very early."

Baby Elizabeth was as dark as Howard was blond. Besides the black fuzz, her skimpy hair was coal black and straight. When she did open her eyes, they rolled so far back that only their whites showed. She rarely cried and otherwise never made a sound except gurgling noises until she was more than eight months old. She was so slow in teething that her mother jokingly suggested they should consult a doctor about getting her dentures.

There was one English custom the Taylors never adopted. They never left their children entirely to the care of servants, nor did they have them live in a separate section of the house, apart from them.

Instead Sara and Francis took their children with them everywhere. They lunched and dined as a family, and if invitations came that did not include their children, they did not accept them.

It was in the summer of 1932, when Elizabeth was still an infant, that the caravan craze first hit England, and the Taylors succumbed to it. The Taylors rented a caravan for two months, to indulge their continuing wanderlust. British caravans were no mere utility affairs like American trailers of that time. They had far more style. This caravan had two good-sized bedrooms as well as a kitchen and dining room. To further cushion their gypsy life, the Taylors also hauled two huge green-and-white tents behind their American Buick. One of the tents served them as a dressing room. The other

3

was a bedroom for their two servants. Years later Mike Todd, Elizabeth's third husband, expected to impress her when he bought her a car equipped with a complete bar and kitchen. It delighted her but did not unduly impress her, and Mike never quite understood why.

In September of 1932 the Taylors, with the children and Daisy, the cook, Hilda, Elizabeth's nurse, and Monty, the family's golden retriever, started out. They bought food along the roads, eggs warm from hens, lobsters just hauled from the sea, vegetables fresh pulled from country gardens. The cook gave them meals wherever they all became hungry. The whole group slept when and where they pleased. Possibly in gratitude for such a felicitous set of circumstances, little Elizabeth chose these two months to blossom forth.

The black fuzz disappeared from her back, arms, and ears. Her practically invisible nose began to assume a lovely shape. She grew sturdy and began trying to walk and talk, and her blue eyes deepened into violet. Now people stopped to stare at her rather than at her brother. "Did you ever see such a wonderful baby?"

It was the first impact of her beauty on the world, and the effect of it, even then, produced action. Her parents immediately decided to take her to America for her first Christmas and show her off, first to her Taylor grandparents in Kansas, then to the Warmbrodts in California. Finally they would take her to her great-uncle Howard Young's estate, Star Island, just off Miami, to celebrate her first birthday.

Sixteen years later Elizabeth would be back at Star Island, welcoming her first love back from Korea while scores of photographers clicked shutters and scores of reporters asked questions. At Star Island she would lose that first love and find a second, lose him, too, and as the most beautiful teenager in the world she would weep heartbrokenly.

In 1933 the Taylors never dreamed of such things. Like any parents they wanted only their little girl's happiness, and Sara Taylor wanted her small daughter to have everything good in the world.

Of course, she did achieve many things, including heartbreak and hatred, fame, fortune, and the wildest happiness.

CHAPTER TWO

It was the summer after her second birthday that Elizabeth first encountered the sea and the Taylors first encountered her fearless love of life.

Baby Elizabeth had developed a kind of gait, a cross between a walk and a gallop. This way she could pretty well keep up with her big brother.

When the English go bathing they go to resorts such as Salcombe in Devon, and there the Taylors repaired. On the first day of their vacation, Howard ran swiftly into the surf. Immediately Elizabeth loped after him. A wave broke over her head and sent her sprawling. On the beach, her mother and Nanny screamed. Her father plunged into the surf and pulled her up. She came up laughing. She had loved the shock of the wave's force, the salt taste of it in her mouth. She had found a new game, the excitement of the water, the sweet security of being continually rescued. She was in love with the ocean from that time on, and no one in the family remembers just when it was that she began really to swim.

People divide basically into two groups: the lovers and the haters. Elizabeth loved everything, always. She loved the sun. She loved the mists of England. She loved birds. She loved animals. She adored her family and she personalized everything. She not only named her dolls and her pets but she gave flowers the names of girls and boys.

Elizabeth was as fearless about food as about everything else. She ate what her Nanny put before her and never balked. Howard was the one who occasionally rebelled. His were never great transgressions, but whatever they were, he found it hard to apologize for them.

Elizabeth would nudge him back into a state of grace. "Say you're sorry," she would whisper as they sat before the jury of their parents. She would poke him sharply in the ribs. "Say you're sorry, Howard."

Elizabeth, when out of line, would instantly admit her own small errors. She could not bear being put in Coventry, as the English call it, being exiled from the room or being ignored. This hurt her much more than a dozen spankings. She could not bear to have love withdrawn from her.

It was the children's nanny, Frieda Gill, who innocently first fostered Elizabeth's acting ability. Nanny began it very simply, merely to provide a diversion at teatime. One gloomy day in the winter of 1934, as she brought Elizabeth and Howard in to tea, she announced, "Mr. and Mrs. Taylor, we shall give a performance for you."

Nanny had never heard of improvisation, in the acting sense, or of theater in the round. The Stanislavsky system, now known as the Actors' Studio "method," had not yet been popularized, but Nanny's productions were "method" just the same.

Nanny cast herself as an oak tree. Elizabeth, she said, was to be a fairy princess, and Howard was to be a mushroom. The Princess would discover him under the tree.

Elizabeth was immediately lost to all reality. Finding Howard behind Nanny's capacious apron, she promptly tried to eat him. He loudly disapproved. This made Nanny switch their roles. Howard became the oak. Nanny became the fairy princess. Elizabeth was the mushroom. Instantly Elizabeth bent herself double, and peered out at her parents between her little fat legs, her pants highly exposed.

Teatime from that day on became Elizabeth's fantasy land, and included such "props" as a crown made of gold papier-mâché. Elizabeth knew, even then, her place in the sex scheme of things. She never wanted to give up her crown, and occasionally Nanny indulged her to the extent of letting her wear it to bed.

Years and years later Elizabeth was to delight Mike Todd by the way she first wore the diamond tiara he gave her. She wore it to bed; she wore it to breakfast the next morning also. The tiara, that is—and nothing else.

There was also ballet school. This was run by Madame Vaccani and all the nicest small fry of London attended it. Sara Taylor had learned of it from her close friend Mollie Cazalet. Both she and her brother were then members of Parliament. He was also the self-appointed godfather of the

Taylor children. Howard and Elizabeth called the Cazalets "Uncle Victor" and "Aunt Mollie," and it was through them that Elizabeth was to make her first acquaintance with royalty, even though it was royalty barely past the teething stage.

Howard, aged eight, took the dancing lessons with Madame Vaccani with considerable aplomb. However, Elizabeth, brought into the ballet world at three, was overcome with shyness. For weeks she hid her face in Nanny's lap, until one threat finally sent her out on the floor. This was the information that Howard, now expert, would be leaving the school the next month. She, Elizabeth, would never be taken there again, and would have to grow up unable ever to be her brother's partner on a dance floor.

Elizabeth couldn't bear to give up anyone she loved, even then. She trotted out on the floor, her small face solemn with resolve. But out on the floor she forgot reality. Swiftly she was the little mushroom all over again, the sturdy oak, the fairy princess. From that time on she could scarcely wait for her lessons.

Madame Vaccani immediately put Elizabeth into a dance recital. It was given at Queen's Hall for the Duchess of York and the two young princesses, one of whom is now the Queen of England.

At the start of the recital there were solo ballets by the older pupils. But the tiny ones, like Elizabeth, came on last as a ballet of butterflies, and after duly fluttering around a bit, their final gesture was to make a deep curtsey to the royal box before exiting.

With the other children Elizabeth made her curtsey, but then the enchantment enveloped her.

Rising to the responsibility of enchanting her truly royal audience, small Elizabeth took a second bow—and a third. Then she heard the loveliest sound any actress ever knows.

Applause!

That instant the first beam of her personal star flashed. The dream was born, and the impossible started to come true. Yet almost at the same time the counterbalance fell, too. A shadow was cast on her glory—the first of her curious near-fatal accidents and illnesses.

The infection in Elizabeth's ear began mildly only a few weeks after her ballet triumph. Nanny was not too worried at the start. Elizabeth was put to bed in the upstairs guest room with its enormous Louis XV bed, which Francis Taylor had

7

picked up in his antique-shop prowling. A doctor was called. By the time he arrived, however, Elizabeth's temperature was 103.

Yet children's temperatures often go that high without too much danger. The Taylors were assured that with proper medication and Nanny's nursing, Elizabeth would soon be back to normal.

Easter was about three weeks away. Nanny, playing nurse, talked to Elizabeth about the various trees they could see out in the garden. Nanny said they must both wait for the first sign of spring, the sign of the flowers and trees awakening. As soon as she got well, Nanny promised, Elizabeth and Howard could go out and pick the primroses and violets that would be popping up in the fields. Elizabeth must hurry and get well.

She did not get well. She became worse. Now Dr. Goodwin was called several times each day. Then a professional nurse came in, and Sara Taylor never left Elizabeth alone.

A week went by. Elizabeth's pain was terrible. A second week went by. Her pain was worse. Her temperature stayed at 103. The danger is great when a temperature stays that high, even for two days, let alone two weeks.

It was Holy Saturday when Dr. Goodwin took Sara Taylor aside. "I have lanced that ear eight times," he said. "I am afraid to do it again. Are you a religious woman? Is this child religious?"

"I've always avoided adopting any special creed," Sara Taylor said, "but Elizabeth and Howard were brought up with religious training and background, and I let Elizabeth choose her godparents, Victor and Mollie Cazalet. She adores them."

"It might help if you could get them here."

Sara Taylor went back to Elizabeth's bedside, while her husband telephoned to Victor and Mollie.

The entire house was hushed. Sara knew everyone in it was praying—her husband, Howard, Nanny, Daisy, the cook, and the various maids. The hours dragged by while Elizabeth slept, sedated.

Then, just before dawn, the Cazalets' car arrived. Mollie Cazalet tiptoed in alone, wrapped Sara Taylor in her arms, and explained that Victor had stopped in the garden.

The two women turned as they heard him enter. He was holding a spray of roses on a single stem, which had plainly just been cut from a bush. "Let me see Elizabeth alone," he said.

8

Later Elizabeth was to know that Victor began talking to her while she slept. He talked softly, persuasively, as he stroked her forehead. Eventually this roused her.

Did he know, that very kind man, that she was a highly suggestible child? Would she in later life respond with delight to direction by such firm male voices?

Victor Cazalet said to her, "See this stem of roses? See how they branch out, one from the other? These come from God, like all living things. These are God's message to you, Elizabeth, because His concern is with the living. So now, I want you to take these roses from Him and get well. Will you promise me to do that?"

She took the roses in her right hand and snuggled her left inside his. Her eyes shone with her trust, responsive to the male order. "Yes, Uncle Victor. But you must stay here by me."

"I am your godfather, dear child. I shall always watch over you."

She drew a contented sigh. She went back to sleep. Victor Cazalet sat absolutely still, holding her small hand. Two hours passed. By then, he knew it was not a trick of his imagination that her hand had cooled and that her sleep had become entirely relaxed.

He stood up, a tall, quiet man, very much the British gentleman. He tucked Elizabeth's hand under the covers. He put the spray of roses where she could immediately be conscious of their scent the moment she woke.

He went down to the drawing room, where the Taylors and Aunt Mollie were anxiously waiting. At that moment Dr. Goodwin entered. "I rather think she will be all right now," Victor Cazalet told the doctor. Then shyly he added, "I lulled her with a bit of private philosophy of mine."

Dr. Goodwin confirmed that Elizabeth's temperature was almost back to normal. The next day her ear began healing.

Later in her life Elizabeth Taylor would suffer from many psychosomatic illnesses. As her second husband, Michael Wilding, said, "If she gets a cold, she reacts so violently she's almost dead from pneumonia. If a bee stings her, she becomes very ill. I remember that during the first year of our marriage, this extreme reaction of hers to illness actually first became apparent to me. I had been lolling by our pool and a bee stung me. I pulled the stinger out and that was the end of it. But at the same time, Liz was stung and though I pulled that stinger out, too, the swelling lasted for a week and a half.

"When she was making *The Last Time I Saw Paris* she developed an abscessed tooth. It should have been extracted immediately, and with the average person, that would have been that. But Liz didn't want to hold up production and naturally the studio profoundly agreed with that.

"So by the time the picture was ended and she got to the dentist, the poison had spread through her entire system and she was ill for more than two weeks. That's the way it is with her, but it's still not proof to me that all her illnesses are psychosomatic."

That was Mike Wilding's reaction, right or wrong. Was Elizabeth's response to Victor Cazalet's talk an example of psychosomatic healing? Was it perhaps an act of faith?

In 1959, when Elizabeth Taylor embraced Judaism, many people assumed it was simply a romantic gesture to please Eddie Fisher.

This was not entirely true. She had thought about adopting the Jewish faith even before Mike Todd was killed. Her conversion was not because of Mike Todd either, much as she adored him. Brought up without any formal religious instruction, she had always felt the need for some religion. In her teens she was briefly a Christian Scientist, and with Nick Hilton, she once hoped for a time to become a good Catholic. In the sophisticated Hollywood climate in which she has always lived, faith is seldom discussed, perhaps is even considered a bit corny. Yet religious faith is high in the category of her complex emotions. When Elizabeth later embraced Judaism, Rabbi Nussbaum congratulated her on her religious training and upbringing.

Late on that March day in 1961, after it had been announced to the world that she had come, almost literally, back from death, the nurses came upon a note she had written during the most dangerous hours. No one had seen her write it. When a nurse showed it to Elizabeth, she did not remember writing it.

Yet there it was in her handwriting. It simply said, "Help me." Obviously, she had never doubted that someone would help her.

CHAPTER THREE

During the Easter holidays of 1939 it became evident that war was inevitable, and that American nationals should get out of England as quickly as possible.

Two weeks later, after a good deal of wire pulling, Sara Taylor with Howard and Elizabeth sailed for New York on the S.S. *Manhattan*. Francis Taylor stayed behind to wind up the affairs of his gallery.

It was May Day, 1939, when the three Taylors arrived in Pasadena, California, where Grandpa Warmbrodt lived. Elizabeth felt it was the luckiest thing that they had arrived too late in the school year for her and Howard to be entered into classes. Still, she and Howard learned plenty from the Pasadena children. With their British accents and clothes, they stood out among the other kids.

Even if she had been a plain little girl, Elizabeth would have been very noticeable in a quiet place like Pasadena if only because of her clothes and her beautiful English manners. She was, even at seven, very beautiful.

To this day Elizabeth ignores her own beauty. Certainly the little girl had no inkling of a fabulous movie career. However, what was in Sara's mind was known only to Sara Taylor.

Sara was relieved, Howard and Elizabeth were wild with delight when they received a cable from Francis Taylor. He had wound up the affairs of his gallery in London. He had a ship reservation. He would join his wife and make a home for the family in Hollywood. Those movie millionaires, he thought, might want to buy some of his paintings.

Sara agreed. In fact Sara, as usual, was thinking far ahead of him. As it turned out, nothing could have worked out better for Sara and her family than the move.

11

CHAPTER FOUR

The Château-Elysée was chosen as the locale for the gallery. The Château-Elysée was a mid-Hollywood address that in 1939 was very chic, though it is passé today. The house they rented for the family was a good twenty-five miles distant and not in Hollywood at all. It was in a then new, luxurious district, down near the ocean, known as Pacific Palisades. Almost all the lovely estates there were occupied by top movie executives.

The dynamic men like Darryl Zanuck, Louis B. Mayer, and William Goetz who lived in that area might be hard-driving studio tycoons by day, but in their leisure they played polo or went surfboarding or worked off their excess energy in hard sets of tennis.

Young Howard and Elizabeth Taylor, going out to play, met these men's children. There were Darrylin, Susan, and Richard Zanuck, children of the man who was then head of United Artists and was about to move to Twentieth Century-Fox. There were Katy and Irving Thalberg, Jr., whose father had been the so-called "boy genius" of MGM and whose mother was Norma Shearer. There were Judy and Barbara Goetz, who were Louis B. Mayer's granddaughters. And other young sprouts with lesser but still important names and backgrounds.

Elizabeth was very shy with the other kids, perhaps because they all loomed so tall around her, she who still was so small for her age. Besides, the children had all known one another for years, and she and Howard were the strangers. Elizabeth felt the same emotions as in London when she was enrolled in an American ballet class.

The year became 1940, and small Elizabeth was both happy and unhappy. She had so much to forget, so much to learn. She must forget everything about England and absorb everything about California. She must remember to say Mother and not Mummie. She must grow accustomed to jeans instead of jodhpurs, and somehow she must survive in the aura of competition she felt around her.

At her new ballet class, besides the Zanuck and Goetz girls, there were other girls such as movie star John Gilbert's daughter and Erin Considine, whose father was a producer at MGM and whose mother was a Pantages, rich and influential in show business.

Francis Taylor's gallery seemed to be doing very, very well in Hollywood. He had gotten out of England on the last regular steamer that was to sail from there until the war would be over, and he had brought out many paintings, particularly his collection of Augustus Johns.

Andrea Berens, who was engaged to marry Cheever Cowden, head of the Universal Studios, was an Augustus John enthusiast, and had once had her portrait painted by him. Hearing of the Taylor collection, she called and made an appointment to come over and see the gallery.

It was that afternoon that Sara and Elizabeth went to call on Francis at the gallery in Hollywood.

When she saw her, Miss Berens acted much like other adults did about Elizabeth. She stood and stared. Then she said, "Mrs. Taylor, I'd like Mr. Cowden to see this child."

Sara flashed her warm smile and said, "You know, Miss Berens, we have still more Augustus Johns down at our house in Pacific Palisades. Would you like to see those? They are really superb. Would next Sunday for tea be all right? And if you'd like to bring Mr. Cowden that would be very nice, too."

Miss Berens accepted.

The screen in 1940 was full of moppets, most of them singing: Shirley Temple was followed by Jane Withers, followed by Deanna Durbin, Jane Powell, and Judy Garland. Sara Taylor had encouraged her daughter to sing. Elizabeth didn't like her own voice, however, and she never once thought of singing for guests.

So the next Sunday when Miss Berens brought Mr. Cowden to tea, Elizabeth just took him into the garden for a few minutes and told him about her pets. The movie executive chuckled at the child's make-believe. Then Miss Berens and Sara Taylor came out into the garden to join them at their tea. Just before Mr. Cowden left, he told Sara Taylor that he would set up an appointment for Elizabeth to see his top casting director, on, let's say, Wednesday. His secretary would call and confirm the date.

"Mummie, Mummie, will I be in the movies now?" Elizabeth cried, as Mr. Cowden's car pulled away from their gate.

"Might I get into movies, Mummie? Like Deanna Durbin?"

"Darling, we'll have to wait and see. Probably nothing will come of it."

"I hope not," said her father.

"Gosh, no," said Howard.

But Elizabeth was already dreaming.

There was no immediate result of the Cowden interview. However, shortly afterward, when Elizabeth went to her dancing class, Mrs. Considine, the mother of Elizabeth's friend Erin, happened to be there and said, "I'd like my husband to meet you."

The fact that Erin was Elizabeth's classmate at this school, attended by so many movie children, was a fateful circumstance and was Elizabeth's first step up the ladder.

Thus her friendship with the Considines' daughter resulted in an actual date at MGM. At the studio first she saw Erin's father; then several other men came in. While they were talking to her, the door was suddenly flung open and a stout but very energetic man came catapulting in.

He looked at Elizabeth only once. Then he turned to the silent men around her. "What are you waiting for? Sign her. Sign her. I've got to get out of here on a plane for New York."

He turned as swiftly as he had entered and left, slamming the door behind him. Sara recognized him. He was the Goetz girls' grandfather, Louis B. Mayer, the King of Hollywood.

But Sara held out. "We must keep our other appointment for Wednesday. We made it before we knew this one was going to come up and we must keep our word about it. We cannot sign anything until after that."

The appointment on Wednesday was quite different. The Universal Studio was far out in the then scarcely settled San Fernando Valley. It was a smaller studio, and the casting director's office was a small, haphazardly furnished room. Furthermore, the casting director was alone. No one else came in to look at Elizabeth or to talk to her mother.

The casting director asked only a few questions. In a very

14

few minutes, he stood up, dismissing them. "You'll hear from us."

Outside, in the dusty road before the tawdry little studio, Elizabeth said, "Oh, Mother, don't let's sign here. Let's sign with Metro. That man in there doesn't like me."

"Darling, don't get your hopes too high. You're probably not going to sign anywhere. But don't be impressed just because Metro is bigger. In some ways, I think a small studio would be better for an unknown youngster."

Eventually Elizabeth was signed by Universal. It was for one year only.

On an empty sound stage, some weeks later, Universal tried out her voice. Her only audience was three bored men who seemed to shake their heads in tired apathy before she had gotten through a single little parlor tune.

Universal, at that time, was producing a row of musicals. They wanted a cutie who could jazz it up. They had no use for a child ballerina with an English accent. So everyone except the bookkeeping department forgot about her.

Then, after two months, there came a call from Universal. They had not forgotten her after all! (Actually it was the bookkeeping department which had brought her small salary to the attention of the production department.) But neither Sara nor Elizabeth knew that.

They were overjoyed at the news that Elizabeth was to come to the studio at once, prepared to go to work.

The film, called *Man or Mouse*, was to star a freckle-faced moppet named Alfalfa Switzer. His specialty was singing off key. Elizabeth was cast to play a brat, and her big moment would be when she would sing, on key, while Alfalfa did a burlesque of her.

Elizabeth worked three days. That was the only film she made for Universal under her contract, which soon ran out and was not renewed.

But just then the family had something more exciting and personal to discuss. At this moment, Francis Taylor's gallery was shifted to the chic Beverly Hills Hotel, and the family was also moving to Beverly Hills.

The house on Elm Drive wasn't grand, but Elizabeth loved it at first sight. It was a big old house, on a quiet treelined street. It had a big backyard, full of trees and flower beds, but no pool, no tennis court. Next door lived a family named Westmore. Yes, Mr. Westmore was in the movie business, but he wasn't a magnate. He was a makeup man.

The day they moved in, Elizabeth saw the girl next door, Anne Westmore, come racing out of her house. She promptly climbed a tree which was between her house and the Taylors'. Elizabeth remembers that Anne flipped herself so that she was hanging head down.

"Me Tarzan," said Anne Westmore. "Want to make believe you're Jane?"

That began her first truly American friendship for Elizabeth. Nine years later Anne Westmore was the maid of honor to Elizabeth Taylor when she married a young millionaire, Conrad Nicholson Hilton, Jr.

Neither of them dreamed that, of course, that first day. Francis Taylor, leaving his home just as the two little girls met in the tree, was even less foresighted. He waved to his small daughter, delighted to see her face glowing again. That night at dinner he said to his wife, "I'm glad all that nonsense about Elizabeth becoming an actress is over and done with. I just want her to have a normal childhood."

The trouble was that the wheels had been set in motion. Elizabeth's chance of ever having a remotely normal life was already destroyed.

CHAPTER FIVE

Louis B. Mayer had not forgotten the beautiful little Taylor tot and in 1942 asked that Elizabeth Taylor be brought to the MGM Studios in Culver City to make a test for *Lassie Come Home*.

No one mentioned to the eager little girl and her mother that already twenty-five other little girls had been tested for the part—tested and rejected. Sam Marx, the producer, looked at Elizabeth sharply, then smiled. "Don't be scared. We'll shoot right now. You have only a few lines to say."

"Oh, thank you. I'm not scared."

Elizabeth was telling the truth. She who was ordinarily so shy felt perfectly poised at that moment. Somehow she knew that she was in her right atmosphere at last.

"This is Mr. Wilcox, the director," the producer said. "Give her the lines, Freddy."

A younger man now smiled at her. "Hello, Elizabeth. This is to be a scene between you and your grandfather and a dog."

"A dog? What kind of a dog?"

"A collie dog, a big beautiful collie dog. Now I'll pretend to be your grandfather, and will you make believe that that spot there is a dog?"

"Yes, I will." Who couldn't make believe a spot was a beautiful big collie dog? It was much easier than making believe you were a mushroom.

"Your grandfather is talking to you. I'll read his lines. You make the replies you see here. Do you want to study them?"

"Hurry up, Freddy," said Mr. Marx. "We've only got ten minutes left."

Elizabeth looked down at the piece of paper she'd been given. She didn't know then that she was—and still is—what is known professionally as a quick study, that she possessed a photographic memory.

"I'm ready now, thank you," she said.

As Freddy Wilcox began speaking in a quavery voice, making like a grandfather, Elizabeth made believe that the spot on the stage which she was patting was a beautiful collie.

Finishing her lines, Elizabeth lifted her head, as Frank Wilcox had told her to, and smiled straight into the camera.

"Cut," yelled Mr. Wilcox. The hot lights on the set died down. She turned to look anxiously at Mr. Marx.

"You're a fine little actress," said Mr. Marx. He looked over her head at her mother. "You'll be hearing from us," he said.

CHAPTER SIX

When Sara Taylor wrote about her beautiful daughter in 1954, she proclaimed, "Elizabeth's childhood is the story of a little girl who loved the simple, fundamental things of life; the love of a dog, the back of a horse, the purr of a kitten; who loved to play with her dolls, ride her bike and roller skate with all the other children of the neighborhood.

"It was a very normal growing up and it happened to Elizabeth just as it happened to thousands of other girls all over the country.

"The only difference was that when the other teenage girls were reading romantic stories and imagining themselves as the heroine, Elizabeth was living in her dreamworld by acting the role of her heroine—that is, at the studio. At home she was just an ordinary member of an ordinary family of four."

In 1954 Sara Taylor was not to be blamed for that delusion. After all, at that time Elizabeth had been married only twice, and as Mrs. Michael Wilding, the radiant mother of two sons, she proclaimed her happiness to every listener.

Yet the ground for the defiant Elizabeth Taylor of Rome, Richard Burton, and *Cleopatra*, circa 1962, was prepared in 1942 when the excited little ten-year-old went into *Lassie Come Home*. To this day Sara Taylor insists that she thought it would just be a glorified kind of game that Elizabeth would play for two weeks.

It was, of course, the beginning of the fateful game she would be compelled to play all her life, the game of all great stars, the lonely bewildered engrossment in self, the what *I* will do; what *I* will say; the restless apartness from the group, forever.

While filming her first scene in *Lassie Come Home*, an incident occurred which altered Elizabeth's prospects considerably. She was to ride down a road into camera range. Nigel Bruce, playing her grandfather, was to ride beside her. They rehearsed the scene several times. Everything went smoothly. However, when the lights blazed up for the actual take, Elizabeth's horse, frightened by a reflector, reared.

All action stopped immediately, while the company held its collective breath for the little girl. But nothing happened— she wasn't unseated, she wasn't frightened. They saw her rein in the animal, pat him, and then bring him to the spot before the camera where she had been told to halt him. The watching MGM brass looked at one another in amazement. By absolute happenstance they had found the girl to play *National Velvet*!

National Velvet was a big property. Virtually every important female star had tested for it.

But the combination of a young star who could act and also ride had seemed, until that moment, impossible. Elizabeth was not yet a star, but one thing MGM knew: whatever their decision, the Taylor child must immediately be placed under long-term contract.

The deal was for seven years, with six-month options, including a tidy weekly salary for Sara to act as chaperone and dialogue coach. No one foresaw that for one reason or another, including suspensions, absences, and two of Elizabeth's pregnancies, the contract would stretch from 1942 to 1959, when Elizabeth would get her first million-dollar chance to make *Cleopatra* and be forced to make *Butterfield 8* instead.

The final day of shooting on *Lassie Come Home* Elizabeth's horse acted up again and set a pattern for her life as definitely as did her MGM contract. The horse stepped on her foot during the last take. Elizabeth insisted she was not hurt. She kept on working until the scene was finally recorded. Then only did they carry her to her dressing room. Her foot by then had swollen so that her jodhpur shoe had to be cut off.

Health was a factor from then on, whether good health or poor, in all the crises of her life.

Life in the Taylor household changed from the day Elizabeth's contract was signed. Now the most important part of her life was lived at the studio.

She made *Jane Eyre*, in which all she had to do was die. She made *The White Cliffs of Dover*, in which about all she did was look up adoringly at the star, Irene Dunne. She was forced by law to go to school, where she managed with great effort to maintain a B average. A C average was all she maintained on the friendship level with the other girls in her class. She was too far out for them, already entering the isolation of stardom. None of them were yet teenagers, but they were already thinking of boys.

Elizabeth wasn't. She had horses on her mind, horses and *National Velvet*. Every afternoon when school was out, she rushed to the Dupry Stables in Hollywood, where she practiced steeplechase jumps.

MGM had given Elizabeth a copy of *National Velvet*. Sara and Elizabeth pored over it.

Then one day at the studio, Elizabeth heard that two other actresses were being tested for the role. Desperate, she invaded producer Pandro Berman's office. She stood before him, a beautiful tiny child, nearly eleven though she was no larger than a six-year-old.

"Mr. Berman," she begged. "I *am* going to play Velvet, aren't I?"

"You're too little, Elizabeth," Berman said. "If you were only two or three inches taller, I'd never dream of anyone else playing her."

This was true. Berman didn't see how he could cast any adult against this tiny Elizabeth, not if she was to play the heroine. He hadn't then thought of using Mickey Rooney in the male lead.

"I'll grow, I'll grow. Oh, Mr. Berman, I'll grow."

"In three months? How can you? Your mother says you haven't grown in three years."

She didn't know how she could grow three inches in three months, but she knew she would. And she did.

And she became *National Velvet*.

With the finish of *National Velvet*, Elizabeth went into *Life With Father* at the request of Mrs. Clarence Day, the widow of the author, and then, *Courage of Lassie*.

It was a happy time for Elizabeth, lost in her world of fantasy. There was an animal trainer on the picture, a salty old character named Curley Twifert, who gave her a trained chipmunk. She named it Nibbles, and she took it everywhere on a scarlet leash. As a school essay she wrote "Nibbles and Me," which was published as a book.

Meanwhile, she was nearing fourteen. She was taking

21

algebra lessons, grammar lessons, and dancing lessons. She was naturally obedient. She wanted to win love and affection and did.

Life would all have been perfect if it hadn't been for boys. Howard had advanced to Beverly High and did his brotherly duty by taking her to several school dances. But—"Why is it that some straggling little boy is always the one who finally comes up to me and asks me to dance?" she asked Betty Sullivan, whose father was then just a newspaper columnist and not yet TV's Ed Sullivan.

There were several reasons, which any mature man could have explained to her; she was too beautiful; she was too famous; she was too eager—she was too much for boys.

The adult males around Hollywood were disturbingly conscious of her, but she was depressingly aware of her lack of boyfriends of her own age.

Sara Taylor, with her highly developed social sense, was determined to do something about Elizabeth's lack of dates. During Elizabeth's fourteenth summer, the family occupied a beach house at Malibu. Sara told her son to tell his friends at Beverly High that there would be open house at the Taylors' every Saturday.

The first Saturday was an amazing success. The high-school boys and girls began arriving at the Taylors' about ten A.M. There was an elaborate barbecue of steaks and hot dogs and various casseroles. Some forty youngsters consumed it all to the last crumb.

But after they had eaten, they began to drift off into the darkness, two by two by two. Only Elizabeth was left, a lonely little movie star. The end of the party was signaled by the ringing of a huge bell.

Straggling, giggling, they went. And that was the beginning and the end of the Taylor open house.

Shortly after, Marshall Thompson, a gangling nineteen-year-old actor at MGM, came to Sara and asked if he could invite Elizabeth to the premiere of *The Yearling*.

Sara barely restrained herself from reaching up and kissing him, the first boy anywhere near Elizabeth's age who had ever tried to date her for anything. Of course, Sara did go along to chaperone her daughter, so it wasn't exactly a lovers' meeting, but it was indubitably a date.

On screen, Elizabeth was portraying Greer Garson's twenty-year-old daughter in *Julia Misbehaves*. She wore custom-made gowns. Her hair was set by Sidney Guilaroff, one of the world's greatest hairdressers. She was on the cover of *Life* magazine.

She envied her brother's going to a public high school. She wanted to attend the proms, the football games, get in on the fun. She wanted her career plus school plus fun plus dates. Roddy McDowall was a beau, sort of. She could discuss acting with him very, very seriously. To Roddy she said things like "I don't think you should learn acting tricks. If a person's supposed to feel one emotion and they do it by some sort of a trick, it doesn't really come from you. The camera picks up something you don't really feel, Roddy. I think you should make a part your own, make yourself the part."

Yet when Roddy McDowall's birthday party came up, she couldn't get a date to take her to it. Her mother stepped into the breach. She got Bill Lyon from MGM's publicity department. Lyon was thirty-five and a bachelor, and there was a good excuse for his taking Elizabeth to Roddy's. The party was for publicity, wasn't it?

"It was a ridiculous situation," Lyon now recalls. "Liz was barely fifteen, but she had blossomed into quite a young lady physically, and any man would have given his left arm to take her out. But he also would have been aware of her age. So, along I went with Liz. I was entirely surrounded by kids of about sixteen. Elizabeth had a great time, but she danced continually with older men. I could see that the boys of her own age were awed by her. They didn't dare approach her because they felt they didn't have a chance with her."

Elizabeth began dreaming constantly about the Tall Handsome Stranger who would walk into her life.

One night after she got home from the studio, she wrote a poem, "Loving You":

> Loving you,
> Loving you,
> Could be such heavenly bliss,
> And, as our hearts would tenderly kiss,
> I would know how happy I could be...
> Happier still, if only you'd love me.
> If only you'd love me.

Before long, the Tall Handsome Stranger not only walked into her life, but fell immediately in love with her—and she with him.

CHAPTER SEVEN

No script writer could have devised the sequence more perfectly.

She was racing along the sands of Malibu Beach. Howard was chasing her.

The Pacific was being true to its name that day. There was no riptide. The surf was gentle. The gulls were honking. Elizabeth had been in and out of the water many times, and her white satin strapless suit clung tightly.

It was all perfect—because in one dizzy instant Elizabeth recognized him, the godlike figure striding down the beach toward her, tall and bronzed, with fantastic shoulders and the slimmest hips. He also happened to be the biggest football hero in the United States. Glenn Davis, the All-American. Glenn Davis of West Point. Now patriot Glenn Davis, heading gallantly for Korea to serve his country.

Of course, he was not there by accident any more than she was. Like many things in her life, this had flowed from her studio life. It was a publicity masterpiece. A football hero, now in uniform, meeting the most beautiful teenager in the world. What more could the papers want?

Glenn Davis was on leave from the Army to play a special football game in Los Angeles. Someone at MGM knew him and proposed to Mrs. Taylor that it would be nice if Davis could come to the Taylors' summer place at Malibu to meet Elizabeth.

So the pigskin prince met the family on the beach. The cameramen zeroed in.

Elizabeth paid no attention to the flashbulbs popping. She was too thrilled.

She dropped her eyes so that he would see how long her lashes were. Her heart thudded. No movie she had ever been in had been half as wonderful. She knew what was

24

happening to her. After all, she had played the scene many times, only this time it was for real. She was falling in love absolutely at first sight.

Introductions swirled around. "My brother, Howard, Lieutenant Davis. Miss Westmore, Lieutenant Davis." Then after a pause, Lieutenant Davis was asked to play touch football on Elizabeth's side.

Glenn grabbed her hand, grinned at her, yelled at her, told her what to do. They all went into the fastest action; became a riot of legs and arms. Naturally, she and Glenn were on the winning team.

Later, she and her football hero circled around a generous buffet.

"I'm playing a game tomorrow. Could you come, be my guest?"

She fluttered her double lashes at him. "Will you ask my mother? Will you *beg* my mother?"

"Wait right here." He got up, big yet graceful, and went over to her mother. Sara smiled and nodded.

Sitting watching the football game that second evening, Elizabeth listened to the crowd. "We want Davis. We want Davis," they were shouting. Outwardly, Elizabeth sat very quietly, very correctly, but inwardly she was crowing to herself. "I've got Davis. I've got Davis." She was in love. At last, she was loved.

She was smiling very dreamily in the shots the cameramen took of her that night.

During the next few days life cooperated with her and Glenn. The studio cooperated. The Army cooperated. Thus Elizabeth and Glenn managed many an hour together during which she lost all awareness of time or other obstacles.

During that ecstatic interval she never once walked. She ran. She sang. For the first time in her life she shouted. If her spirits had been any higher, she felt she would have blown away.

Glenn wasn't aware of it, but he freed her from the last trace of her British reserve. The humiliating memory of those dateless dances at Beverly High was washed out by proof that this absolutely wizard hero found her attractive. She wasn't just a little movie girl to him. She wasn't just a kid in high school. She was a *femme fatale*.

Quite innocently, she used the best trick of a femme fatale—she hung on his every word. He talked of sports. He had been the co-captain of West Point's football team, star of its basketball and track teams, captain of its baseball team. He'd graduated from the Point the year before, and this barred him from professional sports. But he told Elizabeth that when he got free of his Army stretch in 1951, he'd be allowed to go into pro basketball. He might even make a career of it, he said. It paid big money.

He didn't talk only of sports. He knew about war. He knew about politics. He knew about big business and business people, East Coast business people.

Her violet eyes stared at him adoringly. He was twenty-four. Elizabeth thought him very profound.

She didn't mention her salary of twelve hundred dollars a week. There was no need to bring that up. She didn't even talk about acting. She had immediately decided to give up her career when they married. He was the only career she wanted, the only career worth dreaming over. She listened and dreamed as she twirled on her engagement finger the miniature West Point ring he had given her.

The days until he would be shipped out whirled by. Glenn and Elizabeth were never alone, and yet they always were. They played, they flirted, and they were almost part of a crowd, yet they were always alone together.

To this day, Mrs. Taylor says, "Oh, I felt Elizabeth's seeing Glenn Davis was so normal. He was such a football hero, and every young girl in America was crazy about him. When Glenn was shipped to Korea, Elizabeth wore his gold All-American football on a gold chain around her neck.

"I never worried about what would be the outcome. I thought when he did return from Korea, she would have outgrown it. She had to realize Glenn would want her to retire, and I think she knew even then she couldn't give up acting."

The outcome, however, was not innocent. It was to be a hurtful thing. On Davis's first Korean leave a year later, Elizabeth's first love shattered. Shattered, too, was the approval of a section of her public. Until then, she had been its darling child. In 1948 the press began its first carping at her, a steadily mounting indictment that was later to rise to volcanic proportions.

Every newsreel service and every press photographer was alerted the day Glenn Davis shipped out to Korea for his two-and-a-half-year hitch. Elizabeth clung to him while the flashbulbs burned. There practically wasn't a publication the world around that didn't print those romantic photographs of her. And by no accident of timing whatsoever, MGM right then sent her to England to play the wife of thirty-five-year-old Robert Taylor in *The Conspirator.*

That trip was Elizabeth's nineteenth crossing of the Atlantic, but as it was her first as a star, she went in style. Her mother, naturally, was along. For the first time though she had a personal representative, Morgan Hudgins, to handle her press relationships, and Miss Melinda Anderson of the Los Angeles school system to see to it that she spent three hours a day at her lessons. In the hold of the ship there were seventeen trunks full of clothes Helen Rose had created for her.

Elizabeth found that London, when she was working, was no different from Hollywood. The crowded pattern of her days was exactly the same. She had almost no personal time between her acting, her school lessons, the publicity demands on her, and writing Glenn nightly.

The young lovers exchanged daily letters. Twice he managed to get roses sent to her. Once, by traveling over more than a hundred miles of back Korean roads, he was able to telephone her.

After the first day on *The Conspirator* her work went uneventfully. As Robert Taylor's wife, she would play a love scene, then rush from his romantic arms to the austere Miss Anderson, who was about sixty. After parsing verbs or solving an algebraic problem for fifteen minutes, she would rush back to Taylor's embrace. Simultaneously she had to remember her dialogue, remember where she had been standing and what she had been portraying, and also not forget her school lessons.

No one tried to correct the ambivalent atmosphere that continually surrounded her, one compounded equally of adulation and criticism. At all times she had upwards of a hundred people around her, telling her she was the most beautiful girl in the world as well as the most charming and talented. Yet these same adulators ordered her not to rumple her hair or her clothes. They chided her to stand exactly where she was told to stand for the cameras and not to hop around like a common teenager. They ordered her not to eat the sweets she craved. They were enthusiastic over her diction, but told her to keep her voice down, down. She had a tendency to shrill.

She must know her lines. She must be more punctual. She simply must not dawdle around dreaming. That she was at

27

the age for dreaming and dawdling seemed never to have occurred to any of them.

One evening her mother relaxed discipline enough to allow her to go out dancing unchaperoned.

Her escort was her devoted press agent, Morgan Hudgins, a good safe twenty years her senior and very much the Southern gentleman. She loved talking to Morgan. She spent hours mimicking his Southern accent, not dreaming that eleven years later she would use this accent in *Cat on a Hot Tin Roof*.

Besides, that evening was most agreeable since they ran into Gene Kelly and Peter Ustinov, and she got a chance to dance with each of them.

The next morning at the studio she got a real thrill, and she forgot completely the other stars. For there she met Michael Wilding, the most popular actor in London at that time.

CHAPTER EIGHT

Michael Charles Gauntlet Wilding had been born in a small town in the south of England. His father was a captain in the British Army, which means his earnings were never generous; his mother was a warm and witty woman, who had played briefly on the stage, but gave it up when she married.

In the family's ancestry there were two contrasting figures. One was the Archbishop of Canterbury who crowned Victoria. The other was John of Gaunt, though "on the wrong side of the blanket, I'm sorry to say," Mike would explain.

The second of two sons, Mike Wilding came naturally by his good looks and charm. Life in the Wilding household was casual, understated, and very pleasant.

For his elementary schooling, his parents sent young Michael to an institution of learning called, with characteristic British indirection, Christ's Hospital. "My best grades there came from jumping," Mike cheerfully confessed.

He wanted to go on to a university, but there wasn't enough cash in the Wilding coffers to permit it. He had a good legacy, however, the inheritance of always being surrounded by good taste and good manners and by an appreciation of things other than the material. Thus, when he somewhat vaguely announced that he would like to try painting as a profession, his parents, even though he was only seventeen, let him go to Brussels, very much on his own, to study.

Life in Brussels was much as it had been in Britain for him—at once casual, sensual, and intellectual. He thoroughly enjoyed painting, but presently his built-in sense of proportion warned him that he never could make a living at it.

Then, he hit upon the happy thought of painting sets for British films. It wouldn't be hard. It would be a pleasant atmosphere. It would pay him enough to live on nicely, or so

29

he hoped. He no sooner made the decision than he booked passage on a slow Channel steamer.

Quite by accident he applied first at British-International. Quite by accident he arrived at the studio gates just as there was a call out for extras. A casting director spotted him in the crowd, and why not? He was eighteen, six feet one, a lean one hundred and sixty pounds, and clearly a gentleman.

One minute later Mike discovered he was about to be paid a pound for standing around and doing nothing. "I told myself, quite grandly, that in that atmosphere I could learn to 'evaluate' set design," Mike Wilding now says. "The truth was, of course, that sheer luck had made me stumble into the exact milieu for my natural laziness."

He also that day stumbled into exactly the right companion for his dilettante nature. This was another handsome young man named James Stewart. Stewart, however, was much more ambitious than Wilding, and he was to attain fame in America under the name of Stewart Granger. That was far in the future, however, that day in 1930, two years before Elizabeth Taylor was born.

Wilding and Stewart both eventually got into the West End theaters of London and made glittering names for themselves, and they both married shortly afterwards. None of which Elizabeth Taylor knew when she first met Mike Wilding. She was simply aware of his elegant height, his extraordinary good looks. She excitedly noted that his eyes were aqua blue, her favorite color.

Mike Wilding was a man who automatically responded to beauty. He responded to Elizabeth's exquisiteness. He flashed his smile at her, and she was immediately smitten. Glenn Davis, to whom she was engaged to be engaged? He was thousands of miles away—in fact and in her excited thoughts.

From that first meeting, Elizabeth chased Mike Wilding all over the studio. Every morning when he left his dressing room, he found her just outside in the hall. At lunchtime, she was lingering at the entrance of the commissary. When he left for home at night, there she was, just exiting as he did. This kept on for weeks.

Elizabeth was crushed that Mr. Wilding did not seem to notice her after that first meeting.

Actually, he surprised himself by being so disturbingly aware of her. He had discovered that this passionate child was a mere sixteen to his thirty-six. To his inbred British sense of decorum, the only decent thing to do seemed to be to snub

30

her entirely. Except that she would not stay snubbed. She did not know consciously what she was after, but her body knew.

Wilding knew, too. He discussed her one evening with Stewart Granger. "Rather than ask the waitress for some salt," he said, "that Taylor chit will walk clear through the commissary to get it from the kitchen, wiggling her hips. Then she wiggles her way back again, past my table."

"Courage, man," said Granger, smiling. Granger himself had recently met a teenaged actress named Jean Simmons.

"I know it's ridiculous," Wilding confessed, "but this child makes me feel chivalrous. She makes me want to go all the way—marry her, you know."

"Why don't you tell her that?"

Granger had meant it impishly, but Michael Wilding, a few days later, decided to try out the suggestion. As Elizabeth wiggled by him one afternoon, he did tell her that he wanted to marry her.

He did it debonairely. He conveyed the idea that it was nonsense. He didn't kiss her. He didn't even touch her. He simply leaned negligently against his dressing-room door, as she started off the sound stage.

"Someday you should marry me, you know," he said, "but ye gods, we must wait at least two years, until you are eighteen."

Her amethyst eyes blazed up at him.

"Of course," she breathed. Right at that moment she meant what she said, this girl who was almost engaged to a young man fighting in Korea.

"She was very lovely and very busy," Wilding says. "She was working. She was studying. She was writing to her soldier boy, and among other things she was going to balls. Lord Mountbatten gave one for his daughter Pamela, and on that occasion I was very aware of young Miss Taylor dancing with Prince Philip.

"Yet, I managed—I found myself compelled to manage—to see her during the lulls."

During one of those lulls, Elizabeth made her first trip to Paris and forgot all men. For one day, that is.

Now she goes as casually to the City of Light, whether it is by polar flight from Hollywood or a swift hop over from London, as most women go to their favorite supermarket. But in 1948, Paris was all glory and excitement to Elizabeth.

31

The Paris trip was a weekend reward from MGM to its golden girl for her good behavior on *The Conspirator.* That was the way film studios, and particularly MGM, were run back in the forties. Nothing was too good for the personalities who were moneymakers. And if a little glamour and publicity resulted from such handling, that was an excellent by-product, too.

In 1961 Mrs. Taylor recalled that first episode:

"Elizabeth was very excited, flying across the Channel. She had never seen Paris, and Paris had never seen her or any of her pictures. What Elizabeth wanted to do was to go shopping, a young girl's dream of shopping in Paris. What I wanted to do was to go sight-seeing. So we compromised. The MGM publicity woman there, Nadia Markulescu, met us. We did our sight-seeing in the morning, all the tourist thrills like the Louvre, the Arc de Triomphe, and the Eiffel Tower. We planned to shop after lunch, and Nadia took us to a little place along the Seine to eat.

"It was called 'The Golden Coq,' and as we stood waiting to be taken to our table, I felt just like any other eager tourist, until Nadia said, 'Will you look at this room?'

"Elizabeth was standing a little apart from me. As I looked around, I saw that everyone had stopped eating and was staring at her. It was so embarrassing. Just at that moment the headwaiter approached us and escorted us into another room. As we came into the new room, the same thing happened. People just looked, speechless, unmoving.

"They sat us at a table against the wall. There was a French couple sitting across from us. The man kept staring and staring. Finally, his wife said in French, 'Stop staring at that girl. It is very rude.'

"The man retorted, 'My dear, it is no more rude to stare at that beautiful creature than it is to stare at the Mona Lisa. It is like looking at a picture.'

"Of course, neither Elizabeth nor I spoke enough French to understand them, but when Nadia translated what the man had said, I felt much more relaxed.

"After lunch we went shopping first for shoes. That was because Elizabeth has always adored shoes, but in the store the French just walked up to her, staring. I couldn't stand it. We left without buying anything, and then when I saw how disappointed Elizabeth was, I tried to explain my action by saying, 'It must have made you nervous having those people staring at you.'

"Elizabeth, however, didn't take it that way at all. She was absolutely calm. She said, 'No, it's just that they wanted to be friendly.'

"I've always been so delighted Elizabeth could take her beauty so for granted, but I can take no credit for her having this attitude. What she had said the year before, when she was only fifteen, to a photographer, who told her she was the most beautiful woman he'd ever photographed, has been told so many times. Still, it is so like her that I like to repeat it.

"Elizabeth said to the photographer in response to that compliment, 'Why, that's very nice. Thank you.' Then she didn't say a word until he had left, whereupon she turned to me and said, 'Mother, did you hear? He called me a woman.'"

Michael Wilding went further than the photographer. When the Taylors, mother and daughter, returned to London, en route to Hollywood, Mike's reaction to Elizabeth was that of a man to a woman.

"I wasn't yet admitting to myself then how in love with her I was," Mike later confessed. "I simply knew I had to be near her. When I learned she was returning to America, I quickly suggested that I drive her to the airport.

"Her mother and Morgan Hudgins and the schoolteacher followed us in another car. Elizabeth was so radiantly beautiful that day that I had difficulty driving. At the airport, Morgan pulled strings. I was allowed to go through the customs barrier with Elizabeth and out on the flying field. Suddenly, Elizabeth stood on tiptoe and kissed me. Then she ran across the field.

"I rushed after her. I caught her just as she reached the plane steps. That time I kissed her. I kissed her very thoroughly. I knew I would remember that kiss for some time. I stood there and watched her plane disappear in the distance. I had small hope that she would remember it, too."

CHAPTER NINE

Elizabeth did remember Mike Wilding's kiss very well indeed. For weeks, she found herself turning the memory of it off and on, like an electric sign, and being excited by it.

However, landing in New York, she had other things to think about. There were the inevitable photographers and reporters to meet her. There was a message from the Coast that she must fly out the very next morning to make *The Big Hangover*. There was a call from her Uncle Howard that he was expecting her down to his place in Florida for her seventeenth birthday party, two weeks away.

But the most heavenly news was that Glenn was being given a furlough on March 1, two days after her birthday, and would meet her at her uncle's house.

The thought of seeing Glenn so soon exhilarated her so that she practically flew to the Coast under her own power. Michael Wilding was forgotten—for the time being.

The Big Hangover was a stupid picture and she couldn't have cared less. Pandro Berman, the producer who has spanned her career from *National Velvet* to *Butterfield 8*, says today, "Elizabeth was a worry then to all of us. We recognized her beauty, but she didn't have the strength of voice at sixteen or the personality to go with her face. Today, she is a great technician, a great actress, and a great businesswoman, but at sixteen she was half child, half adult, and she was actually not as good an actress as she had been at the beginning, making *Courage of Lassie* or *Life With Father.*"

Elizabeth couldn't have cared less how the studio felt, because she knew her career was just about over. The moment Glenn was out of uniform they'd be married, she'd be the perfect wife and the most wonderful mother, and there would be nothing in her life but love, love all the time.

The night *The Big Hangover* finished, she flew to Florida. Her seventeenth birthday party was a smash. A society band played all evening. The governor of Florida, Fuller Warren, stopped the music just long enough to make her an honorary lieutenant colonel. Later the governor of Kentucky was more gallant. He made her a full colonel.

Men cut in on her every few minutes, but to her every man holding her in his arms was Glenn.

But the next day she met William Pawley, Jr., son of a millionaire, former American ambassador to Brazil and Peru. Young Bill, after getting out of the Air Force in 1945, had represented his father's enterprises for a while, but was currently head of his own business. Uncle Howard had invited him to lunch.

As Elizabeth came down into her uncle's sitting room the next afternoon at one, Bill Pawley's back was to her. She coughed politely. He turned and both of them stared. He was staring at her beauty, but Elizabeth was enraptured by his being so wonderfully mature at twenty-eight.

Bill wasted no time. He not only took her out to lunch that day but to a debutante dance that evening. And when he brought her back to her uncle's house, his kiss made her think of Michael Wilding. It had that sort of emphasis to it.

But the next day Glenn Davis returned. The news photographers and reporters were all around Glenn's plane as it touched down. Microphones were everywhere, broadcasters were everywhere. Elizabeth flew into Glenn's arms. Her lipstick smeared his face. They clung to one another as the flashbulbs blazed.

"Glenn, hold your head back a little. You're putting a shadow on Liz's face. Hey, Liz, look this way. Smile, Liz. Atta girl. One more now. Kiss her again, Glenn."

They kissed again and again, Glenn's face red with embarrassment.

Liz took her handkerchief and rubbed her lipstick from his cheeks. "Hey, Liz, do that again," the cameramen immediately shouted.

Glenn ran interference on the Miami crowds, but they could not be alone. They ducked out of crowded rooms only to find cameramen covering the exits. They hurled themselves inside taxis and found cameramen shooting at them from beside the driver. They dodged the "spots" and sought out hideaway restaurants.

It was useless. Wherever they went reporters were asking them questions or cameramen were saying, "Hey, Glenn, give her a big smooch."

The bitter frustration of her first, lost love is still vivid to Elizabeth Taylor. She says, "We positively fought, Glenn and I, to get even a half hour alone together but we couldn't," Elizabeth said later. "Even though I thought myself so worldly and mature, I simply didn't know how to handle it all.

"We were romantically in love, and when we got back together again, we wanted the chance to get to know one another. But the pressure was impossible."

Glenn Davis reacted like any very male and very young man. He was a Korean War hero, therefore an idol. On the athletic field he had been a winner. He could not make the swift adjustment to being an also-there in a crowd, waiting while his girl signed autographs. It was humiliating to kiss your girl, not for the thrill of it, but because some cameramen wanted another shot.

Still, when Elizabeth had to return to Hollywood, he followed her. They both hoped to recreate the happiness of the hours they had shared that first summer in Malibu.

However, it was Academy Award time in Hollywood. Glenn, very handsome in his uniform, escorted Elizabeth, magnificent in a jeweled gown which Helen Rose had especially created for her.

The young lovers were again mobbed by the autograph fans, by the photographers, by the press. Glenn was ordered to stand nearer Elizabeth, then farther back, then to look this way, that way. Again, he was just the fellow who was escorting Elizabeth Taylor.

He had a free week before he had to return to the army, but Elizabeth was working. On the set, everyone was extremely polite to Glenn, but there is a kind of suave Hollywood politeness that can be smothering. It suavely smothered Glenn Davis.

Neither Glenn nor Elizabeth was detached enough to recognize the forces that were alienating them. They quarreled when they meant to make love. They were angry when they intended to be romantic.

The night before Glenn was due to leave, they had a bitter quarrel. With shattering dignity Elizabeth took off the emerald earrings he had given her and returned them to him. She pulled his miniature West Point ring off her engagement finger and handed him that.

She hoped he would take her in his arms and kiss her until her teeth rattled. Either that, or slap her hard. But he wasn't that wise to women. The angry lines of his face did not relax.

She reached up, found the clasp on the chain holding his golden football around her neck. Slowly she unfastened it, dropped it into his hand. She just had to hold on to herself, be dignified, be a lady, until she could go into her own bedroom. Just hold on that long. Make-believe. It was just make-believe.

She heard the door slam behind him. He was gone. She rushed to her room, and by lying face down in the pillows, she managed to keep her mother from hearing her sobs, which were real.

The next day MGM issued a dignified statement for her. Miss Taylor's life and Lieutenant Glenn Davis's life were too different to assure their future happiness, it said.

The headlines played it big, and two days later she received an airmail letter from Bill Pawley—a love letter. Bill had read the news about her. She had another love letter the day after, too, and the day after that. Then Bill wrote that he was arriving in Hollywood the next week.

Would she marry him?

CHAPTER TEN

Would she marry rich, intelligent, handsome William Pawley, Jr.?

Elizabeth was quickly in a glow, her self-esteem restored. This was more like it! This wasn't being engaged to be engaged. This was true love!

She had to be in love. She wasn't alive otherwise. And this time she was in love with a mature, understanding, rich man. If some critics called her fickle, she was simply in the same romantic confusion as many of her elders, and she at least had the excuse of being only seventeen.

All around her on the MGM lot were great stars in the ferment of instant love. Joan Crawford had just become the bride of Phillip Terry, whom she had known only six weeks before their marriage. Greer Garson was the wife of Richard Ney, so many years her junior that Ronald Colman, encountering them one morning as they gazed passionately at one another, acidly murmured, "Madonna and Child." Lana Turner had just sworn her undying love for her third husband, and Arline Judge was about to discover undying love with her sixth.

Elizabeth answered Bill's proposal within ten minutes of her receiving it. Would he please not give out their joyous news to the papers? Would he please let her mother announce it, and not from Hollywood, but from Florida? Wouldn't it be more correct that way?

Bill phoned her the next evening. He told her how madly he loved her. She told him how madly she loved him. He said he would be on the Coast the next weekend and he could bring her engagement ring, but he'd slip in so that the papers would never know a thing.

The ring Bill brought was a solitaire diamond that weighed

38

three and a half carats, set between two half-carat diamonds. Her left hand shook as he slipped it on her third finger.

"This must be forever, darling," he said.

"Yes, yes, oh, darling, yes."

She was going to be married!

Bill flew back to Florida Sunday night. She went back to the studio school Monday for three more weeks. Bill phoned her every night, and they planned out the details of their announcement—Bill planned, that is, and she said, yes, darling.

Bill said they would not give a big party to celebrate their romantic announcement. Rather, they would spend the evening alone together. They would dine at a small inn that was his favorite eating place. They would go lazily sailing afterward. Then they would come back in and dance a bit. No photographers, no reporters, nothing but the perfection of being near one another, knowing that they were to belong to one another always.

Did Elizabeth agree? Her happy squeals of assent carried over the wires for more than two thousand miles. Did Mrs. Taylor agree? Completely and utterly.

On the sixth of June, released from school, Elizabeth and her mother planed to Florida. But for Bill Pawley to dream that such a beautiful, sexy celebrity could slip into Miami unnoticed was like expecting a second full moon to rise unobserved in a clear sky. The moment Elizabeth and Sara Taylor stepped off the plane in Miami they were mobbed.

Nonetheless, Bill Pawley was not Glenn Davis. He managed the press so he and Elizabeth were able to follow out some of their dream plan. Reporters and cameramen dogged them everywhere, but they did dine. They did go sailing. Very late they did go dancing, and as they danced, Bill Pawley whispered, "Darling, it's midnight. I promised your mother I'd get you back to the house by midnight every night." She and her mother were his father's houseguests.

She wanted to keep on dancing. Still, she must obey her almost-husband. She looked up at Bill and smiled. How very conservative his clothes were, not a bit like Hollywood, solid suits and dark, one-color ties. She wondered if he would laugh if she bought him a really crazy tie.

"Let's go," he commanded. The thrill of his orders shook her—love, honor, and obey—but the flashbulbs burned as they went to his car.

He kissed her passionately before they slipped into his father's house. She clung to him, wishing he would never stop, but upstairs he kissed her very quickly and went down the hall away from her.

Next day at noon a maid woke her. Bill had come back from his office to take her to lunch. Elizabeth flew around the room trying to hurry, and she would not have taken more than an hour to dress except that she couldn't quite make up her mind what to wear. After trying a dozen outfits, she finally donned a low-cut peasant blouse above a petunia blue skirt and cinched it with a wide, white belt.

It was ten after two when she went downstairs. Bill, who was pacing up and down, held out his arms to her and then recoiled.

She saw that her extreme décolletage shocked him. Where Hollywood men would have grinned and leered, gentlemanly Bill Pawley was disapproving.

She put her hand to her mouth in startled dismay. "Oh, Bill, I forgot my pin for this blouse. Just one sec." She rushed back to her bedroom, spent ten minutes looking through her costume jewelry to find just the right pin to fasten the neck of the blouse up tight to her throat. She felt positively muffled, but she saw Bill's face relax as she reappeared. That night, when he took her fishing, she was smarter. She wore a sweater buttoned up to her chin, though she felt like an Eskimo in tropical Florida.

In the month that flew by, Elizabeth learned also that Bill did not like the bright colors she adored, and that he brooded when he was angry instead of letting his temper flare out as hers did sometimes.

Meanwhile rumors about Elizabeth leaving the screen had reached the executive councils of Metro. It didn't want its million-dollar child taken away from it. A Metro executive arrived in Miami and asked Elizabeth to lunch to talk about a new picture.

That night Bill called what was virtually a board meeting, of Elizabeth and her mother and his parents and ordered a vote on what Elizabeth should do after their marriage. The vote was carried that she should retire and have at least five children. Elizabeth was ecstatic.

Yet next morning when MGM called Elizabeth back to Hollywood to get ready for *Father of the Bride*, Sara Taylor did not protest.

Elizabeth found herself happy back at work, too. *Father of the Bride* was fun. Spencer Tracy, playing her father, made her feel actually like an adored young daughter. In spite of the hours of school on the lot, Elizabeth rather hated to see each day end—because her evenings were now dreary.

Bill Pawley phoned daily. He wrote daily. Whenever his business could spare him, Bill flew to Hollywood. But whether by phone, mail, or in person, his conversations all emphasized one promise: Elizabeth would give up acting.

Then came the showers for radiant Jane Powell. Janie was marrying her one and only love, Geary Steffen, on September 17, and everyone knew they would live happily ever after. Elizabeth, who was to be one of the bridesmaids, couldn't figure out why love was so simple for other people but never for her.

Then on September 15 Elizabeth received a piece of news that startled her as much as it did all Hollywood. MGM had just loaned her to Paramount for a highly dramatic role in George Stevens's production *A Place in the Sun* opposite Montgomery Clift.

Overnight Elizabeth Taylor's whole status was changed, as the wires carried the announcement. The movie colony sat up, startled by the fact that Stevens, the great starmaker, had seen something important behind this girl's beauty.

In Florida Bill Pawley sat up and did not like what he saw in the headlines. He telephoned immediately. He wanted Elizabeth to name the exact date when she would give up her career, the exact date when they would marry.

Elizabeth was bubbling over with excitement. Her other roles had been fun, really fun, but to be in a Stevens picture was a challenge. "Bill, just as soon as I get this picture finished, then we'll get married. But just think, Montgomery Clift—and Shelley Winters. And I'm the third side of the triangle and . . ."

"I thought you wanted to give up your career for me."

"Oh, Bill, I do, I do, the moment I finish this picture."

"I thought you were bored with your career."

"Bill, I am. I truly am. But you don't know what it is to work for somebody like George Stevens. Why, he's the best director there is, an absolute king, and you don't know what he does for a player . . ."

"No, I don't. I thought you loved me."

"Bill, I do. I love you more than anything in the world. Oh, Bill, wait, Mother wants to talk to you."

Sara Taylor said, "Bill dear, listen. It won't take Elizabeth any time to make this picture, not more than five or six months at the most. And after all, she is only seventeen, and to make a picture with George Stevens, well, you wouldn't want her to miss such an opportunity, I know, and..."

"I'm flying out there tonight," Bill Pawley said. "I want to get this settled face to face."

He was in a black mood when he arrived the next morning. In vain he was urged to consider that *A Place in the Sun* was just a trifle, that after it Elizabeth would be his entirely.

Bill flatly demanded that she give up her career right then.

"But you can't say that and love me," Elizabeth sobbed. "You can't refuse and love me."

The choice was impossible. Bill was being impossible. She had to have love. She must have a husband. But the opportunity to be in a George Stevens picture, to discover if she could really act, such an opportunity would never again be hers if she turned it down now.

The tears rained down her face, but Bill did not yield.

"Okay. There's a late plane east this afternoon. I'll be on it. Good-bye, Liz."

Walking up the aisle at the Steffen-Powell wedding, Elizabeth held her head erect, but her eyes were downcast to hide her tears.

Bill Pawley bowed out of Elizabeth's life that September. He never did quite recover from her. He said for publication a good dozen years later, "I spent two years trying to get over it. To me, Elizabeth was... well, what can I say? I never have married."

CHAPTER ELEVEN

Montgomery Clift, in 1949, was expected to be Hollywood's next great star. He was young, and handsome in a very sensitive way. He had had a great deal of stage training. He had made only two pictures, *The Search* and *Red River*, but his work in each of them had been so distinctive that the film exhibitors had tagged him "The Star of Tomorrow." The exhibitors were wiser than they realized. Monty Clift was the forerunner of a whole new breed of stars, but Hollywood didn't know it then.

Clift in *The Search* registered persuasively as a romantic intellectual. Then, in *Red River* he gave a vivid portrayal of a fighting cowboy. It was this latter performance which most impressed Hollywood, since it knew Clift had virtually never seen a horse before, let alone ridden one. What's more, he had stolen the picture from its real star, John Wayne.

Then, the news flashed that George Stevens wanted him for *A Place in the Sun*, the screen version of Theodore Dreiser's *An American Tragedy*, and Monty Clift became the hottest property in movieland.

But Monty Clift was of a new breed—the "Method" actor. His wardrobe in 1949 seemed to be limited to cords or dungarees, rumpled white shirts, and old tennis sneakers. Occasionally he wore socks. Against the private grandeur of the established stars of Hollywood, his official Hollywood residence was in an old apartment hotel in the seediest section of the city.

Monty lived in a single, cheap room. He had a fetish about privacy and would never permit his friends to write down his telephone number for fear some unauthorized person might come upon it. He made them memorize it but changed the number constantly. Above all things he did not want personal publicity.

Elizabeth Taylor in her oversheltered life had never encountered anyone like Monty Clift, and she was wildly excited when she received the word that he was to escort her to the opening of *The Heiress*.

Monty could barely wait for it to be over. He was going to the opening of *The Heiress* and he was taking Elizabeth Taylor because Paramount had flatly ordered him to do so. Paramount had spelled it out. Paramount had made *The Heiress*. Paramount was making *A Place in the Sun*. Beautiful, unwed Elizabeth Taylor, aged seventeen, was going to be his co-star in *A Place in the Sun*. He was handsome and unwed. It was a publicity natural. See?

Mr. Clift saw and put up considerable resistance. He didn't have a tuxedo. Paramount said it would hire one for him. It would also provide a limousine.

Elizabeth spent all day long getting herself ready for *The Heiress* preview, and the moment Monty stood in the doorway, she felt her heart begin to race. How handsome he was! He beamed at her! She beamed back at him. It was high approval at first sight.

They made a wonderful entrance into the theater, those two talented young strangers. But as the house lights dimmed and the film began, Elizabeth was startled to discover that Monty was shaking with nervousness. He slid down in his seat so far that he was practically sitting on his shoulders, while he stared balefully at himself on the screen.

She was accustomed to the professionalism of stars like Spencer Tracy and Clark Gable, who on the surface, at least, viewed their work with nonchalance. Monty Clift, however, clutched her hand, holding it with a desperate intensity. Tenderness stirred her. She leaned close to him and whispered, "You're great. You're really great."

His eyes did not move from his screen image, but she saw his mouth relax a little. "Oh, God, it's awful, Bessie Mae."

After that she only half-watched the film, saw only his tremendous work, hardly noticed Olivia de Havilland, the real star of *The Heiress*. She could barely wait for the film to be over, to ask him why he'd nicknamed her. While the preview applause was ringing in the theater, she did ask him.

He smiled down at her then. People were swarming around them, calling out congratulations to him. His mood had changed; he was no longer afraid. "I won't call you Elizabeth Taylor," he whispered. "The whole world calls you that. But only I can call you Bessie Mae."

William Wyler, the director of *The Heiress*, got through the ring around them and asked them to a party at his house after the premiere. Monty accepted, and in the lovely Wyler living room, he kept her close to his side as he received more and more congratulations. People began dancing and she longed for him to ask her, but he did not.

It was nearly two in the morning when he brought her home in the studio limousine. He kissed her lightly on the forehead. "Sleep well, little Bessie Mae," he said.

She walked into the house, bemused.

The next day was Thursday, and Elizabeth stalled around the house all day, expecting Monty to call her. He didn't call, not that day or Friday. Saturday, with her mother, she was due to report at George Stevens's office at noon. *A Place in the Sun* was going on location at Lake Tahoe the following Monday, and she and her mother were to get the final details at the Stevens headquarters.

Monty Clift was just exiting as they entered, and Elizabeth sailed right by him. She was hurt. But when she and her mother emerged from Stevens's office, Monty Clift was still there, his long legs stretched out before him. He grinned up at her. She tried to snub him again.

"Why, Bessie Mae," he said, "you can't have forgotten me already. Let me introduce myself to you. I'm Montgomery Schwartzkopf."

George Stevens spoke warmly about Elizabeth on the set of *A Place in the Sun*.

"I can't recall now," he said, "whether or not I had seen Elizabeth in a picture before I cast her. I may have seen something of *National Velvet* some years before. I knew I wanted her because she was this extraordinary child of great beauty and sweet personality.

"She was a teenager, but she had all the emotional capabilities. She had the intelligence, sharp as a tack. She had humor and lightness that kept her from burdening herself with misconceptions about her place in the world. She had enormous beauty but she wasn't charmed by it. It was just there.

"She was seventeen and she had been an actress all her life. So there was no problem there. The only thing was to prod her a bit into realizing her dramatic potential."

Some directors berate their players to get performances out of them. Some clown with them. Some argue. George Stevens

45

cajoled, confided, urged, and then *became* the player himself.

Elizabeth had never consciously thought about acting until she began working for him. Until that time she still responded as she had originally at ten when they pointed to a spot on the sound stage and told her that was the dog, Lassie. Maturing, she could be told she was Robert Taylor's wife or Spencer Tracy's daughter, and she simply was.

In *A Place in the Sun* the first scene she was to play at Lake Tahoe was a lightly flirtatious one with Montgomery Clift. Elizabeth knew every word of its dialogue when she and her mother arrived in Lake Tahoe early Monday evening, and she thought that was all there was to it.

Monty Clift was checking in just as the Taylors arrived. Beside him was Miss Letts, his ever-present drama coach.

Elizabeth awoke Tuesday morning eager for work, only to give a deep sigh of disappointment as she looked out the window. Lake Tahoe was blanketed with snow.

Elizabeth turned to her mother with a sigh. "We can't shoot," she said, just as a wardrobe woman knocked at their door.

"Mr. Stevens told me to bring these dungarees and sweaters over to Elizabeth," the woman said. "She's to put them on over her bathing suit. He'll be ready to shoot the scene in an hour. The makeup man's on his way over."

"But there's snow all over the lake shore," said Sara Taylor.

"Mr. Stevens is having a patch melted and having smudge pots put around where the players will be sitting, off camera," said the wardrobe woman calmly.

In an hour Elizabeth went out into that bit of make-believe summer. The air was bitterly cold. In an instant she felt as though her mouth were frozen under her lipstick and her hair frozen tight to her head. The dungarees she wore were much too big and lumped around her hips. The sweater hung on her like wet wash. As Monty's eyes met hers, she was tempted to throw off all those outer wrappings and let him see her figure at once, revealed in her bathing suit. So what if she got pneumonia!

He reacted too quickly. His eyes twinkled as though he read her mind. He stretched out his arms. "Tondeleyo, my siren!"

He capered about her then, doing other poses of the infatuated lover. Quickly Elizabeth fell into matching poses, laughing.

46

"Okay, kids, get into the boat," called Stevens's voice. "Let's get to work."

Basically the scene was simple. She and Monty, in a rowboat, had just touched the shore. They were playfully flirting with one another. As she tried to dodge his kiss, he was to throw a handful of lake water on her. She would squeal and shiver. He'd then bundle her up in a towel and rub her down.

Elizabeth tossed off the dungarees and the sweater. Monty tossed off his topcoat, and she looked at him swiftly, excited by his height and his excellent figure. But the shock of the icy air upon her was less great than the sight of his face at that moment. It was the face of a stranger, the half-crazed look of the story's George Eastman, who would love her, Angela, enough to commit murder to get her.

His voice, as he spoke, was not Monty's voice either. It was a cheap voice, somehow, but she recognized at once that George Eastman would have a cheap voice. Nevertheless, involuntarily, she pulled back a little from him.

"Cut," called George Stevens. "We'll try it again."

She drew a relieved breath. It was only a rehearsal. She wasn't wasting film. They tried it again. Still rehearsing. And again and again. Still rehearsing.

Each time Monty's intensity bore down upon her. Each time when Stevens stopped the scene, she felt that he approved of Monty, but that she was the one at fault. Yet Stevens was speaking to her each time, gently, persuasively. They broke for lunch, but she was not aware of what she ate. The sun was warming things up a little as they returned to the lake shore, and the snow was beginning to melt. That made it much easier to pretend it was midsummer.

Stevens now stood quietly beside her. "We'll shoot it now, Liz," he said. "Look, dear." Elizabeth looked at the big man and she suddenly saw herself. She found herself holding her head as he held his. "All right, Monty," Stevens called, stepping back.

She looked up at Monty. She was in love with him.

She was in love with Monty Clift. She was in love with George Eastman Montgomery Clift. She longed to kiss him.

How many takes they did she didn't know after that. How many times she was soaked with that icy lake water, rubbed down by Monty's quick hands. And still unkissed. She came off-camera, dried off, re-dressed in a little tent with the

47

wardrobe woman's help, fast, fast into fresh, dry bathing suits, had her makeup touched up, her hair combed. Then she was on camera again, but still unkissed. It all went by in a blur. She was in love with George Eastman Montgomery Clift, so terribly, and he loved her so frighteningly.

"That's it," shouted a big voice somewhere near her. "That's my girl. We've got it." Big arms were around her. She came out of the daze. They were George Stevens's arms. It was George Stevens's big face looming down upon hers. "You're a great actress, Liz my child," he was saying. "You're a great actress."

Color burned in her cheeks. He had to be kidding her. "Was I really all right?"

"All right? You were wonderful. Honey, you are going to be the greatest actress on screen. That's all for the day, now. You go rest."

Suddenly Monty was walking away with his drama coach. How could he, when she was still standing there, so in love with him?

"Come, Elizabeth," said her mother, who swiftly was beside her. "You must be cold and hungry."

"Yes, Mother," she said. "Yes, Mother."

The next morning Stevens kept them busy. As the day advanced, Shelley Winters came on the set to watch them, too. Shelley was demanding and loud, but Elizabeth felt at ease around her. In between the takes, they all talked and Elizabeth listened, feeling very young and silly.

It was a revelation to her to hear Monty saying that he had wanted this role of George Eastman since he had read the book five years ago. She had never read books like *An American Tragedy* or thought about roles in them.

It was another revelation for her to hear how Shelley had fought for *her* part in the picture. Shelley had read the book, too.

Seventeen-year-old Elizabeth felt very stupid. She hadn't fought for her role of Angela. She had just taken it because it came to her.

Her days on *A Place in the Sun* grew steadily more arduous. Before the camera, she and Monty had intense moments together, like the day when they had to ride into the scene down a narrow mountain ridge. Monty's animal was fractious. Monty was riding on the outside of the trail, on the side of the big drop. She was frightened, and she sensed that Monty did not know how to control the beast. Instinctively she reined in her own mount, then nodded to Monty to do what she was doing. Monty's hand responded on his reins. She sat utterly still, utterly erect, keeping her horse still. She watched Monty stiffen into the same posture. His horse responded to the new mastery.

"We're safe now," she whispered. "Follow me." She gently tapped her horse's flanks with her heels. Monty copied her. They walked the horses into the close-up. There, they could not speak as the cameras were rolling, but his eyes communicated his gratitude to her, she the expert horsewoman, he an actor who had ridden only once before and then for the camera.

"Great, great, great," Stevens shouted to them as the arcs faded.

She slid from the saddle. She said, flicking her lashes at him, "You learn things so fast, like controlling a horse."

"Only in scenes, dear Liza."

That was true. The next day they had a scene where they danced together. He danced flawlessly, but when the scene was over, he confessed, "Bessie Mae, the reason I didn't ask you to dance after *The Heiress* is that I don't know how. I can do it only when it's an act."

Day by day, with Stevens's demands and Monty's reserve, she found herself flaring up occasionally into what Stevens called "distemper." "If we had a little something that would disappoint her, if she thought I was more severe in my aim than a scene needed to be in a make-believe thing like a movie, she'd spit fire. But the following morning she had forgotten it completely. Liz simply couldn't bear a grudge. What a lovely child she was. Every morning, she was ready to take the light approach again."

This ability to take that light approach, Elizabeth came to realize, was one difference between herself and Monty. As the picture progressed, she could feel his steadily mounting intensity in all their scenes, and she felt herself responding to it. But when the scene was recorded to Stevens's satisfaction, she could let down. Monty could not.

She would start running around, joking with her mother, joking with Stevens, but Monty would remain tense, sunk in a brooding silence.

The company moved back to Hollywood to work in the Paramount studio. This meant she did not see Monty for dinner each night, along with the rest of the cast.

So she could barely wait to get to the studio every morning. Because it was so completely unrequited, her passion for Monty intensified. She tried all the wiles she remembered trying on Mike Wilding in London, the trick of being wherever he was when he was free from the camera, the trick of standing too close to him, the trick of hanging on his every word. It did her no good at all. He laughed at her, but kindly. He called her his Bessie Mae, his Tondeleyo, his little Liza. But kiss her he did not, except sometimes lightly on the top of her hair or on her forehead after a particularly good scene.

Nonetheless, when they were acting together they were in complete communication. Then his kisses burned on her lips and his hands on her body were disturbing.

The picture was drawing to a close, and the thought of their separation made her desperate. Surely, surely, loving him as she did, he had to love her, too, even a little. They still had two very important scenes together and the mood of these was entirely downbeat. One was the scene where the police would come to arrest Monty for murder and she would not know the reason for it. The other was when she would call upon him in the death house, just before he was due to be electrocuted.

Elizabeth approached the arrest scene without nervousness. It was Monty's scene really. She knew every word and movement of it. Outside of what was supposed to be her family's rich house, two policemen were waiting. She and Monty were to walk into camera range, and she was to stop with surprise at sight of the law.

Monty was to turn to her then and say, quickly, "Go into the house, Angela. I'll join you in a minute." She was to smile up at him, turn, and exit. The moment she was out of sight, however, Monty had to turn back to the policemen. The way in which he turned was to reveal that he knew his crime had caught up with him. It was all over and he was heading toward his doom.

Stevens insisted upon a very positive contrast between her innocence and Monty's guilt. Her part of it was easy, but Monty's agony in the scene frightened her. They worked all one day, shooting and reshooting, then a second day and a third. Through take after take after take, his hands were icy when they touched her. The terrible pitch at which he kept himself communicated to her more and more, until by the end of the third day, when the scene was finally finished, she felt shattered.

She drew a long breath when Stevens yelled, "Print it."

Then, stunned, she saw Monty turning away from her without a word. Looking neither to the right nor the left, he stalked straight to the sound-stage door and exited.

Elizabeth stood still, shocked. Then she felt her mother's arm around her shoulders. She managed to smile. She said, "Let's go, Mother. I'll take my makeup off at home."

It was so late the Paramount lot was practically deserted. Mother and daughter walked across the lot. Monty Clift was nowhere in sight. At the Paramount gate there was a newsstand. Both of them stopped, staring at the same headline on the evening paper.

Montgomery Clift to Marry Elizabeth Taylor.

The Paramount publicity department had done its work well. The story was one of those iffy ones, those maybe-perhaps affairs that Hollywood would know was entirely studio inspired. But there were big photographs of Elizabeth and Monty in love scenes together. There were lavish credits to *A Place in the Sun*. It was good publicity for the picture, all right.

Elizabeth felt humiliated, afraid Monty might think she had cooperated on the publicity. "Mother, what can I say to Monty in the morning? How can I face him?"

"Immediately, honey, we must think what we will say to the reporters. I'm sure they will be calling."

They were. Both telephones were ringing as Sara and Elizabeth entered the Taylor house. One wire-service reporter said, "We've talked to Clift, Mrs. Taylor, and he says there's nothing to this, that he and Liz are just good friends. What's Elizabeth saying, or what are you saying for her?"

"I'm saying exactly the same thing. She and Mr. Clift are good friends. They are making a fine movie together. That is truly all there is to it."

"Well, would you want to guess..."

"There's nothing to guess about it. Truly, there is no story here."

The calls came in all evening, many of them from overseas. The phones were still jangling the next morning when Elizabeth and Monty faced one another on the set of the prison death house. As Elizabeth walked in through a barred doorway and heard it being locked behind her, the sinister atmosphere engulfed her.

The man standing there turned and faced her, and she nearly screamed. He wasn't Montgomery Clift at all. He wasn't even George Eastman, the character. He was a man

51

about to be electrocuted. His dreadful pallor, the tragedy in his eyes, the tension in his body were almost unendurable to see.

She began to sob.

"Hey, now, Bessie Mae, you save those tears. You're going to need them for this scene," said Monty. He was the real Monty as he came over and put his arm across her shoulders. "You realize this is our last day's work? What are you going to do for a rest? Me, I'm getting out of here tonight, flying down to South Carolina to see Libby Holman."

Her mind spun. Libby Holman? Why, Libby Holman must have been a star before he was born.

Elizabeth felt a dull, sullen anger stirring within her. He was just friends with her. He was just friends with Libby Holman. Just friends . . . Wasn't he even going to *mention* that "engagement" of theirs?

The lights of the set flamed up. "All right, children, let's get to work," George Stevens ordered.

It was a heartbreaking scene, the scene where Angela said good-bye to George Eastman, just before he was to die. But it was also she, Elizabeth, saying good-bye to Monty, saying good-bye to her dreams.

She began to sob. Stevens spoke to her softly, and she heard herself answering. Yes, she could do it again. She drew in her shaky breath. Yes, she was all right. She was ready now.

They did it again, and then just once more. Her throat ached from holding the tears back between those takes, and she was almost screaming in the final take as Monty's icy hands caressed her. She was so desolated.

"Strike it," called Stevens. The lights faded. "I don't see how any scene could be better than what you two just did. Are you all right, Liz?"

She nodded and then ran off the set. It was all over, her part in the picture, her part in Monty's life. Right then she thought Montgomery Clift was the villain in her life. She was too young then to know the real villain was George Stevens, who had turned her into an artist.

(It would be several years before Elizabeth understood why Montgomery Clift never responded to her as other men did; that he couldn't, because he was struggling with his own bisexuality—in an era when any hint of this nature spelled doom for an actor's career. Yet there was never any doubt that Monty did love Elizabeth very much—in his own way.)

*   *   *

"Hi, there, Elizabeth."

The male voice roused her from her melancholy. She saw Pete Freeman standing before her grinning. Pete Freeman's father ran Paramount, and she was immediately conscious of her tear-streaked face.

"Excuse the way I look," she said. "We just finished the death scene, Monty's death scene."

"I know. I hear you were super, too. I have a proposition which I hope will cheer you up."

"What?"

"Have lunch with me at Lucey's, right now. That will get you out of this mood."

"Would you wait till I do something to my makeup and my hair?"

She managed with the aid of only one wardrobe woman to use up an hour, while Pete lounged outside the trailer that was her dressing room. She had put on a simple dress, just a violet sheath with a round white collar. She had a sudden yearning for simplicity.

"Wow," said Pete Freeman as she came out.

She giggled, despite her depression.

"Mind if a friend of mine joins us?" asked Pete. "Nice guy. Adds to any group."

"I like nice guys who add to any group." She wondered if she really did. Monty was a genius, probably. But a nice guy? No, he'd never be called that. He was too complicated.

All the heads swiveled around to watch her as she entered Lucey's, but she saw only the nice guy who stood up as they entered. He was tall. Six feet, anyhow. Cute, darkish hair. Blue eyes. Terrific smile with very white teeth.

Said Pete, "Miss Taylor, may I present Nicky Hilton?"

Well, now really! This was certainly something. Nicky Hilton. The son of the man who owned all those hotels all over the country, including the Waldorf-Astoria in New York! Elizabeth looked up with sharp interest at him through her eyelashes. She felt his blue eyes burning holes through her.

Startled, she felt a blush rising, spreading all over her face. She dropped her lashes, but it was too late. She had, in that instant when love was something she wanted to forget, found a husband.

CHAPTER TWELVE

It was almost inevitable that Conrad Nicholson Hilton, Jr., should fall in love with Elizabeth Taylor. Glamour beguiled him, a characteristic he inherited from his father.

He was twenty-three when they first met. He was the oldest son of a self-made millionaire. He was completely spoiled, completely charming, and he had grown up in an atmosphere as colorful as Elizabeth's without one trace of the discipline of hers.

During his boyhood, Nick lived alternately in Texas, New York, and California. He grew up in luxury hotels, where he was kowtowed to before he could walk.

During the Depression, Conrad Hilton was, by his own confession, "going broke by inches." In the mid-thirties, the Hilton hotels were either already lost or going into bankruptcy. All that kept Conrad and Mary Hilton, with their sons, Nicky, Barron, and Eric, from starving was the rent from some small flats.

But Conrad Hilton was a natural fighter, and steadily, from 1929 to 1936, he traveled from one side of America to the other, struggling to keep his empire. That meant the boys and their mother saw very little of him. They were all devout Catholics, and so eight-year-old Nick was considerably shaken when Conrad and Mary Barron Hilton divorced.

The divorce at least gave Connie Hilton his entire time to devote to his hotels. By 1940, he, like most of America, was well on the road back. Connie, in fact, was once again a millionaire. His divorce, however, had made Connie react as do most divorced fathers: he felt guilty, and he tried to hold his children's love by overindulging them.

He also gave his sons, when Nick was sixteen, a really dazzling stepmother, Zsa Zsa Gabor. Zsa Zsa of the diamonds, the lure, and the man-catching line. She adored being

54

photographed with her handsome young stepsons, and they didn't mind it, either.

Nick, steadily growing taller, handsomer, and more charming, began to acquire his father's romanticism, dash, and taste for glamour. Once, his father, trying to bawl him out for some escapade, asked plaintively why Nick acted so wildly. Said Nick, grinning, "The trouble with me is that I have a millionaire dad."

Then in 1948, he saw his dream girl's photograph. After that, for one whole year, he acted like a typical movie fan. He was driven to meet Elizabeth Taylor, but he found that was not too easy. Her mother was her guardian. There were the headlines about Glenn Davis and then Bill Pawley. Elizabeth Taylor was in Longon, Elizabeth Taylor was in Florida or New York. She was seldom at Hollywood parties and never alone.

Nicky Hilton discovered, however, that he could learn from the gossip columns where she might be going on some occasions, such as premieres and official parties—and he got himself invited.

It was this dogged following of Elizabeth that made Nick turn up stag at the Mocambo the night of Jane Powell's wedding, the night that he never once took his eyes off Elizabeth. But to meet her in person he had to wait until that lucky day when Pete Freeman phoned him that Elizabeth was at the studio alone.

He found her even more beautiful than on the screen. He wanted to marry her. He wanted her children, a dozen children. She wasn't a Catholic, but they could fix that. She would be the most beautiful wife any man could have.

"May I call you, Elizabeth?" he asked with a formality that delighted her.

"I'd like you to," she said, feeling shy, feeling giddy.

There was a long florist's box waiting for her when she arrived home that afternoon. Three dozen long-stemmed yellow roses. Who had told Nicky Hilton that those were her favorites? She buried her face in them. She wouldn't be going back to Paramount again. She wouldn't be seeing Monty again. And she just wouldn't let herself think of him again, with Libby Holman or any other old woman.

She grinned at her mother, who was standing watching her. She held out the card that had come with the roses.

"Nicky Hilton!" her mother cried. "Nicky Hilton! Oh, Elizabeth."

* * *

It was two days after their first meeting that Nicky came calling in person. Sara Taylor quickly asked him to stay for dinner, and he more quickly accepted. Sara Taylor was delighted with him, and he gave every evidence of being delighted with her, with Francis Taylor, Howard Taylor, Elizabeth Taylor, and the Taylor dogs, cats, and kittens.

They had beef and kidney pie for dinner. When he saw Elizabeth push the kidneys aside and hunt about for the beef, he did the same thing. They laughed across the table in unison.

Did Nick drink? asked Sara Taylor. Elizabeth was too young to drink. "Oh, once in a while," said Nick.

Did he smoke? "Mildly," said Nick. He grinned across the table at Elizabeth and his eyes told her he was playing it down, for her mother's benefit. She smiled back at him, part of his conspiracy of youth.

Before noon the next day Nick was on the telephone, inviting all the Taylors to a dinner party at his father's place in Bel-Air the following Saturday. It was just a family party, he explained, for his younger brother Barron and his wife, Marilyn visiting from Chicago. The Taylors accepted.

Sara Taylor loved the whole Hilton atmosphere, the sweeping driveway up to the great house, the house itself with its high-ceilinged rooms. The dinner was superb, the service flawless, and yet it was truly a family party. Barron and Marilyn Hilton and their two small children, Conrad Hilton with his guest, dancer Ann Miller, and the Taylor contingent. It was all so very, very homey, so very, very correct, and so very, very rich.

After dinner they repaired to the Mocambo for a few glasses of champagne and some dancing. Sara permitted Elizabeth to have some of the wine, for you couldn't call sipping champagne drinking. There was a movie premiere the next Tuesday, and Nicky asked Elizabeth if she would like to go with him.

"Janie Powell and her husband Geary Steffen are going to it," said Sara Taylor quickly. "It might be fun if you and Elizabeth made up a foursome."

They did go as a foursome, and her mother was right: it was fun. The next weekend Marsh and Barbara Thompson asked them to a football game. That was fun, too. Then her brother, Howard, and his one and only girl, Mara, took them out to dinner. Elizabeth could feel her whole level of happiness rising.

Christmas was coming. Conrad Hilton phoned her mother. He'd just taken over the management of a hotel up near Lake Arrowhead. There was lots of space up there, he said, and winter sports, dancing, all kinds of entertainment. Why didn't the Taylors join the Hilton clan and spend the holidays together? The Taylors eagerly accepted.

Their hotel rooms proved to be simple but very comfortable. The food was excellent. The Hilton suites were close to theirs, and while there was a huge Christmas tree for guests in the lobby, Connie Hilton had one almost as big in his own suite, which was just for his family and the Taylor family.

Nicky had diversions provided for every minute. Elizabeth had to keep off skis. Suppose she broke a leg? But Sara agreed that she could go up in the ski lift, which was scary and wonderful, particularly with Nicky there. She went down the toboggan run, with Nicky holding her close. With assorted Hiltons she went sailing on the big, lovely lake, and at night they all danced and danced and danced.

Yes, it was fun. She screamed with delight when she found Nick's gift for her among the mound of packages at the base of Connie's tree. Diamond earrings! Dangling diamond earrings surrounded by pearls. She put them on immediately, and kept swinging her head so that she could feel them touching her cheeks.

It made her present for Nick seem very meager—a gold identification bracelet. Nick said he adored it, though, and he did wear it constantly.

Christmas afternoon, Nick got Francis Taylor aside. "Have I your permission to marry Elizabeth, sir?" he asked.

Francis Taylor gave a long sigh. "I guess I don't have to ask you your prospects, Nick. But can I ask you to wait until Elizabeth is graduated from high school?"

Elizabeth's graduation was only four weeks away, January 27, 1950.

Graduation night, Nicky took her to the Mocambo, the stylish, expensive Mocambo. "A toast," he said, raising his glass of champagne, "to your brains and my beauty."

"Yes, master," she said.

"What I want to be," he said, "is your *husband*. Will you marry me, Elizabeth?"

Nicky Hilton was proposing to her. Did she love him? Why, of course she did. What girl wouldn't?

"Nicky, I . . . I . . . Nicky, there's my career . . ." That had spoiled everything with her and Bill, with her and Glenn.

"I like your career. And I love you, Elizabeth. I told your father I was going to ask you. I'll bet he told you, too."

She giggled and nodded.

"Oh, you little ham, acting so surprised! Why can't we set the date right now, say next week?"

"Why can't we dance right now till I get a chance to, well, think?"

Actually, she wanted him to hold her for that was when she was sure she loved him, when his hands were on her and he was kissing her. Now they stepped out on the handkerchief-sized floor and into one another's arms.

He held her close. He was whispering to her. "When is Elizabeth Taylor marrying Nick Hilton?"

"In May," she heard herself saying dreamily. "In May. Early in May. Say the fifth. Is that okay?"

Dimly she heard him saying, "May fifth it is then, sweetie, and I get the most wonderful girl in the world."

"We've never had a moment when we disagreed," she whispered. "We've never had one quarrel, one moment of disagreement."

"We never will. We never will, sweetie." She felt him stiffen a little and his voice grew more serious.

"You know when you marry a Catholic, it's forever, Elizabeth."

"Yes, I know. Forever and ever. That's the way it would be with us if you were a Hottentot, darling. I'm going to become a Catholic just as soon as I can. Will you arrange that for me?"

He kissed her then, right there on the dance floor with everybody in the Mocambo looking on. Somebody started to applaud.

"We'd better get out of here," Nick said. "Let's go tell your mother the date."

Louella Parsons was on the phone before noon the next day. "Oh, Elizabeth, don't be cross with me," she said. "Don't be cross with your future father-in-law either. He didn't really tell me. When I sort of guessed the right date, he just didn't deny it."

Elizabeth laughed. "I'm not cross, Miss Parsons," she said.

58

"I think Mother is more disappointed than I am because you scooped the news. But I'm too happy to care."

She drew in a long breath and rattled on, not waiting to be questioned. "Your heart knows when you meet the right man, doesn't it? There's no doubt in my mind but that Nick is the one I want to spend my life with. We met last October, and we've never had one moment of misunderstanding. Every day I love him more. I wouldn't be marrying him in the Church if this weren't true."

"Then you are joining the Church?"

"I'm taking instruction. I'm deeply interested in Nicky's religion. I want this marriage to last forever."

After she had hung up on the Parsons call, the phone never stopped ringing. Marjorie Dillon, her stand-in, called. Then Barbara Thompson. Then Mara Reagan, Howard's girl. Then Betty Sullivan, and after that Nicky's sister-in-law, Barron's wife, from Chicago. Instantly, Elizabeth asked them all to be bridesmaids. She was going to have a traditional wedding, six bridesmaids, six ushers, the best man, Nicky's brother Barron, and her maid of honor, Anne Westmore.

New York called. That was a jeweler offering her a forty-five-piece sterling silver tea set as a wedding present if she would only pose in a picture with it. She squealed with pleasure as she agreed.

New York called again. Sam Chapman, husband of the designer, Ceil Chapman, offered her a complete trousseau and the gowns for her bridesmaids. Of course, they'd like a little publicity. "Of course, of course," Elizabeth said.

Helen Rose got through then with the exciting news that she had already begun Elizabeth's wedding dress of white satin and seed pearls. Yes, fabulously expensive, but Elizabeth was not to worry. MGM was paying for it.

Right after Helen, Edith Head, who had the same job at Paramount that Helen had at MGM, called. Edith's news was that she was already designing Elizabeth's going-away costume and Paramount was footing that bill.

Nick called with word that his father was giving them three months in Europe with all expenses paid as a honeymoon gift. Then he called back to say that his father had just set aside the most expensive suite in the elegant Bel-Air hotel for their official residence when they returned. Then he called again to say they could also live in any Hilton Hotel anywhere else, if they preferred, even in the newest one in Puerto Rico.

Janie Powell was giving her a shower. Helen Rose was giving her a shower. All the bridesmaids were giving her showers.

The days raced by. Late afternoons she studied with Monsignor Concannan at the Church of the Good Shepherd, and would sit listening to his Irish brogue, tears in her eyes, visualizing herself and Nicky being married by him.

January, February, March, April flew by. The studio wanted her to work in *Father's Little Dividend* before she went on her honeymoon, and when this was accepted, MGM gave her and her mother a trip to New York as a reward.

But her time in New York was just as jammed. There were interviews and photographic sittings and fittings.

However, just before she was due to return to Hollywood, she managed to slip away from everyone for a moment. She slid into a public phone booth and called Monty.

Something stabbed through her at the sound of his voice. "When I'm married, will you come see us?" she asked.

"I don't think so, Bessie Mae. I don't know—somehow I don't think Nick's my kind of guy."

Anger seared through her. "I thought you were always going to be my friend, my good, good friend."

"That's what I intend to be. I hope you'll be very, very happy."

She slammed down the receiver, and all the way across the country she thought of how she would never think of him again.

Father's Little Dividend necessitated her getting up at five A.M. This, together with her hat and shoe and glove fittings, her religious instructions, and the parties and showers—she was lucky if she got to bed by one A.M. But no matter when she came in, she always stopped to check the rising mountain of wedding gifts, taking up so much room that all the Taylor furniture except their beds and the kitchen stuff had been sent into storage at MGM till May 7.

Her mother did most of her packing, and soon there were twenty-two trunks ready for the *Queen Mary,* on which she and Nick would sail. One trunk held nothing but hats. Another had only shoes, a third was jammed with purses, a fourth held her negligees and underwear. All her negligees had matching nighties, one in cloth of gold. Her bathing suits took up another, some of those in cloth of gold, too. In all, she had forty outfits with everything to match, besides her free mink coat and two mink scarves.

As May fifth grew nearer, she and Nicky never had a second alone, but she did not fret. She pointed out to everyone, "Nick and I think as one person."

The day before the wedding, Elizabeth began running a fever. The doctor put her to bed, and she liked being alone for the first time in months.

The ceremony was set for five in the afternoon, but the mob at the Church of the Good Shepherd had grown to thirty-five hundred by the time the bride arrived. Her veil caught and tore on the limousine door as she stepped out. The police linked hands to hold back the fans. She got into the church safely. The vestry was noisy and crowded with the yellow-organdy clutter of her bridesmaids, who all swarmed up to embrace her.

The organ pealed. The bridesmaids took their positions. Elizabeth and Anne Westmore gave one another one final kiss as she saw her father extending his arm to her. Somebody handed her her bouquet of white orchids, and for one fleeting instant she nearly panicked.

Then she felt herself falling into step with her father, going up the center aisle of the Church of the Good Shepherd, going to meet her husband...

The mob was still around the church as she and Nicky came out. As they posed on the church steps for the photographers, the crowd pelted them with rice and flowers, called out half-ribald greetings to them.

Elizabeth was joyous. Her handsome husband smiled. He waved. Once inside the limousine, heading for their wedding reception, he sent her into cascades of giggles by murmuring under his breath as he kept bowing and smiling to the throng. "Here we are with this damned reception to go through and I can't even hold your hand."

It took five long hours for the reception line to pass them. She stood beside her mother and father, next to Nick, who had his mother and father there together, even if they were divorced.

Elizabeth kept shaking hands, newspaper hands, movie-star hands, just-people hands, businessman hands—these latter were Nicky's friends, she supposed. She kept saying, "Oh, thank you so much. Oh, I saw your adorable wedding gift, and I will write you a proper thank-you note for it soon,

61

but right now, thank you so much." She watched the guests drinking champagne and feasting on crabmeat and turkey and oysters. She kept saying, "How very sweet of you. Yes, I'm sure we are going to be very, very happy, but you are very kind to wish the best for us." She kept wishing she could slip her feet out of her shoes, but she stood straight, smiling.

As the crowd began to thin a little, she leaned forward, so that she could smile right into Nicky's mother's eyes to tell her how grateful she was because she'd brought Nicky into the world.

Right at that moment Conrad Hilton was talking to his ex-wife. It was well that Elizabeth couldn't ever hear what was being said.

Conrad Hilton said, "They've got everything, haven't they, our boy and his wife? Youth, looks, position, no need to worry about where their next meal is coming from."

"Maybe they have too much. I don't think it is going to be easy for them."

"Nonsense," said Conrad Hilton.

CHAPTER THIRTEEN

The newlywed Mr. and Mrs. Conrad Nicholson Hilton, Jr.,
arrived at Del Monte Lodge at Pebble Beach, some four
hundred miles north of Beverly Hills, just before four in the
morning. Their blood was too eager for them to feel tired.
They blazed by the three waiting photographers, flashing
them quick smiles as the camera shutters clicked.

They went to their suite, redolent with flowers, its curtains
drawn and its great bed already turned down. Nick tipped
the bellboys and snapped the outer lock and they were alone,
finally.

They did not emerge until the afternoon. There were
photographers waiting in the dining room for them, and
movie fans wanting autographs. Elizabeth gave Nicky an
anxious glance, but she saw he liked all the attention and she
relaxed, sighing with gratitude.

How perfect he was. How lucky she was!

But their real honeymoon began on the *Queen Mary*.
Quite by accident, their first night out, they met another
famous pair of lovers: the Duke and Duchess of Windsor.

The Hiltons and the Windsors were quartered in the same
section of the great ship. One day they happened to exit from
their cabins at the same moment. Elizabeth was fascinated by
the sight of a man who had given up the world's greatest
kingdom for love. Then she blushed as she saw him smile at
her and knew he had recognized her. An aide, stepping up
quickly, made the proper introductions.

What did one say to royalty? The Duchess, with quick tact,
stretched out a hand in greeting, murmuring that she was
having guests in for tea the next afternoon at four, and would
Mr. and Mrs. Hilton care to join them?

Being news, being young, and passionately in love, and rich and beautiful, Elizabeth and Nicky Hilton were bound anyway to be social lions in Europe. But when the word sped that the Windsors had taken them up on board the *Queen Mary*, the whole giddy international set flocked toward them.

Overnight Mr. and Mrs. Conrad Nicholson Hilton, Jr., aged twenty-three and eighteen respectively, became everyone's pets. They had little more than checked into the elegant George V in Paris when the fabulously wealthy Maharajah of Baroda invited them to fly to England with him and the Maharanee as his guests at the Ascot races.

After that they were due at a party Elsa Maxwell was giving them in Paris in three days.

At Elsa's party they were surrounded by dukes, barons, other maharajahs and maharanees, Maurice Chevalier, and magnums of champagne. Orson Welles, one of the guests, reminded Elizabeth of his having been in *Jane Eyre* with her. He was going to Rome, he said. Why didn't she and Nicky come along?

"Let's go, let's go," said Nicky.

In Rome, the MGM man said, they were shooting *Quo Vadis*. For kicks—and of course, it also made wonderful publicity—Elizabeth let them make her up as a slave girl, a Christian martyr. She mingled in the crowd of extras and nobody knew it was she—except everyone connected with the entire production. Nicky wouldn't agree to be a slave. He waited, laughing, behind the camera with Mervyn Le Roy, the producer-director.

They did the scene five times before director Le Roy okayed it, and by that time Elizabeth was exhausted. She had been dropping weight steadily for six weeks. She was homesick, homesick for her mother and her work and familiar faces about her. She did not want to be on the go any more, entirely surrounded by strangers, glamorous though they might be.

Headed back toward Paris after *Quo Vadis*, due to be the guest of honor at a ball there the following evening, Elizabeth found herself quaking. Nicky had bought her a magnificent gown at Balmain. A Parisian jeweler had insisted upon loaning her $150,000 worth of diamonds to wear.

"Would you want to go home—I mean back to California— after the ball?" Elizabeth asked Nicky.

"No, I don't want to go home for another month yet. All

that ails you is that sad movie scene." He leaned down and kissed her. "Snap out of it."

She was suddenly in tears, crying out that he was selfish, that he thought only of his own pleasure, that he did not care whether she was tired and fed up with bars and drinking.

He responded just as hotly. They went to bed without speaking. The next morning, Elizabeth begged Nick to forgive her.

They were, of course, booked for dinner before the ball, and Elizabeth saw that whenever Nick looked at her, there was a challenge in his eyes. She was aware of something she had been trying not to admit for weeks: Nicky was envious of her. In some subtle, unexpressed way, he had come to be in competition with her.

She was too naive to realize that adroit flattery would have solved the situation. She was also too accustomed to being flattered herself.

The ball was to begin at eleven. At midnight exactly, Elizabeth entered the great, mirrored drawing room. The crowd gaped. She was the perfect dream queen, Nick the flawless consort. But she did not feel like a queen. She was too tired, too bewildered.

The orchestra began to play, and Nick started out with her on the dance floor. They were cut in on immediately, and then she seemed to be changing partners every two steps. Strange men held her too closely, whispered to her too ardently, while she made herself laugh.

The hours dragged by. Once in a while Nick got back to her, but they were not permitted to stay together. He was beside her when breakfast was served, but they were jammed together in a throng and could not talk intimately. It was close to dawn as they headed back to the George V.

Nick wanted to go gambling.

She was so tired she was shaking. "Oh, Nicky darling, I don't think I can go on anywhere else tonight, please, sweetie."

It was then that she learned that women of her age are not permitted in French gambling rooms.

That meant she would be left alone.

She knew better than to cry in the lobby of a spotlighted place like the George V. There was bound to be a photographer around somewhere.

There was. But she could not hold back her tears as Nicky took her up to their suite. The papers around the world printed the pictures.

The next morning, when they ordered breakfast sent up, the papers were sent up, too, and in them were long accounts of their quarrel, some with quotes from both of them about their differences.

"How dare they?" said Nick. "I never talked to any reporters."

"Oh, Nicky, I know that. But they just do that. I didn't talk to any of them either. But if you don't say what they want you to, they make it up."

Nicky retorted that it was all her fault. Had they ever been left alone, had they ever had a meal without its being publicized, ever gone dancing unnoticed just once?

"I know," said Elizabeth. "But you must have known it would be this way when you married me."

Nick had discovered his weapon against her. That night he went gambling again. That night she went along with him hopefully. But Nicky played on and on, and the most beautiful bride in the world sat and sobbed, as hundreds of newspapers told their readers the next day.

Sara called from California. Elizabeth felt guilty. She had written her mother only once and had not answered any of Sara's letters or cables.

For the first time in her life, she lied to her mother. "Oh, you know how the press exaggerates, Mummie. We'll work this out, Nicky and I. The first year is the hardest, you know. Don't worry. Please don't worry. We'll work it out."

But they didn't.

They sulked and snarled and made up and battled through two more weeks and a dozen more headlines before they decided their marriage was over. They returned to New York to separate there. Nick was staying to check out some matters at the Waldorf-Astoria. Elizabeth was flying straight to the Coast.

At her request, an MGM man promised to call Hollywood and have Bill Lyon meet her on the plane's stopover in Chicago, so that she wouldn't have to come into Hollywood alone.

Bill Lyon, her old party escort. Elizabeth smiled for the first time in many days. She was going home to friends, like Bill and Helen Rose and all the studio. She was going to her parents. Such love, such undemanding love she was sure of. Soon she would be with Janie and Anne and all her girl friends. Soon she would be talking to her brother.

She slept all the way to Chicago. However, as she came

down the steps at the airport Bill Lyon was not there to meet her.

Nicky was. Nicky was standing there, holding out his arms to her, and she ran straight into them.

CHAPTER FOURTEEN

In the euphoria of lovers who have parted forever and then discover they do not have to take their separation seriously, the young Hiltons worked blissfully on the future details of their life as they flew from Chicago to Los Angeles.

Primarily each promised to be perfect. Nicky, the perfect husband, Elizabeth, the perfect wife. Nicky would limit himself to two drinks at most per evening and no gambling. Elizabeth would learn to cook. She'd learn to run a house.

Nicky said it would be best if they didn't rush into buying a house. Buying was serious. They would rent while they looked for their ideal home. They'd start with a little one-servant house.

Her parents met them at the airport, along with Nick's father and several people from the studio and, of course, cameramen. Everyone was tactful about Elizabeth's thinness.

They found a house, and Nicky found a good maid somewhere in the Hilton organization. But soon Elizabeth was back at the studio, doing retakes on *Father's Little Dividend*, discussing her next picture, *Love Is Better Than Ever*, and hearing lavish praise for her work in *A Place in the Sun*.

She was finally attaining artistic status, which, for all of its love of money and power, Hollywood respected above every other quality. Although *Love Is Better Than Ever* would be just a light, romantic picture, Elizabeth was exhilarated because the studio implied that she would soon be given much more important films. On the MGM lot, late that summer of 1950, she was a junior goddess, babied and flattered by everyone at the studio.

Nick was back at work, too, the boss's son, the rising young executive, the heir to a great fortune.

In the evenings, young Mr. and Mrs. Hilton found it took

great tact to be entirely happy in an atmosphere where each of them expected praise constantly.

She became a chain smoker, and for the one and only time in her life had no appetite. Even the simplest food upset her. She suspected she might have an ulcer but was afraid to go to a doctor and have it confirmed.

She was accustomed to going to bed by ten when making a picture, but Nicky pointed out that if they lived by her rule of never going to parties while working, they would never go anywhere at all. Thus, night after night, she went out, got to bed at midnight if she was lucky, and was up again at six. Her weight kept on dropping.

She discovered that the parties she enjoyed were bores to Nicky. Janie Powell gave them a welcome-home evening. All Elizabeth's closest friends were there: Anne Westmore, Betty Sullivan, Mara Reagan, who by that time was officially engaged to Howard Taylor, the Marshall Thompsons. The homey food was served buffet style, and they ate it sitting on the floor. After dinner, they played charades. There were similar parties at Marjie Dillon's and then at Mara's.

Fresh from the great galas of Paris and Rome, Elizabeth knew how naive such evenings were. Yet, when Nick said they were drags, she angrily defended them.

The morning of a party that Anne Westmore was hostessing, Nicky suddenly refused to go.

"I'm fed up with kids' games," he said.

Elizabeth was furious.

"Does everything but a—a maharajah bore you?" she screamed.

"This bores me, I can tell you. You go to the party. I'm flying to Las Vegas."

In a rage, she said the first thing that came into her mind.

"Then I'll go to Palm Springs!"

"Happy landings," said Nick.

She drove to Palm Springs at a furious pace and checked into the luxurious Miramar. No, she said, she was not expecting Mr. Hilton. She was just taking a tiny weekend rest, that was all.

Then she was in a vast suite. It was four in the afternoon, and although the late October sun was already down behind Mount San Jacinto, the sky above was still brilliantly blue. Outside, Elizabeth could hear people splashing about in the pool, hear friends calling to one another.

Only she was alone. Only she was alone in this romantic setting meant for lovers. And she was alone in a way that a single woman can never be. She was alone as only a wife can be when parted from her husband—lopsided, incomplete, insecure.

She threw herself across the king-sized bed and began to sob.

A knock sounded on the door. It had to be the boy with her bags.

"Come in," she said, in a small, unhappy voice.

"Thanks, darling, I will," said Nicky.

She was in his arms. He was kissing her. It was all so silly and too dramatic.

"You didn't go to Las Vegas at all?"

"Yes, I did, but the moment I landed I knew I had to be where you were. I've discovered one advantage in your being Elizabeth Taylor. You're easy to track down, and I could fly faster than you could drive."

Passionately, they remained in Palm Springs for several days. Even when they came back to Beverly Hills, they remained felicitous. For almost a month. Then they had another of their infantile spats. Elizabeth flew at Nicky, in a rage, like a furious bantam.

With a harsh laugh, he easily overpowered her. Elizabeth pulled free. "I'm going home to my mother," she sobbed as she rushed out of the room.

"That's okay by me," Nick yelled after her.

It was utterly childish, of course, but even there Nick wasn't going to let his wife beat him. Mary just happened to be in Los Angeles at that moment. So Nick went home to *his* mother.

For one whole day, Elizabeth basked in the warmth of her mother's adoration, the delight of her mother's waiting upon her. She was giddily happy.

The second day she found herself restless, and by the third day, she knew that she was no longer a child. She was a woman. She was a wife.

"I must go back to Nick."

"Of course you must, Elizabeth, but I'm so glad you made up your own mind to it." Sara was relieved.

She phoned home, discovered her husband's whereabouts, and phoned Mary's. Nick answered. She whispered, "Nicky?"

"Oh, sweetie, sweetie. Can I come and get you?"

"Right away. Right away fast."

Home again, they told each other they would stay home nights, would settle down. They did so and neither would admit to the other how dull they found it. Then Elizabeth, most innocently, accepted Marsh and Barbara Thompson's invitation to a picnic supper at the beach.

Nick looked at her scornfully. "You go. It sounds like your kind of sweet event. Count me out."

She began to cry and he stalked across the room.

"Nicky, where are you going? What are you going to do?" The door slammed behind him.

Elizabeth stood stock still. Her tears stopped as swiftly as they had come. She realized that she was feeling nothing at all.

Suddenly she ran into the master bedroom. She pulled a weekend case down off a closet shelf, threw in some cosmetics, a dressing gown, a nightdress and slipped noiselessly out of the house. She got into her car and drove to Anne Westmore's.

By the time Nicky tracked her there that evening, she had slipped away again, this time to Helen Rose's.

After that she turned up at one friend's household after another. She talked to none of them. She was like a wraith. Whether she was at Marjie Dillon's or the Thompsons' she only stayed one night. No one could make her eat but she smoked incessantly, pack after pack. She paid no attention to her appearance, and wore the same dress day after day— something she had never in her life done before.

Marjie, Helen Rose, Jane Powell, Barbara, Anne Westmore stopped trying to question her. For she would weep soundlessly, the tears pouring down her face. She was on the verge of a nervous breakdown, but none of them could get her to a doctor.

Nick pursued her but she kept moving too fast for him. Everywhere she found phone calls from him, boxes of yellow roses from him. She did not return the phone calls. She did not open the boxes of roses. She couldn't sleep, and dark circles appeared under her eyes. Finally, she turned up at the house of her agent, Jules Goldstone. Mrs. Goldstone was a warm, maternal woman.

Elizabeth stayed there for a week, and this time Nick caught up with her. White and defiant, she faced him across the Goldstones' living room. "It's all over," she said, tonelessly. "I'm divorcing you."

Nick was enraged. He began shouting, and Jules Goldstone

ordered him to leave. As Nick went thundering out, Elizabeth collapsed.

To Goldstone she sobbed, "Get me an apartment, Jules, I've got to have a place of my own, where I can be alone and think this out. I must be alone. Jules, I'll go mad if I don't work this out."

Jules was accustomed to star temperaments.

"Honey, you can't live alone," he said. "The papers will harpoon you, once your divorce news leaks out. You can't face all that alone. Once you're free, the wolf pack will close in. You don't know how to handle that. Let's face it. You don't know how to handle anything."

"Don't be cruel to me."

"I'm not cruel to you, Elizabeth. I'm just telling you some facts. It's not your fault if you don't know how to do anything, even make a cup of coffee. Now listen to me. I know a girl who used to be Bob Hope's wife's secretary. Nice dame, kind of a society girl. Her name's Peggy Rutledge. Let me hire her for you—to be your secretary, that is. She'll rent you an apartment today. She'll go get your clothes. She'll move you in. She'll look after you and won't make any demands on you. She'll be there when you want to talk—you do understand, don't you?"

When she didn't answer, he turned to face her. She had fainted.

The doctor did not hospitalize Elizabeth, but he said she must not be alone, and he approved of her moving in with a young woman companion. So Peggy Rutledge was hired.

Elizabeth liked Peggy from their first meeting. Peggy could make good coffee. Peggy was neat and tidy. Peggy could chatter, silly girl-talk, or remain quiet, as Elizabeth might wish.

The doctor called daily, and she began to eat a little. She wasn't permitted anything but baby food, mashed vegetables, occasional bits of chicken. She didn't care. She just didn't care, period.

When Peggy answered the phone, the caller usually hung up without saying a word. When Elizabeth answered, the callers were various but all male: Orson Welles, Ted Briskin, Lin Howard, Jr., the millionaire's son, Tommy Breen, plus others whose names meant nothing to Elizabeth. The two most persistent callers were Howard Hughes and Nicky.

Nick kept calling, kept sending her roses, notes, and

telegrams. But she knew she could not go back to Nicky's love games.

The days dragged by, wintry as her own mood. She hoped that the studio would start *Love Is Better Than Ever* soon. She needed to get back to work. She had been off salary for seven months, and she was having to be thrifty, a new and dreary experience to her.

Her doctor bills were tremendous. Peggy's salary was no pittance. She mildly thought of redecorating the apartment until she found out the cost of it. She had never had to worry about the cost of anything before.

So she would sit in the living room with Peggy and not see it while she watched television. And look at those damned yellow roses Nick kept on sending.

Finally, a month and a day before her nineteenth birthday, on Friday, January 26, 1951, she crept into the divorce court. Her voice was so weak that the judge ordered her to speak louder. She testified that Nick "had left her alone many nights." Her charge was that convenient California one of mental cruelty. She refused alimony. "I don't want a prize for failing," she whispered.

The court gave her her freedom. Her "perfect marriage" had lasted only eight months.

When she came back to her apartment, she found a message from the studio. She was to report the following Monday to start *Love Is Better Than Ever*.

CHAPTER FIFTEEN

Stanley Donen, who was to direct *Love Is Better Than Ever,*
like every other male on the MGM lot, had been aware of
Elizabeth ever since she had blazed into adolescence. But
she barely knew him before their first meeting on the set of
their mutual picture.

Gene Kelly had brought Donen to Hollywood—they had
met when both of them were in the Broadway hit, *Pal Joey,*
Gene as star and Donen as a chorus boy. When *Pal Joey*
closed, Gene went into *Best Foot Forward* and had Donen
stage his dances. When MGM bought the film rights to that,
Kelly made Donen part of his team, then got him a codirecting
credit on *Anchors Aweigh.* Donen finally branched out on his
own with Fred Astaire's *Royal Wedding. Love Is Better Than
Ever* was to be his third picture.

Elizabeth felt shy and awkward at their first meeting. Her
doctor had insisted she be accompanied by a nurse. She still
had a tendency to faint without warning, and she was to play
a ballerina in *Love Is Better Than Ever.*

"I know you are an expert choreographer, but I'm no
ballerina," she told Donen.

He smiled. "Don't worry about your dancing," he said.
"That's my worry. As a couple of friends working together, we
can lick it. We can be friends, can't we?"

That word "friend" struck a response in her. Just to talk to
a man, really talk...She smiled at him. "I'd like us to be
friends," she said.

"Wonderful. Look, there's a preview Thursday of a really
good ballet film. Want to go?"

She smiled at him again. He wasn't even offering to buy
her dinner! Why, bless him, he wasn't on the make. All he
did want to do was to take her to a movie.

She gave him her address before she went into makeup.

The script of *Love Is Better Than Ever* was certainly a light one. Her co-star, Larry Parks, was an amiable actor. The three days before her date with Donen flew by agreeably.

Thursday evening they went to the movie, and later had coffee at a small restaurant. Then Stan brought her back to her apartment at eleven o'clock. That was all.

But they had been seen together. She had just got her divorce. He was separated. One newspaper said the next morning that Elizabeth Taylor was obviously a girl with no feeling for the sanctity of marriage. Another tagged her and Donen as two callous divorced people contemplating a new union.

It was embarrassing. But they quickly forgot it as they began working the next day, and at lunch Elizabeth came up with what she naively considered the ideal way of stopping the gossip. "I'd like you to meet my mother and father," she said.

Elizabeth felt she had the right to invite Stanley to her home. But Stanley Donen wasn't a football hero like Glenn Davis. Or rich like Bill Pawley and Nicky Hilton. He was a recently divorced, second-string (at that time) movie director. Sara just didn't consider him good enough for her daughter. That night, Donen became the bystander in a bitter difference between mother and daughter.

Elizabeth had never gone through the normal teenage revolt against her mother, but, standing there on her mother's doorstep, with Stanley Donen beside her, Elizabeth went into her delayed revolt. She screamed at her mother. Her mother snapped back at her. They had never before lost their tempers with each other. They had never made the commonplace adjustments of parent and child. But there, in Stanley Donen's presence, they spewed out at one another all the repressions of nearly nineteen years.

As Sara Taylor slammed the door, shutting herself in and her daughter out, she was weeping. But Elizabeth took her suffering in another way. As they drove away, she began shivering. Donen noted her pallor. He started to talk to her, but she did not seem to hear him. He speeded up his car, got her back to her apartment. She fell in a faint as Peggy opened the door.

The doctor hospitalized her, and for days Stanley Donen was the only person she wanted to see. It did not help their personal publicity any when the news got out.

However, somewhere in that four-day retreat from reality,

Elizabeth had changed, had hardened. When she left the hospital, she stopped paying any attention to the papers. She made no attempt to make up her quarrel with her mother. She was with Donen constantly, on the set of their picture by day, seeing movies with him almost every evening, spending Saturday and Sunday afternoons at the beach.

Stan Donen sensed in her what none of the wolf pack ever would have realized. She was not a sophisticate. For all her exotic face and form, the warm winter sun of California, the salt spray rising from the Pacific beguiled her as no nightclub ever could. To be taken to a zoo made her happier than being escorted to a hundred cocktail parties.

Stanley also stimulated her mind, a new experience for her. He represented a completely different culture from any she had ever known—he was Jewish. She was to say later, "I asked him a lot of questions and I was fascinated by his religion. He brought me books and I did some reading, and I guess I identified with him as an underdog."

What might have resulted from their compatibility will never be known, for they were parted by an unexpected blow. Larry Parks was accused of Communist leanings.

Since Parks wasn't really a star—he had clicked initially because he had Al Jolson's voice on the sound track of his first picture, *The Jolson Story*, but didn't quite have the impact to make it on his own—Hollywood had no wish to fight for him. MGM shelved *Love Is Better Than Ever*, which as far as Elizabeth and Donen were concerned meant all their work together had come to nothing.

MGM did, however, know how to care for and feed stars. Their prescription for Elizabeth Taylor was one they had used before. They cast her in another picture with Robert Taylor, a picture to be made in London, just like *The Conspirator*. *The Conspirator* had been quite successful in putting a dent in the Glenn Davis romance.

The new picture was *Ivanhoe*, and Elizabeth's role in it was so small she could have phoned it in. This she realized the moment she read the script, just as she realized that the studio was trying to separate her from Donen. Her ire was sufficient to get her out of bed. She went raging to MGM. Pandro Berman was the producer, the same Pandro Berman of *National Velvet* and the same Pandro Berman who battled her again in *Butterfield 8* in 1960.

Elizabeth screamed at Berman that she would not go to London. He calmly told her that she would or go off salary.

He knew she was broke. So did she. So she yelled that she would just walk through the part and what would he do about that?

"I knew she wouldn't," Berman says today. "I knew even at nineteen she was actually too much of an artist to deliberately ruin a part. When in 1960 she threatened to sabotage *Butterfield 8* I knew just the same thing. On *Butterfield 8* she really tried to be impossible, but I still stayed calm. I knew her artistic conscience would thwart her and besides that crazy defiance of hers was just what the role needed."

In the spring of 1951, just as in 1960, finances forced Elizabeth to give in, but she didn't give in gracefully. For the first time she asserted her power. She demanded that the studio send Peggy Rutledge to England with her. The studio agreed.

Next she demanded that a woman publicist at MGM, Malvina Pumphrey, be her publicist and, further, that Mrs. Pumphrey should bring her husband abroad with her, too.

The studio submitted. Elizabeth was dazzled with such concessions. Nine years and hundreds of similar whims later, was it any wonder that she knew perfectly well that Twenti- eth Century would give in to all her demands on *Cleopatra*? Both times it was a matter of protecting an investment on the part of the studios, but to the 1951 Elizabeth it also proved she was becoming adult, running her own life.

When she changed planes in New York, Monty Clift was waiting.

She was pleased. For Monty to submit himself deliberately to a crowd was the most flattering visible proof of his friend- ship for her, possibly even of his love for her. He must have run the gauntlet of all the photographers who had been outside, waiting for her. Yet, her new awareness of herself as a self kept her from throwing her arms about him.

"Hello, Bessie Mae," he said. "You're all right?"

Monty was the one person in the world she could tell all about Nicky. He'd said Nicky wasn't his type of man. Nicky hadn't been her type of man either. But she was conscious of all the listeners packed tight around them. "I'm fine, Monty."

He lowered his voice. "You're sure?" It was just like Monty's awful honesty to let her know he was noticing her thinness, her pallor.

"Yes, Mr. Schwartzkopf, I'm sure."

The nickname made him smile. "Okay. Now what's with you and Stanley Donen?"

She drew herself up. "We're just friends, Stan and I," she said. She looked Monty straight in the eye. "Does that sound familiar to you, my dear, dear friend?"

She knew it was a good curtain line, and she took advantage of it, turning and walking into the customs room before Monty could even say good-bye.

Arriving the next morning in London, Peggy Rutledge hated it, but Elizabeth discovered herself rejoicing. This was the land of her childhood. This was remembrance of things unspoiled.

She told Peggy she was going to make both of them relax. She described the weekends they would spend in the country, planned tours they would make when she wasn't working.

They were still unpacking that first morning when Michael Wilding called. "Welcome home," he said. "Are you by any miracle available for dinner?"

Evening after evening, in all the tiny luxurious eating places of London, she and Mike Wilding dined together. Her appetite revived. She ate everything set before her, Mike always flawlessly ordering the meals without even consulting her, yet always pleasing her.

Elizabeth forgot she had ever been ill. She was not conscious that she had found what she was seeking, but she had. She had found the man who could be her father and her lover, too.

She put on her lost weight, and a bit more. Copying Mike, she learned to drink champagne.

Every day in the studio, where *Ivanhoe* took so little of her time, she thought of the evening before her. Mike was finishing up a picture, too, a light comedy. When she asked him about it, he said, "It's nothing to be taken seriously. I'd rather talk about you."

It was his complete lack of conceit that enchanted her, his lack of demands, completely different from Nicky. He loved the theater, and took Elizabeth to the various hits on which the curtain rose at seven, while the sun was still shining. They would be out by ten, in the gentle English twilight. "We English come to realize, perhaps through this twilight of ours, that things are more than black or white," Mike said to her. "We come to appreciate the grays in everything."

The summer flew by for Elizabeth. If she and Mike went to the theater, they would go to a supper club later. But many an evening they ate early and separated early because of their work schedules. On weekends, they sometimes pub-crawled, but on other occasions, Mike would take her for a sail down the Thames.

Mike's constant wit, his constant understatement, taught her how to laugh, and gradually she was able to laugh at herself for the things she had taken too seriously or too dramatically. Nevertheless, she was dismayed when she discovered Mike had never seen her on screen. Impishly she arranged for MGM to screen *National Velvet* for him.

That was almost a mistake. For after the showing Mike looked at her uneasily. "It is unbearable that you were that young merely eight years ago."

Her heart raced with the sudden fear that she might lose him, now that she had become so dependent upon him.

"Oh, Michael," she said, "I'm almost twenty. That's old for a girl, really old." She drew in an excited breath and focused her violet eyes on him. "You haven't proposed to me," she said, "so I'm proposing to you. Please marry me. Marry me as quickly as possible. Oh, Michael, I've found out in this past year that happiness is such a fragile thing. We have so little time, all of us, for happiness or love."

He did not speak for several minutes. Then, "You are much too young, my darling, to marry me. I'm twice your age. You'll change your mind."

"I won't, Michael, I won't. Remember how we kissed two years ago when I was going home? That proves we were in love even then. Now I'm so much more grown up. You are everything I admire. Oh, I do love you."

"I'm dead broke," he said. "I work continually, but I have no talent for hanging onto money. I can hardly afford to buy you a dinner, let alone an engagement ring expensive enough to be worthy of you. I should like to give you the darkest sapphire to match your eyes. I'd like to give you the whole damned earth. But I'm still married, and so are you, and even if I had the price I haven't the right to give you anything."

She was too much a creature of Hollywood to listen to such an argument.

Elizabeth said to Michael Wilding, "I'm getting my final divorce decree. You must get your divorce. You must marry me, Michael. I need you. I need you very much."

She did not question that her need was the clinching argument. Neither of them realized how prophetic was the

79

fact that she was the one who had done the proposing, that she was the one issuing the orders.

She telephoned him the next morning and told him he must meet her at eleven at one of Bond Street's most chic jewelers.

"Look, darling," she cried when he arrived. "Look at these two rings. Which do you like best?"

They were the darkest sapphires, and they did match her eyes.

"The small one."

"No, stop that. I'm buying myself a gift. Which do you like best?"

"Better. The larger one, then."

She quickly purchased it. "Please get a cab. Can we go to Rule's for lunch? It's a celebration."

There was a cab at the curb, and Elizabeth sprang into it, pulling Mike in after her. She threw herself back in the seat, her eyes shining. She held out her left hand, separating her fingers so that the third finger stood alone. "Put the ring on, darling," she commanded. "Put it on quickly, please."

Against his better judgment Michael Wilding slid the ring on her finger.

"Now we are engaged," she said. "We wind up *Ivanhoe* tomorrow. They have ordered me home—the studio, I mean—and I'll announce our engagement from Hollywood the moment you are free. Michael, can we have a big evening on the town tonight?"

They did have a big evening on the town that night, making a party of it with Malvina Pumphrey, the press agent, and her husband, Kenny. They danced and ate and drank champagne until the sun came up, and sometime in the night, exactly when none of them remembered too clearly, they sent a cable to Sara Taylor.

It read: *We are all thinking of you and wishing you were here. We are all having a wonderful reunion together, all very happy. Can't wait to see you in Beverly Hills. All our love, Elizabeth, Malvina and Kenny and Michael Wilding.*

It was the first time Elizabeth had been in touch with her mother since their quarrel over Stanley Donen. That cable healed the breach between them. Nonetheless Sara Taylor was never again going to dominate. Her daughter ruled herself from that time on.

Elizabeth flew home two days later by way of New York. At the same time Michael Wilding called on his wife, Kay

Young, and asked for his freedom. Miss Young behaved flawlessly. She not only put the divorce proceedings immediately into the works, but as soon as the decree was handed down, she immediately became engaged to another actor.

Elizabeth, to her delighted surprise, found her parents and Montgomery Clift at planeside in New York to meet her. Her parents explained that they were in New York to celebrate their twenty-fifth wedding anniversary. They brought the news that the studio didn't need her for a week.

She kissed her parents happily. "I'll stay here then and celebrate with you. Oh, darlings, I've got such a big secret to tell you."

Then she kissed Monty very quickly on the cheek. She drew him aside, and, not caring that the photographers were snapping them together, she whispered so that her parents would not be able to hear her.

"Oh, dear Mr. Schwartzkopf, when do I get the chance to ask your advice—advice about love? You do know about love, don't you?"

"I'm a tower of knowledge, Bessie Mae, a leaning tower, maybe, but a tower. Shall I buy you your dinner tonight? But meanwhile can you tell me if you are still in love with your perfect friend, Mr. Donen, or have you a new candidate?"

"Monty, you are a monster. If I accept your invitation, do we dine in one of those dives of yours?"

"Indeed not. I'll make the supreme sacrifice. Is the Pavillon classy enough for your amorous confessions?"

He was still Monty. She couldn't anger him. She couldn't stay angry at him. "Love that Pavillon—but just us, Monty."

They dined that night. They dined every night for the rest of the week, while the papers buzzed with it. In California, Nicky Hilton, who hadn't given up at all, read about them. He wired Elizabeth and said he was eager to see her in New York regarding their property settlement.

In London, Mike Wilding, who was wise though infatuated, read about them and telephoned Elizabeth that his picture was finishing before the weekend, and he'd fly out immediately and join her in Manhattan.

Hearing his charming voice, Elizabeth knew that she loved Michael more than anyone in the world.

Still, she was only nineteen. So she wasn't able to resist those everyday rendezvous with Monty, particularly when he took her to places like the Maisonette at the St. Regis and 21 and Voisin. And she was thrilled when her ex-father-in-law,

Connie Hilton, took her dining and dancing one evening, which, of course, made all the papers, along with the fact that she was staying at a Hilton Hotel.

Then when Nicky arrived and, in his most charming way, asked her if she knew any spot where they could talk quietly, she suggested her Uncle Howard's house in Connecticut, some forty miles away from New York.

It was autumn in New York, the leaves turning to red and gold, the air crisp, the sky unclouded. Nicky was looking at her with those terrific eyes of his. She forgot all their quarrels. He really was wonderful.

"Sweetie, why don't we drive to Connecticut, just lazy and just us?" he asked.

Excitedly, she agreed. Just before they reached her uncle's house, his car broke down on a lonely country road.

Four small disillusioning experiences, following one immediately after the other, helped right then to shape her life.

The first was set in motion by the State of Connecticut, or more exactly a state trooper who came cruising along, heard from Nick about his car trouble, and offered to take them on to Howard Young's house, which was nearer than any garage.

By way of being a good host, Howard Young offered his niece, her ex-husband, and the trooper something to drink, which with Elizabeth meant champagne. Because she was feeling giddy, Elizabeth perched on Nicky's knee as she emptied her glass, and Nick leaned toward her a couple of times as he emptied his and kissed her. And the trooper, upon leaving, phoned the New York papers all about it.

The second thing was that Nicky, when the trooper left, proved that even if he was being adorable, he still was very sharp about money. So he and Elizabeth didn't settle their property, after all.

The third experience took place the next day in New York. With Mike Wilding arriving, Elizabeth asked Monty Clift how he'd feel about going with her to meet him. Monty felt fine about it and was obviously not in the least jealous.

The fourth event was the afternoon papers printing a dispatch from Hollywood: Nicky Hilton was engaged to Betsy von Furstenberg, a society girl turned actress.

It all made Elizabeth appreciate Michael Wilding very, very much. He registered at the Hotel St. Regis. Elizabeth was at the Plaza, a Hilton hotel. When she had checked in, she had been told she was a guest of the management and had been installed in a tremendous suite.

The studio called her back to Hollywood for retakes on *Ivanhoe*. Her parents were due to visit Howard Young. "I'll fly back with you," said Michael Wilding. "I don't want you traveling alone."

"But Michael, you have to return to England so soon."

"I know. Don't worry, my pet."

And when she went to check out of the Plaza, she discovered she was not a guest of the management after all. Her bill was twenty-five hundred dollars.

But she had a lovely flight west with Mike Wilding taking charge of everything, never worried, always beside her. In Hollywood, Elizabeth found she need not have hurried. The retakes were trivial, and once they were made, the studio didn't have a script ready for her. But the studio was against her marrying Michael Wilding. He was much too old for her.

Mike took her to visit his best friend, Stewart Granger, who had just married Jean Simmons. The age difference between them was just exactly the age difference between her and Mike, and they were ideally happy. Mike also completely charmed Sara and Francis Taylor.

Mike was with her for a week in Hollywood before he had to go back to London for his next picture. When Elizabeth saw him off at the airport, the tears streamed down her face.

"Don't be blue, darling," he said. "I shall phone you every day and the very moment I am free in February, we'll be married."

He did telephone her every day. She called him sometimes twice a day. MGM still had no picture for her. Her friends kept on saying she must not marry a man twice her age.

The very fact that her love had no expression made it increase. The day she knew Michael was legally free, she determined to wait no longer. She did not want a big wedding such as she had had with Nicky. She yearned for the simplest possible ceremony, at the earliest possible date. Accordingly, one February day she flew alone to London, and as she came into the airport she saw Michael outside the customs barrier, completely relaxed, waiting, her lover, husband, her friend.

CHAPTER SIXTEEN

She ran wildly out into Michael's arms.

"Here, here," he said. "Calm down. Give me those thousands of baggage checks. Give me your passport and while you are about it, you might as well give me all the documents."

Her violet eyes widened with something close to fear. Then she began to giggle. "Oh, Michael," she gasped.

"Oh, no!" he said. "Does that levity mean you have none of them, not your divorce papers nor your birth certificate? My girl, I cabled you about them. This is not Hollywood, remember? This is jolly old England, where we are formal about such things. That's why we couldn't be married in the Church of England, as you wished. Stuffy about divorces here."

"I know. Oh, Michael." She took his arm and hoped he wouldn't be angry.

He wasn't even ruffled. "Come along," he said, laughing. "Once we've registered you into the Dorchester, we'll start on our rounds. We'll have a lot of oaths to take to satisfy the registry bureau."

She knew it was no accident that she was registered for the same suite at the Dorchester she had shared with Peggy when she had been making *Ivanhoe*. It was like Mike to remember she had loved it, to reengage it for her. But she also knew that the hotel's management remembered that it was the same suite from which she had watched the coronation of George VI when she had been a tiny girl of seven. The British were all like that, thoughtful. That was why she would be so happy as the wife of an Englishman.

Later, dressing for dinner, Elizabeth read the statement which Mike had given out about them. "Elizabeth wants to be married to someone who will love and protect her," he had said, "and that someone, by some heaven-sent luck, turns out to be me. I won't let her down."

Actually, Mike Wilding never did let her down.

The morning of her second wedding day, Elizabeth was proudly ready on time, dressed in dove gray with white collar and cuffs. Driving with Anna Neagle to the registry office in Claxton Hall, she saw the street filled with movie fans.

The chauffeur circled to the back of the building. There was a mob there, too, Mike in the middle of it, laughing, trying to reach out to help her and Anna. No one could move until presently a solid line of bobbies created a path for her and Anna.

She ran up the steps of Claxton Hall toward her future husband, and she was so rapturous that she turned to throw a kiss toward the crowd before she went into the little brick building.

Blessedly, however, there were no crowds in there, no cameras, no lights. She drew a long, delighted breath. This wedding wasn't a news event. It was just a wedding such as any girl could have.

She went into another room, square and plain, and saw Mike's mother and father waiting there beside Mike, and near them Herbert Wilcox, Anna's producer-husband. Six people only, including herself.

She found herself standing beside Mike and facing a funny little man with a voice exactly like that of the British comedian, Richard Hayden. She realized that the little man was reading the service, but uncontrollably she started to giggle and could not stop.

She saw Michael grow pale. She saw the little registrar staring at her angrily. She knew she was half hysterical but she could not stop giggling.

Then she heard her own voice say, "I do." She had not heard Mike's voice, but she knew he must have spoken. She waited, and in the silence she realized that she was now legally Mrs. Michael Wilding.

The realization made her giggles stop as quickly as they had begun.

She threw herself into Mike's arms. "May I kiss the groom?" she cried. "May I kiss my darling husband now?"

The mob had grown to nearly three thousand delirious fans when the bridal party tried to leave the registry office. But now the bobbies knew how to control the mob. Elizabeth saw that she and Michael could make a path through to the car easily, and she stopped on the steps of Claxton Hall. "I hope you will all be as happy some day as I am right this moment," she said. "This is, for me, the beginning of a happy end."

The next morning Elizabeth Wilding felt she was newly born, because for the first time since *Lassie Come Home* she could "forget." To "forget" was the phrase she had always used mentally when she tried to get away from being Elizabeth Taylor and just be a girl. It had never once worked during her first honeymoon, during her marriage to Nicky.

But with Michael Wilding it did work. She could "forget" because Mike had planned it that way. First they flew to Paris.

"We are headed for a ski resort called Val d'Isère, my darling," her new husband told her. "I confess I've never been there. We have to take a train from Paris to Grenoble. Then we have to drive three hours up into the French Alps. I am simply trusting to Mike Rennie that it is all right. He recommended it, and he is a lad who loves the pleasures of life."

"Does he now?" said the bride. "What I love is you. Pour me more champagne."

That was the sort of mood she was in.

It was late afternoon when they finally got into Grenoble. There, as promised, a car was waiting for them. They started off merrily, but soon, awed and frightened, Elizabeth huddled silently in Mike's arms.

The road along which they were being driven was so narrow no car could pass them. On the inner side, the cliffs of the Alps rose, continually higher and higher, magnificent under their cover of snow. The outer side of the road dropped off sheer.

The sun set. The dark fell swiftly, so that it seemed very late when they finally reached Val d'Isère, though actually it was only eight o'clock. The exterior of the inn was not reassuring. Neither was the lobby. As Mike registered for them, they saw a few dignified middle-aged French couples sitting dully in a downstairs salon.

There was nothing impressive about their suite, either, though it was scrupulously clean, and in both the tiny parlor and the big bedroom fires were burning in small fireplaces. The bedroom was dominated by a tremendous bed on which a feather coverlet puffed up like a golden soufflé, over just as high a featherbed mattress.

The honeymooners grimaced at one another. "Don't unpack," Mike said. "We'll go back to Paris in the morning. Meanwhile, I'll have more champagne and sandwiches sent up. Right?"

It would have been all right to Elizabeth at that moment if he had suggested they stand on their heads. She was relaxed as she had never been since *National Velvet*. She was safe. She was loved. Ah, how she was loved for hours after they finished that final bottle of champagne.

Proof of her happiness was that she was the first to wake in the morning—she who hated early rising. Though the wooden shutters were tightly closed, there was an unusual light in the room. She bounded suddenly up across the icy floor. She threw the shutters open. Her cry of delight woke Mike, who sprang instantly to her side.

In that instant they knew why Mike Rennie had recommended Val d'Isère. It was like a jewel in a setting of mountains that completely ringed it about. From the cloudless, sharply blue Alpine sky the sun gleamed down upon the snow, white and untrammeled, that covered everything.

Mike said, "Go unpack, my bride. I now venture to say that this may be perfect."

And it was perfect. They had merely eight days of it before Mike was called back to work, but they did not waste a second of them. The days warmed up to eighty degrees. The evenings went down to zero. The Wildings rose with the sun and went to bed with it, too, and in between they skied, they ate, they frolicked, and they made love. For hours on end they made love.

They were the only English-speaking guests at the inn, and no one recognized either of them.

Since dinner was served at one big, common table, Mike would tease Elizabeth, by telling jokes to the French couples. His French was excellent. Then he would tease her by refusing to translate them. But she loved his teasing. In every way he treated her both like an indulged child and a passionate woman. He skied expertly, but he didn't mind holding her up, so that she got some sense of the sport.

He never told her to hurry. He never told her to eat less. He neither advised nor criticized her. He simply loved her, and she adored him in return. When she took hours to dress, he waited, at complete ease, for her. When finally she was ready, he would look at her, smile, and say, "Why, Mrs. Wilding, I had heard that there was a girl named Elizabeth

Taylor, who was the most beautiful girl in the world, but you are much more beautiful than she."

What's more, Elizabeth knew this was true. Elizabeth Wilding was more beautiful than Elizabeth Taylor. There was a glow on her skin and hair, a light in her eyes she had never possessed before. This, she told herself, was the happiest time in her life.

When they returned to London for Mike's picture, she entered into another happiest time of her life. She was not working, and she got her first opportunity to be merely a wife.

Mike had a flat in Mayfair, that most chic of London's very chic sections. It was rich in comfort and taste. Mike had been collecting antique furniture for a long time, and among his most priceless antiques were a devoted old couple who had served him for years. These factotums made it easy for the young bride to entertain, and from their first party the doting Mrs. Wilding discovered that her husband was a fine and witty host.

Except for Jean Simmons, who never visited them except with Stewart Granger, and a very handsome young actor named Richard Burton (yes, *the* Richard Burton), all the Wilding guests were nearly twice Elizabeth's age. They represented all the arts. Their get-togethers were totally unlike Hollywood parties.

The men did not separate from the women and solidly talk business. The women did not solidly discuss babies or servant problems. Neither did the guests play cards or games.

They talked.

They were all talkers, and they talked about everything. Elizabeth listened, hanging on Michael's every clever word. He was an omnivorous reader, a natural dilettante, but he wasn't consciously highbrow or avant-garde. He was an appreciator, and he appreciated music, women, books, food, the theater, wine, all equally. He had very little money. He didn't really need it. His wealth was his delight in the pleasure of living.

Among his group few thought that Elizabeth might have a good mind, she least of all. And, in a sense, she didn't have a mind of her own at that time. She craved the very anonymity of her existence with Mike, her nonthinking, her lovely drifting.

Mike continually indulged her. One Sunday, by way of diversion, he started an oil painting of her. For all of his studying in Brussels, he had never tried working in oil, and he labored over the portrait on several Sundays, abandoning it weekdays for his film work.

It was nearly completed when Elizabeth, puttering around the flat one day, noticed that he had not painted in the lace on her dress. She decided to do it herself.

She liked her handiwork. She backed away from the portrait and decided Michael hadn't put her eyebrows in quite correctly. She wanted them more heavily indicated. She was just finishing when the phone rang. It was Mike calling her from the set, as he did at least every hour.

"What are you doing, my darling?" he asked.

"I'm painting."

"Are you? Good. What are you painting?"

"Me."

"Are you really? What decided you to do a self-portrait?"

"It's your painting, darling, yours of me. I've finished it."

He slammed up the phone not even saying good-bye. She was shocked and scared. She quickly dialed the studio. She was told he had just left. Minutes later she heard his key in the lock. She stood in the middle of the room, rigid with fear. He strode by her wordlessly and looked at the portrait. Then he began to laugh. He threw his arms around her and fiercely kissed her. "Wouldn't you know it?" he said. "You've improved the damned thing."

That incident was prophetic, too, though neither of them recognized it. Elizabeth was better than Mike Wilding in every way. That was her blessing. That was her handicap.

Then MGM cabled Mrs. Wilding to return to Hollywood for *The Girl Who Has Everything*. She was so well disciplined she started packing at once. Mike helped her pack. It occurred to neither of them that she could refuse to return. But she was happy that her contract was running out. She did not mean to sign up again. She would give up her career, just be Mike's adoring wife.

Mike could not go to Hollywood with her. His film was still shooting. She was a bride of nearly three months, when, her face wet with tears, she kissed Mike good-bye at the London airport.

"Without you I don't feel like the girl who has everything," she sobbed.

The studio was playing it very shrewdly for *The Girl Who Has Everything*, as they had when she had loved Bill Pawley. They never mentioned her commercial value to them, but they surrounded her by all the people she loved professionally: Helen Rose to design her clothes, Sidney Guilaroff to do her hair, and on the set the crew members of whom she was most fond. Then MGM, following the theory of its former head, Louis B. Mayer, that you treat an emerald and a movie star like nothing else, offered Elizabeth a new contract for five thousand dollars a week, ten per cent of which was to go to her mother. They also offered Mike Wilding a deal, not at that figure but still rich, and told him he was exactly the type of romantic, drawing-room-comedy actor they needed on their then great roster of fifty-three star names.

Wilding accepted. Swept up in the sentimental tide around her, Elizabeth re-signed. The negotiations took a month, and by that time Mrs. Wilding's mind wasn't on her work at all. Michael had made another of her dreams come true. She was pregnant.

The obstetrician, Dr. Aaberg, told Mrs. Wilding she could expect her child the second week in January, 1953. The radiant Mrs. Wilding telephoned her mother from his office. "Start knitting, Grandma, dear." Then she phoned Peggy Rutledge. "Peggy, huddle with the real-estate agents. The Wildings have to have a house of their own and pronto."

Only then did she call Mike. He was on the set. "Hello, expectant father," she said. "I have a news flash for you."

Mike was forty. This was his first child. His yell of delight alerted the whole acting company, even before he explained it. Greer Garson was a much more important star than Elizabeth Taylor at that time, but she proved herself a romantic, too. Even if there were only a couple of hours' work to go that afternoon, she insisted upon having scenes substituted so that the excited near-father could rush home.

Mike swung Elizabeth into his arms the moment he came through the door and deposited her in his Jaguar, which was still running.

"Let's rush to a store and buy this impending genius a gift." With that he drove at dizzy speed to I. Magnin's, Beverly Hills's most expensive emporium, and bought just what an unborn baby did not need—two huge Teddy bears.

He did not have to work the next day. Elizabeth did. So Mike was the one, aided and abetted by Peggy and realtors, who found a house for them.

It was situated high in the Hollywood hills on a ridge above all its neighbors. This gave it great privacy. Nothing was above it but the sky. Nothing was on any side of it save beautiful vistas. It was very representative of Mike Wilding's taste, carefully casual and expensive—seventy-five thousand dollars back in 1952 when California prices were a fraction of what they are today. It was all in fieldstone, and it was really in three units, connected by roofed walks, around an open patio that contained a heated swimming pool.

One unit held three guest bedrooms and baths. The second was the work unit of kitchen, laundry, and servants' rooms. But it was the main section that had captured Mike, since it was merely two huge bedrooms and two baths plus one enormous L-shaped living-dining room dominated by a tremendous fireplace. Its windows overlooked spectacular views in all directions, to the west row upon row of the Santa Monica mountains falling down to the blue Pacific, to the north the snow-capped Sierras visible between rose gardens and orange groves. Spread out beneath them in all directions were the twinkling lights of Los Angeles. Or as Mike told Elizabeth, "Darling, when we sit up in bed, we will be able to see either Catalina Island or the theaters where your latest films are playing, whichever you prefer."

"You're sure they can't see us?"

"Let's check that out together right now."

There were only two slight stumbling blocks. The Wildings didn't have seventy-five thousand dollars. Neither did they have any furniture.

"I know how to solve part of that," Elizabeth said. "There are the bonds from my child labor. I'll cash them."

"How much do they amount to?"

"I don't know. I'll find out tomorrow."

"If we use those for the down payment, my darling, do you suppose your fine studio would lend me the balance on my contract?"

"Why not?" asked Elizabeth.

That was exactly the studio's attitude the next morning. Why not, indeed? They revised the schedule on *The Girl Who Has Everything* to beat Elizabeth's battle of the bulge, adding an hour on either end of her usual day's work.

Her bonds proved to amount to forty thousand dollars, and the studio readily agreed to advance Mr. Wilding thirty-five thousand dollars, which he was supposed to pay out of his salary when he had it. So Elizabeth did not demur over her extra hours for the same pay. She was too content.

It was like her morning sickness. Every day she awoke with it, but watching her from the huge nine-by-nine-foot bed they had in their otherwise empty dream house, Mike said, "You are actually enjoying your wretched ailment, aren't you?"

"That I am, my angel. It's wonderful to be sick and like it. I like it because I know what it's for. I feel like a contented cat, nice and warm and feminine."

She still felt nice and warm and feminine until the day *The Girl Who Has Everything* wound up, and MGM put her on suspension. To be put on suspension is Hollywood's euphemistic way of saying a person is off salary. Within the next year she and Mike were to be suspended for a year and seven months between them, which is a record even now for one acting family.

Mike, with their unpaid bills piling up, made a joke of it. "We'll call our palace 'Suspension House,'" he said, "and feel like bats hanging from the rafters."

Elizabeth chuckled. For one thing, except for her small flare-up of independence before *Ivanhoe*, she still had no sense of her power over the studio. Her new love and her approaching motherhood were fully occupying her emotions. She was completely in love. Everything was fun to her then.

She and Mike purchased a big curving sofa to be placed beside the living-room fireplace, and a big dining table for the far end of the room. Fortunately the kitchen was fully equipped. They gradually got themselves twin bureaus, twin chairs for their bedroom, and two TV sets against the unlikely time when they might want to watch different programs simultaneously. They purchased a canopied bed for the baby's bedroom and became their own interior decorators.

It was the companionship Elizabeth had always wanted, a domesticity and leisure she had never experienced with Nicky. Together she and Mike bleached down the mahogany walls in the living room, hung drapes, and stretched carpets. Weekends they spent swimming and trying to develop a garden by the pool. Almost every night they ate their dinner in their huge bed, watching TV or the landscapes outside their windows, or, more delightfully, each other.

It was the most relaxed time Elizabeth had ever known, or ever would know again. Except to work, they seldom went out, and except for Stewart Granger and Jean Simmons or the Marshall Thompsons, they seldom had guests. Mike did their cooking. Elizabeth could not even fry eggs.

Many a week went by when by blissful choice they saw no

one save one another. "Darling," said Elizabeth on one of those quiet days, "a year ago, when I was groping for something—I didn't know what—I thought I enjoyed the gay night life. But now that I have you, Michael, I know you are all I need in the world."

She probably did not recognize that one of the reasons for her love of him was that he never demanded anything of her that she did not wish to do, including dieting. Her pregnancy was a continuation of her honeymoon, a flawless time when never a discouraging word was said to her.

She was eating not merely for two but at least for four. She went around barefooted and without make-up in black velvet slacks and a turtleneck sweater. Like most mothers-to-be, she ignored her burgeoning figure and paid attention to her head, and one day she chopped off her hair unevenly, and thus gave herself the first poodle haircut in the film colony. Her face grew increasingly beautiful as her girth increased. There wasn't a day when Mike didn't bring her some present. On the day he brought her a tiny gold cross and chain, she discarded all her jewelry except that and her wedding ring.

Elizabeth quickly discovered all she had to do to get her way with Dr. Aaberg was to bat her double eyelashes. In vain did the obstetrician demand that Mrs. Wilding control her milk drinking. She beamed on him and said, "But I love milk so"—and kept right on lapping it up.

By her eighth month she had put on forty pounds. Daily Mike took snapshots of her. "I want to remember your figure, my darling, as it was the first year of our marriage," he told her, grinning.

She curled up in his arms and giggled back at him. She was beautiful. She was twenty. She was pregnant and totally happy. Mike was totally happy, too. He also was on suspension. They had no income, but they ignored that, and Mike waited on Elizabeth and measured practically to the inch the ten miles that lay between their house and the hospital.

Again and again, alternating between her Cadillac and his Jaguar, he drove the route to time it at different speeds. He kept a suitcase in each car, packed with everything she might possibly need for any emergency. At the hospital he engaged two adjoining rooms, so that Elizabeth would never be separated from her baby. They had agreed on the child's name. A boy would be Michael, a girl Michele.

The baby was due the second week in January, and on the

sixth of January Elizabeth went to see Dr. Aaberg for her next-to-final visit. It was then that Dr. Aaberg discovered that the baby had turned.

"You must go to the hospital this evening, Mrs. Wilding," he said. "I will deliver the baby by Cæsarean section tomorrow morning."

He called the hospital then and found the operating room was not available the next morning. He would have to wait until the next afternoon, either that or operate within a matter of hours.

"We really must not wait that long," he said to his beautiful patient.

"Okay," said the beautiful patient with perfect serenity. "Call my husband, please. Tell him to call my parents and let's go. I'm tired of not knowing what kind of a baby this one is anyhow."

It was five o'clock in the afternoon when she checked into the hospital. Mike was there, pacing up and down. Her mother was crying, and her father was so nervous that he talked incessantly. She smiled at them. She smiled at the attendants getting her ready for the operation.

Not a bit frightened, she said, "Good-bye, my darlings," to the three anxious people leaning over her as she was being wheeled away. "See you in a minute."

Her son was born three minutes before midnight, weighed a tidy seven pounds and three ounces, and a moment before she fell into a profound sleep she named him for the two males she loved best in the world—her husband, Michael, and her brother, Howard.

It was just after dawn that she regained consciousness from the spinal block. Today, she still has total recall of that moment.

"I saw my son and he was purple," Elizabeth says, "purple, my favorite color. On his tiny wrist he had a tag: 'Boy Wilding.' I was so happy that I went back to sleep immediately. It was mid-morning before I woke up again. I looked at my son, and now he was all pink and white with no wrinkles in his skin. He had a beautifully shaped head. I reached for him. His eyes were blue, just like his father's, and I was sure he smiled at me. The nurse put him into my arms. I shall never forget that feeling. They had told me all about those 'baby blues' I might have. I never had them, never for one moment. I had only baby joys."

94

Then she looked up and became aware of her husband, anxiously watching her. "This young man's name is Michael Howard Wilding," she said.

"Yes? Well, personally I shall call him 'Boy Wilding,' as the hospital does. How can I call him Michael? I'll think I'm talking to myself."

Michael had made her laugh as always. "Oh, my darling," she said, "smell this creature. Now I know that the two most beautiful smells in the world are babies and bacon."

"That settles our problems. Let's bottle him and call him Chanel Number Five Hours."

Actually within the next few days they nicknamed him Britches.

Elizabeth, however, had not come through her childbearing as easily as she thought. Dr. Aaberg hospitalized her for five weeks, with only Mike and her parents permitted to see her. She went home by ambulance, and for another three weeks, with day and night nurses in attendance, she had to stay in a hospital bed rented for her.

But she was home again with Mike. She was home with her son, who was completely healthy. Her fans, fortunately, had sent her masses of diapers, booties, blankets, sheets, and bibs, and she was grateful because she and Mike had never thought to buy them. She was able to keep the nurse who had been with Britches at the moment of his birth.

The first day that she was permitted to get up was February 27, her twenty-first birthday. She was on a diet, which, with massage, she hoped, would make her lose a pound a day. Joyously that day she lay out in the sun beside their pool while the masseuse slapped her around.

She started laughing.

Mike, stretched out beside her, holding her hand, asked, "What's so funny?"

"Everything."

"I agree, but what in particular?"

"I was just thinking that here I am, a wife and a mother, having fat pounded off me like a dowager, and today I'm eligible to vote for the first time."

"You are also eligible to be sued, run for office, and be hanged for murder, if that's any comfort." Mike leaned over to kiss her. "Happy birthday. I also think you are eligible to be taken out to dinner tonight, Romanoff's, let's say, with champagne and everything."

"Very reducing, darling. I accept." She felt a stirring of a

95

special excitement. It would be pleasant to go out and see the world from a new mother's eyes.

They took her brother, Howard, and his wife along with them that evening. As she walked proudly through the Romanoff room, she heard the whispers, "So young. So young." She turned back and smiled adoringly at her husband, knowing he must have heard the whispers, too. "You really are so young, you know," she said.

The next day MGM sent her back to work. They had farmed her out again at a great profit, but she got nothing but her regular salary, which by then she very much needed.

A crisis had developed at a rival studio. Vivien Leigh had suffered a nervous breakdown while shooting *Elephant Walk*. Paramount was forced to shut down the picture. There was no chance of Miss Leigh's immediate recovery. Laurence Olivier wanted to get her back to their home in London. To achieve that, Lady Olivier had to be drugged and taken on a stretcher to the plane.

Paramount rushed to MGM to borrow Elizabeth Taylor, and that made one phase of her life come full circle. For the resemblance that could have let her play Miss Leigh's child in *Gone With the Wind* now enabled her to be Miss Leigh's substitute in *Elephant Walk*.

Elizabeth had no power to refuse, and *Elephant Walk* proved to be the toughest acting assignment she had ever encountered. She could do nothing in her own way. To match the actual Vivien Leigh in the background shots, Elizabeth in close-ups had to discipline herself to walk like her, sound like her, look like her.

It was exhausting and unrewarding. Elizabeth hated it, knowing that the public was being half-deceived, since the finished picture would star her, with no mention of Vivien Leigh. There she was, artistically shackled, not getting an extra cent for it, while MGM waxed rich. She simply couldn't give a good performance. But the sense of proportion Mike Wilding had taught her came to her rescue, and she realized she wasn't nearly so irked by the picture as she was by not being able to see enough of Britches.

Daily she left home before he was awake and returned after he was asleep. She lived for Sundays. That was the nurse's day off, and no matter how early the baby woke, she had orders to bring him to his parents' bed.

The moment she left, Mike and Liz began giving Britches his bath. They alternated in feeding him. They would all go swimming together, Britches held in their arms, so that he presently had no more fear of water than he had of air or sunshine.

Working as hard as she did, Elizabeth had little time to study baby books, but presently she solved that problem in her own way. She began inviting to dinner all the young parents she knew. Of course they discussed their wonder children. She rarely joined in the talk. Curled up against Mike, she listened and absorbed. Then on Sunday she tried out the various theories she had heard.

Mike was deeply impressed with the growth of her personality now she was a mother. He told Stewart Granger, "She spends every spare minute with young Mike, and when he's asleep, and she's been away all day, she pores over the hourly charts the nurse has made up.

"And the bedtime stories she tells the boy! He's much too young to appreciate them, but they thoroughly enchant and frighten me. They're a marvelous blend of the classics and her own improvisation, a sort of Jack and the Beanstalk combined with Dragnet."

Granger laughed. "What I should like to watch is Elizabeth's performance."

Mike Wilding stretched out his long length and laughed. "Isn't it fortunate that I am mentally backward and Liz is bright enough to be incapable of worry? Already she's discussing our having another child. She wants to have them close together. She even says she'll arrange to have them between our studio suspensions, so I expect any morning now the MGM accounting department will call to give us the date when we can have another." As Granger laughed, Mike said, "Two more days and Liz will be through with *Elephant Walk*. We plan to become beachcombers, all three of us then, with the Thompsons down at Laguna."

But that day one of Elizabeth's freak accidents happened. They were faking a storm on the *Elephant Walk* set, and a steel splinter from the wind machine flew into her right eyeball. She felt a sudden eye irritation, blinked several times, then went on with the scene.

The next morning, at five thirty when she woke for her studio call, her eye was matted shut. Mike was frantic. He drove her to the specialist's office, held her hand when the ophthalmologist froze her eyeball and made her keep both eyes wide-open as he removed the steel splinter.

"You mustn't work for the balance of this week, and don't

97

bump your head," he instructed Elizabeth. Since it was Friday, Elizabeth had no worry about holding up production.

The following Sunday was Mother's Day. Capering around the pool, little Mike escaped from his parents' grasp for one instant and slipped into the water. Elizabeth and Michael made a dash for him. Their heads banged together. They both saw stars, but laughed as they caught up the baby. They had forgotten all about the doctor's warning.

By mid-afternoon Elizabeth had a towering headache. By late afternoon the eye was steadily tearing. They called the specialist again, who not only immediately hospitalized her, but ordered an immediate operation.

Both realized she could lose not only her sight, but her beauty and her livelihood. Once again, as only four months previously, when Britches had been born, Mike and her parents saw her being wheeled away toward an operating room. Mike saw her lips moving.

"I'm praying with you, too, my darling," he said.

"Don't leave me, Michael."

"Never, my darling."

He stayed beside her all that night after they brought her down. Only at daylight did he slip away to sleep in another room. When he woke and went in to see her, he found that she was awake, though with her eyes bandaged she could see nothing.

"Please notice how clever I am, darling," Elizabeth said. "I've been practicing all morning while you have been doing nothing but sleep. Now watch. See, this is my Kleenex. This is the telephone. There's my radio, and see, I can turn it on. And here's my perfume—no, no, it's not there. Where is it?"

Apparently someone had moved the perfume bottle. Elizabeth sent it shattering on the floor. Michael saw her lips tightening, and he wondered whether under the bandages she was crying. He knew then that she believed she would be blind and was preparing herself for it. He steeled his trained voice to be flippant. "I'm not supposed to tell you this yet, but the hell with it. The doctor says you'll be home by the end of this week, bright as a daisy," he lied.

Mike only lied by three days at that. Elizabeth was home within ten days, and she never mentioned her moments of terror, but she used the memory of them five years later, when she played the insane scenes in *Raintree County*.

MGM put her back to work immediately in a picture called *Rhapsody*, which was finished in midsummer, after which she was due to make *Beau Brummel* in London. For tax reasons, Mike could not stay with her in England but would live temporarily in Paris, and they would meet each weekend.

"I have a large plan in mind," said Michael when they received Elizabeth's schedule.

"I agree to it."

"Without hearing it?"

"Without hearing it. Only what is it?"

"Well, I thought we'd close up this house. We'll take our flawless son to meet his flawless grandparents in England. We will have him christened, and high time, too, if you ask me. Then we'll leave him with his doting grandparents..."

"You are sure they will be doting?"

"Without one moment's doubt. Those magnificent elder Wildings will keep the youngest Wilding while the middle Wildings betake themselves on a second European honeymoon to places like Spain and Italy and even Scandinavia. The idea appeals to you, my exquisite consort?"

Elizabeth wasted no time on words. She answered him with kisses.

Thus, on the afternoon of October 13, 1953, Michael Howard Wilding was christened in fashionable Grosvenor Chapel, Mayfair. Presently his parents, by themselves, were being awed by the vastness of St. Peter's and Vatican City, they were having their fortunes told by Spanish gypsies, and Elizabeth was hiding her eyes against Michael's shoulder so that she wouldn't have to look at her first bullfight. Next they were boating in Stockholm and then dancing together in the beer gardens of Copenhagen.

In Copenhagen Elizabeth said to her husband, "There is only one very little thing lacking in all this heaven."

"I know. Why don't we have him flown over to us?"

"Oh, Michael, can we?"

"I've already arranged it. I knew we couldn't go any longer without seeing the tooth Britches is reported to have cut. He'll be coming over soon with his nanny."

Elizabeth was so excited at the thought of having Britches back that she caught a cold and went to bed for a day. The Danish press called it a nervous breakdown, which naturally made the world press pick up the yarn and caused Sara Taylor to phone from Hollywood. Elizabeth was too content even to deny it. Instead she told her mother her real news: She had just discovered that she was pregnant again.

This time she knew she would be in no hurry to let the

studio know about it. She had been notified to report for *Beau Brummel*, to start the next week. She needed her salary, and she didn't intend to be put on suspension as long as she could hide her condition.

That was the small cloud beginning to develop on her personal horizon. She was becoming aware that Mike had even less money sense than she. She had turned him down when he wanted to buy her a sable coat which he could get at a bargain through a friend. But she knew that even with her salary and his they didn't really have a bean between them.

They were broke because they could not resist giving presents to one another and to young Mike. They were, for instance, always buying one another cars, so that at one point they had six between them. Mike could not resist buying his wife jewelry, particularly when he saw necklaces set with diamonds. He didn't have much resistance when it came to emeralds, either.

As for toys, they both bought everything they saw even though some of them little Mike wouldn't be able to use until he was ready for school.

Still the awareness that they should begin to save some money niggled at the back of Elizabeth's mind. Mike's ability to make life glamorous, while never criticizing her kept her from bringing the matter into the open. When *Beau Brummel* began, they started their weekend holidays. She flew to join Mike in Paris or he flew to meet her in London.

But her emotional calendar began to send out warnings. Small illnesses began. One weekend when Mike met her in London, she caught the flu and was very ill for two weeks. *Beau Brummel* was finished during that time without her. The English papers asked their readers in twenty-four-point type, "Why is Liz so pale? Why are the Wildings having trouble?"

She was so pale because she was actually very ill, she was afraid of miscarrying, and she was overworked. At this moment MGM cabled her to return to Hollywood to go into her fourth picture that year, *The Last Time I Saw Paris*.

The reporters caught up with her at the airport as she bade Michael farewell. Instead of snapping at them, she quipped, "The influenza made me lose twelve pounds. It's better than dieting." She was already learning how to be impervious to press criticism.

In New York she was introduced to Richard Brooks, who was to direct *The Last Time I Saw Paris*. Brooks, a dynamic,

100

brilliant man, thought of her as an important artist. "My first impression of her was that she was the most beautiful woman I had ever seen. But once I began to talk to her, I saw that she was also intelligent and quite disarmingly honest.

"What impressed me was that the real Elizabeth was not the publicity figure that had been created. She had a knack of looking at herself in two lights—at what she was supposed to be according to the press, but also with the honesty and cynicism that comes from disappointment. Her disappointment was that she was not regarded as an actress, but merely as a beautiful girl.

"Actors require love on many levels, and Elizabeth needed more than the love of her husband and child, and even her parents. She needed more than the love she had from her fans. She needed the love of critical approval and I made up my mind that if I could do it, she'd get it for *The Last Time I Saw Paris*."

Of course, the moment she went to Helen Rose to get her dresses for *The Last Time I Saw Paris*, her condition was apparent. Again the picture schedule was adjusted to get all her close-ups done before she would "show."

Mike had nothing to do during this tight shooting schedule. Yet she was working virtually day and night.

She would come home from a particularly hard day at the studio and find big Mike and little Mike lolling by the pool. She realized that such sloth was not her husband's fault. Still, she was enraged when he bought an elaborate set of cameras, meaning to study photography, but then abandoned all the equipment because it was difficult to put the film in.

She was too tired and too emotional to face the fact that his lethargy might be due to frustration. She began losing her temper with him quite regularly, and Mike angered her even more by ignoring her rage. He still loved her as completely as he had from the day of their marriage. It was Elizabeth who was changing. She was beginning to mature. That is one of the dangers in May-and-December marriages. The young change and mature while the mature, fight as they will, age.

Christopher Edward Wilding was born on his beautiful mother's twenty-third birthday, February 27, 1955. Like Britches he had been delivered by Cæsarean section, and she had a bad time with him. Dr. Aaberg warned her against ever attempting motherhood again.

Chris was named for a Wilding ancestor of Charles the Second's reign. Ever since, there had always been a Christopher

Edward in the Wilding line, Mike explained, and in the British Museum there was a medal bearing the original's likeness. There also had been preserved a ring of his, bearing his coat of arms, two shields, and an apple tree. Mike ordered four such rings, tiny ones for each of their sons, and large ones for himself and Elizabeth.

She was very pleased with such sentiment, and she marveled at the increase in love that Chris brought her. In *The Last Time I Saw Paris* she had been playing intense love scenes, and she hoped that her performance conveyed the new feeling she had about love, her wonderful discovery that the more love one gave, the more one had.

She did love Mike and their sons. Yet she discovered she was very eager to get back to work. She told herself that it was probably because they needed cash so desperately. Her second pregnancy had cost much more than her first, the new nurse was very costly, the price of everything seemed to be climbing. Her tax situation was terrible, and Mike wasn't working. It wasn't, of course, his fault, but he got a salary only when he worked. She found herself bickering with him.

When she was able to return to *The Last Time I Saw Paris*, she began hearing, even before the picture reached the public, the kind of critical acclaim she had not received since *A Place in the Sun*. On top of that she learned that George Stevens was borrowing her again for *Giant*. After that, the studio told her, she was going into one of its own super-shows, *Raintree County*, with Montgomery Clift as her leading man.

MGM also found work for Michael Wilding. It lent him to Twentieth Century-Fox for the role of the Pharaoh in *The Egyptian*. The leading role of *The Egyptian* was played by a young unknown named Edmund Purdom. Mike Wilding's role was so small as to be virtually an insult to a man once considered a great English star. But Mike, being under contract and still being so in debt to MGM, could not refuse it.

Knowing how embarrassing such an assignment had to be, Elizabeth was glad that she and Mike did have one great new enthusiasm in common. That was Monty Clift. Monty had returned to Hollywood to make *From Here to Eternity*, had called her, and they had picked up their ironic, emotional friendship right from where they had left it three years before.

Monty and Mike were compatible from the moment she

introduced them, and immediately the Wilding house became Monty's second home. There was always a welcome for him there, there was always food for him there, and good talk. He took to dropping in almost daily, and frequently he brought friends with him. Once he brought Rock Hudson, and this occasion was the beginning of another friendship for the Wildings. Most frequently he brought Kevin McCarthy, his closest pal from Broadway.

Presently the press began asking what was going on between Monty Clift and Elizabeth Taylor. Next they were asking what was going on between Kevin McCarthy and Elizabeth Taylor. *Giant* began, and she went to Marfa, Texas, on location. Rock Hudson was her co-star, and the new sensation in the movie business, James Dean, played the second male role in the production.

Now the press wondered what was going on between James Dean and Elizabeth Taylor?

Elizabeth didn't bother to answer. Her role in *Giant* was the most demanding of her whole career. She was portraying a woman's whole life from girlhood to grandmotherhood, and George Stevens was as severe a taskmaster as ever.

Mike Wilding frequently came down to Marfa, a tiny town in an inaccessible part of Texas. Almost all the time Elizabeth had Britches and little Chris with her.

Stevens had fixed her with a steely eye when she arrived on location with her sons. "Do you have to do this?" he asked her.

She fixed Stevens with an equally steely look. "Yes, I do have to do this. I know how hard you are to work for. Michael is being sent abroad to make a film with Anita Ekberg. I'm not going to have my boys left just with servants. You see, dear George, I know that I won't always be camera-beautiful or camera-young, and I am not going to lose my hold on things that are real."

George Stevens, recalling *Giant*, said later, "Elizabeth had been associating with older people all her life, and there was great maturity about her. But in *Giant* I was asking her to play long scenes that had to do with the heroine's grandchildren. Imagine, at that time of her life. She did it. She got hold of it. So did Rock. They were playing scenes way beyond their years, but they made it work.

"It occurred to me, there at *Giant*, that Elizabeth probably knew a lot more about how to live her life than people with less courage did, in which group I might include myself."

She did have to test her courage, not telling anyone her wretched secret.

She and Michael had had a real quarrel a few days before she had left for Marfa. Mike had begun it by saying, "The happiest years of our marriage were when you were dependent on me."

"Oh, Mike, I'm not your daughter. I'm your wife."

"Yes, darling, I know. But you used to follow me around, and now I either tag you or I'm left alone in a corner."

"Mike, don't be so silly."

"I thought I'd guide you. Now what am I? I am simply Elizabeth Taylor's husband, which is fine work but still..."

She had laughed in response to his deliberately light tone. "Oh, Mike, shut up."

"Yes, my love," he said.

From that day on, they had been friends. Loving and adoring parents to their sons, but only friends.

Mike went abroad while *Giant* was shooting, to make *Zarak Khan,* and returned before her picture was finished, and they were still only dear friends. Her subconscious reacted. She had a series of illnesses and accidents. She was hospitalized for a blood clot on her knee, the result of wearing too tight jodhpurs in *Giant*. She developed a sciatica that made her limp when she walked on location. Later she was hospitalized with what was diagnosed as a twisted colon. For two days following Jimmy Dean's death in an automobile accident, she was so hysterical that Stevens had to shoot the scenes around her.

In the final scenes of *Giant* she played an old woman. Off camera, too, she projected herself into her middle age when she might be plain of face and when no man would desire her. She thought of Britches as possibly a businessman and young Chris as attending college. What of their future? What, what of them? What was she providing for them? What was Mike providing for them? Just charm?

She felt used up. She still loved Michael. She respected him, her very best friend. But a husband was not supposed to be one's best friend. The situation between them was humiliating.

Giant was finished. She returned home, and now almost nightly she and Michael were surrounded by Rock Hudson, Monty, Kevin McCarthy, and often by Humphrey Bogart, the Grangers, and the group Bogie called "The Holmby Hills Rat Pack."

When *Giant* was released, she was widely acclaimed. She was pleased but not thrilled. Her relationship to her work had changed. She was no longer the naive little girl of *A Place in the Sun*. Now she watched her own work and saw how very much more she had to learn.

Spring in southern California is often a foggy, dreary season and the month of May is the gloomiest. May, 1956, was no exception. *Raintree County* was about to shoot in Kentucky. It was Monty Clift's idea that he and Elizabeth rehearse some of their scenes together with Kevin acting as their dialogue coach. Kevin was not getting on well as an actor and had settled for being one of the assistant directors on a film that the Broadway showman, Mike Todd, was about to make in Hollywood, *Around the World in 80 Days*.

Around the World in 80 Days was already shooting in other parts of the globe, but its Hollywood sequences would begin in June. In the meantime Kevin was happy to coach Monty and Liz nightly at her house, with Mike Wilding sitting in as a kind of charming critic on the hearth.

Being such a good host, Mike Wilding was generous with the drinks, which meant the co-stars of *Raintree County*, plus Mr. Wilding and their drama coach, often got slightly loaded.

This was the case on the night of May 14, 1956, when shortly after midnight, Monty in his car, with Kevin following in his, took off down the winding road from the Wilding hilltop. It was one of the California May's foggiest nights and you could not see a fender before your face.

Elizabeth had just snapped off the lights in her living room when she heard the crash. She and Mike stared at one another for one horrified moment, and then catapulted out into the fog and rushed down the hill.

Monty's car had struck a tree head on, and he had been hurled head first into the dashboard.

Kevin was unhurt. He was, in fact, in Monty's car, trying to lift him. Instantly Elizabeth pushed Kevin aside. Monty's face was covered with blood from his broken nose and numerous cuts. But she noticed something even more threatening. Monty, gasping for breath, was choking on his own tongue.

Instantly, she plunged her hand into his mouth and got his tongue back in place. "Call Dr. Kennemer," she ordered her husband. "Wipe the blood off his face," she ordered Kevin.

She waited to faint until after the ambulance had taken Monty away to the Cedars of Lebanon Hospital.

The next day the start on *Raintree County* was delayed several weeks. Rex Kennemer assured Elizabeth that Monty would survive, though he would have to undergo considerable plastic surgery to avoid prominent facial scars.

Visiting Monty daily at the hospital, Elizabeth shuddered at his bandages, thinking that such a wreck might have happened to her on that twisting road. She wanted to get away from that road. She wanted to get away from her home. She was in a mood for escape, yet knew she had no excuse for escape.

Suddenly all her new friends bothered her. She stayed home night after night with her children and her husband, but alas, after the babies were asleep, she and Mike had nothing to say to one another.

They didn't quarrel. They were too fond of one another. They were too polite.

Monty slowly recovered, and the studio started the scenes of *Raintree County* in which he was not needed. Elizabeth found her escape in them, but since she was playing a half-crazed girl, she was not made happy by them.

On June 29 Kevin McCarthy asked the Wildings whether they would like to be guests on Mike Todd's yacht when some scenes of *Around the World in 80 Days* were being shot near Santa Monica. Todd's idea, McCarthy said, was that he would have ten guests. Yes, the yacht was big enough to sleep ten. They would sail up the coast for dinner in Santa Barbara and could drive home from there if they wished.

"I hear this Mike Todd is a very colorful character, a kind of theatrical pirate, and a fine host," said Michael Wilding. "Shall we go, darling?"

"Why not?" said Mrs. Wilding.

CHAPTER SEVENTEEN

If his name had been Lorenzo de Medici and he had been born in fifteenth-century Florence, the bold spirit who called himself Michael Todd could not have been more complex, more flashily creative, nor a greater lover of beautiful objects.

He put women first on his list of beautiful objects.

His real name was Avrom Hirsch Goldbogen. He was born in Minneapolis, Minnesota, about 1908, give or take a year, and he was to become the most dynamic American showman since Barnum.

He never was ashamed of having no schooling. He was always proud of being a Jew. Poverty couldn't scare him. He was raised in it.

But he always lied about his age. He hated growing old, which was just about the only thing in life he did hate.

He didn't know that he was a natural-born dream merchant until he reached the advanced age of seven. A pitchman came through Minneapolis, unloading fake gold watches, and hired the bright-eyed Avrom as shill, to make the first buy so that the gullible crowd would follow his example.

The Goldbogen family needed any extra dimes that Avrom might bring in, but that was not why the boy took the pitchman's job. A slum child soon accepts realism—such realism as prostitution, alcoholism, thievery, and prison stretches. He was being given a chance to sell illusion. The idea enchanted him.

Avrom made a great shill. He used his youth to persuade people to buy the fake gold watches. He used pathos, enthusiasm, or whatever mood was needed. He and the pitchman hit a dozen locations in Minneapolis one breath ahead of the cops before the pitchman skipped town.

After that Avrom attended school only when the law drove him to it, but even at such times he found out how to turn a quick buck. When he was in his early teens, the Goldbogens moved to Chicago. Wacker Park High School was indicated for Avrom. Actually he liked learning, but between classes on the playground he made more than books pay off.

The other boys, at recess, got into crap games. Avrom stayed out but took 10 per cent of their action for acting as lookout. He'd hiss "John Law" at exactly the right moment, and it was a poor day when he didn't net five bucks at least.

At seventeen he married a sweet Jewish girl named Bertha Freshman. There would be other girls in his life, and eventually they separated, but Bertha adored Avrom until the day she died.

At eighteen Avrom retitled himself Mike Todd and became president of a two-million-dollar construction company. Two years later he didn't have the money to pay his rent.

He had an idea, though. The Century of Progress Fair was opening. It needed shows for its Midway. Mike's idea was to have a beautiful girl, half-dressed, do an exciting dance, stepping in and out of real live flames.

He had the girl, too—a girl willing to die for him. And she nearly did, several times when the flames got out of control.

Mike loved the Midway. The Midway made him flush again. Mike was so grateful to his flame girl he wanted to marry her.

Bertha wouldn't hear of it. She had borne him a son, and she allowed him to be named Mike Todd, Jr. Mike was crazy about his son. When the Chicago Fair closed, he closed the file on the flame girl, too.

New York had announced a World's Fair for 1938. As befits our largest city, this one, the management said, would be long on culture. Mike began to dream about it. Privately he approved of culture. Years later the critic George Jean Nathan said, "Mike's an Oxford man posing as a mug." Mike Todd's enemies phrased it differently. They said, "Mike Todd's a con man who wants to be an artist."

In a way both points of view were accurate. Mike was a confidence man who sold people on the idea that every day was Christmas. But he made his own life come up that way, too—all tinsel and lights and gift-giving and gregariousness. The more people there were around him, the more he loved it, and if some of them turned out to be enemies, they only stimulated him. Naturally he exasperated many people, skyrocketing up as he did, from no background, no ancestry, no education.

Mike went to New York. There was a girl there, too. She was leggy, witty, intellectual—and a stripteaser. Her name was Gypsy Rose Lee. Mike, who perceived that most of the culture at the New York World's Fair was laying a bomb, decided to give the people a long look at beautifully bared Gypsy.

Mike wanted to marry her. That was one of the interesting things about him. Considering his environment and opportunities, he was nevertheless very conventional in his attitude to love.

So once again he asked Bertha for his freedom and once again she refused, and Mike couldn't force her, because of young Mike. But Mike told Gypsy he was going to conquer Broadway.

And he did. With his profits from the New York World's Fair, Mike tackled the Big Street. He went into a dozen enterprises and often was wealthy on Friday and stone broke by Monday, but he kept on trying, and presently "Mike Todd Presents" blazed in lights atop four hits—*The Hot Mikado*, *Star and Garter*, which starred Gypsy, *Mexican Hayride*, and *Up in Central Park*.

How to use money was instinctive with him. He could always get it, but he didn't keep it. Bertha Todd blossomed out in mink coats of every color. Young Mike Todd, Jr., attended the best prep schools. The romance between Mike and Gypsy waned. Joan Blondell, the golden-haired, curvaceous movie star, took her place. Mike offered Bertha any price for his freedom. Bertha wouldn't budge.

Then suddenly, under mysterious circumstances, Bertha was dead. She had been discovered by a neighbor, lying in a pool of blood on the floor of her kitchen. After she was rushed to the hospital and into surgery, the doctors saw that the tendons of her right hand had been deeply severed. They stopped the loss of blood. They sewed up her hand, but it was too late. Even as she lay on the operating table, her life flickered out.

The police came after Mike. It was easy enough to prove that he had been calling on Bertha just a few hours before the accident. Mike was held for hours and given the third degree until the word came from the coroner. The autopsy proved that Bertha had actually died of a heart attack, there on the operating table.

So Mike was released, but it was never clear whether Bertha had cut herself by accident or design.

Mike was free to marry Joan Blondell, his heart's desire. But like many another forbidden love, their infatuation lasted longer than their marriage. They were married in 1947. They were divorced in 1950. They had no children.

Then Mike fell for another love, Lady Luck. Maybe that was an expression of disillusion with real women at that time. He was worth a couple of million when he started courting Lady Luck. Night after night he was at the gaming tables. It didn't matter what the game was, or the setting. He would take anybody's bet on anything. So Lady Luck took him.

He lost his millions. He lost his credit. His enemies along Broadway grinned with delight. They forced him into bankruptcy. He owed $1,100,000. Broadway decided it had buried him for good.

It hadn't. Lighting his last fifty-cent cigar, not knowing where his next meal was coming from, Mike said, "I ran a million dollars into a shoestring." He grinned. "I've often been broke, but I've never been poor. Now I've got to earn me some new money."

It took him two years before he made enough cash to pay off the last dime of that $1,100,000.

In 1955, clear of debt but flat broke, he decided to invade Hollywood. It was, to his mind, the logical next step. He had never made a movie. He decided his movie would be a big show. The biggest, the costliest, with the most stars in it, and it would make more money than any other movie ever produced.

So he started on *Around the World in 80 Days*, which did have a host of stars, and which won the Academy Award.

What did Mike Todd use for money when he started the film?

Illusion. He sold illusion to the stars whom he approached. He didn't promise them fabulous salaries. After all, they were used to fabulous salaries. He sold them on the idea of what he called "cameo portraits," small, artistic appearances that would be quite unlike anything they had ever done before.

Prosaic producers called such small roles "bits," and no star would do a "bit." But cameos were different. He said he would pay them off in paintings by Picasso or automobiles by Rolls-Royce, or something equally unusual. He didn't insult his stars by talking money. He flattered them by recognizing how cultured they were, even if sometimes their culture was very, very new.

Next Mike sold illusion to the bankers who loaned him the

110

money, to the writers who did his script, to the directors, to the music men. They fell for it, from Sinatra to Red Skelton, from David Niven to Marlene Dietrich, and some thirty other top personalities in between. Marlene even fell for Mike himself, and he returned that interest until Evelyn Keyes came along.

A note on Miss Keyes: witty, intellectual, beautiful. In 1956 she was Mike Todd's favorite girl. She was definitely a free soul. She had been married to and divorced from two of Hollywood's most talented directors, Charles Vidor and John Huston. Superior men were always attracted to her, and she to them.

On the thirtieth day of June, 1956, when Mr. and Mrs. Michael Wilding went with their friend Kevin McCarthy aboard Mike Todd's rented yacht to watch a scene being made for *Around the World in 80 Days*, Miss Keyes was very much the lady in possession.

That particular day was one of the many, many days during the picture's making that Mike Todd was one jump ahead of the sheriff. But no one would have guessed it from the gala atmosphere.

Mike's guests were Mr. and Mrs. Art Cohn (Mr. Cohn is Mike's official biographer and the author of *The Nine Lives of Mike Todd*); Kurt Frings, the agent, and his then-wife, Ketti Frings, the author; Richard Hanley, Mike's secretary, who now is Elizabeth Taylor's secretary, and Evelyn Keyes.

Actually, according to Mr. Cohn's book, the Wildings did not mingle with the other guests. They sat apart with Kevin and imbibed a goodly amount of Todd's champagne. But there was a moment when they were all disembarking for Santa Barbara, when the eyes of Mike Todd and Elizabeth Taylor met for the first time; and the man who loved beautiful objects looked at the most beautiful woman in the world.

She had changed into skin-tight flamingo pants and a simple cashmere sweater that exactly matched her eyes. Mike Todd and Elizabeth Taylor, as they looked at one another, didn't say a word.

Nevertheless, in that moment, they had communicated.

Two weeks later in his vast rented mansion Mike Todd gave a dinner for Ed Murrow, the news commentator, and his wife. It was a simple Todd party of two hundred guests, among whom were Mr. and Mrs. Michael Wilding.

Evelyn Keyes was distinctly dressed down for this occasion, wearing a casual Mexican skirt and blouse. Just why no one ever knew. The other ladies wore formal dinner dresses. Mrs. Michael Wilding was in white satin, very décolleté, her dark hair, her dark tan very much in contrast. She wore diamonds about her throat.

Mrs. Wilding and the host exchanged no more than a few words. But again their eyes met. Mr. Wilding was his most charming self. If he saw that glance between his wife and his very new friend, he did not show it. In fact he went home early, leaving Mrs. Wilding to be brought home around two A.M. by Kevin McCarthy.

A few days later at another party Evelyn Keyes said to Pandro Berman, "That poor little Liz Taylor. I'm so sad for her. She's so unhappy."

Berman said, "Don't worry about Liz. Don't let it concern you. If she's unhappy, she will find her way out of it very quickly. She always has."

One week after that, on July 19, 1956, the papers headlined an item that must have intrigued Evelyn Keyes. It was the announcement of the formal separation of Michael and Elizabeth Wilding. "To give us an opportunity to work out thoroughly our personal situation," they were quoted as saying.

Hollywood buzzed. In Hollywood's experience it is a rare woman, let alone an actress, who separates from one man unless she has another within her sights. That is, unless she is forced into it. By 1956 Hollywood knew that Elizabeth Taylor was not to be forced into anything.

That afternoon Mike Todd telephoned Elizabeth Taylor for the first time. He asked when he might see her. He wanted to discuss something serious. Caution held her. The sound of his voice brought back to her that moment on the yacht when her eyes had met his. But suppose she had read more in his eyes than had actually been there? Suppose he was calling her just to try to get her to go into *Around the World in 80 Days*? Marlene Dietrich was in that. Evelyn Keyes was in that. Elizabeth Taylor would not be in that, not even if the studio lent her out for it.

She said, to keep it on a business level, "Could we meet at Benny Thau's office tomorrow, say, three o'clock?"

"Great," said Mike Todd.

She was scarcely late at all for their appointment. She found Mike Todd chatting easily with Benny Thau. She also discovered that he had an office at MGM, which he used for conferences on *Around the World in 80 Days*.

"Let's go over to my office and talk, shall we?" he asked.

She smiled her lovely smile at him. "Lead the way, sir." She said it laughingly. He did not respond with laughter, however. He simply walked ahead of her. And she followed.

His office was only a few steps from Benny Thau's. As they came into its anteroom, Elizabeth was impressed by its relaxed and friendly atmosphere. This she had not expected. A couple of writers were sitting in one corner, playing gin rummy. A music man was there with a song he wanted to discuss. Mike's secretary smiled and said, "Boss, there are a thousand phone calls for you."

"No calls," said Mike. "No interruptions."

He opened the door to his private office, ushered Elizabeth in, and closed the door quietly. Then he sat behind his desk. There was a couch against the opposite wall, and with her trained grace Elizabeth sank down knowing the easy skirt of her dress would swirl around her. She snuffed her cigarette out in the ash tray on the coffee table before her. She waited.

The silence lengthened. When he finally spoke, his voice was gentle.

"I love you," said Mike Todd. "I am going to marry you."

She sucked in her breath. No buildup. No "by your leave." Just "I am going to marry you." How did this man dare to talk to her that way? But how wonderful the assurance and boldness of him. What could she say? "Take me"? What should she say? "This is so sudden"?

She was mesmerized. This was a man such as she had never encountered. If he moved toward her, should she submit?

But he did not move. He stayed quiet behind his desk.

She lifted her eyes and felt the shock of his honesty, and she knew that she could not be phony with him. She wouldn't dare. He was too powerful.

"I love you," he repeated. "I'm going to marry you."

There were no fireworks when, three days after she had seen Mike Todd at the studio, it was announced that Elizabeth and Michael Wilding had decided to make their separation permanent. When the reporters went inquiring, they discovered that MGM, with unprecedented efficiency, had wound up the studio shooting on *Raintree County* and had already flown Elizabeth Taylor to Danville, Kentucky, for the location scenes.

What was the sense, the studio pointed out, in chasing Elizabeth down there when Mike Wilding was still around, and ready, as always, to answer any questions?

The debonair Wilding received the press in his hilltop home. He gave the reporters the courtesy of not beating about the bush. He said, "Liz and I sat down and decided that we would sell our house. We will divide the money and share the custody of our boys. Liz is to have them nine months of the year, and I will have them for three."

Before the reporters even got a chance to ask the question, Mike added, "I don't feel bitter. I am adult enough to reconcile myself to circumstances. Elizabeth and Mike Todd did not see one another alone until we were separated, and I wish to say that Todd's conduct in this whole thing has been above reproach."

He crossed the length of the beautiful room and poured the reporters another drink. The lightness came back into his tone.

"Tomorrow I shall be gone from all this. As perhaps you've heard, my father has been living with Liz and me since my mother died. So now I'll see him settled in a London flat, after which I'm off to Sweden to make a film.

"I can't tell you just when or where Elizabeth will file the divorce action. With both of us working, we may have to juggle our time a bit, but she knows I am always available if she needs help in expediting any legalities."

He paused. The reporters couldn't think of a question to ask. Every newsman knows there is nothing quite so defeating as everyone in a headline position behaving well.

Thus, gracefully, Mike Wilding bowed out of Hollywood, and Elizabeth's life.

CHAPTER EIGHTEEN

Mike Todd left for New York almost immediately after his proposal to Elizabeth, but distance proved no obstacle to his lovemaking.

Over three thousand miles he courted her like a combination of emperor and Cyrano de Bergerac. There was no hour of the day when he did not either telephone or wire her, write her a love letter, or send her a gift, and there were many hours when he did all four.

The day of the official Wilding parting MGM adroitly slipped Elizabeth into Louisville, to dodge her fans as well as to avoid inquiring reporters. But there was no way of slipping her away from Mike Todd.

Very secretly a chartered plane brought her in, far down the Louisville landing field, an hour before the time the studio had rumored she would arrive at the airport proper. Monty Clift and a chauffeur met her, with a disreputable old sedan. The plan was to drive her swiftly by back roads to the sleepy little village of Danville, where she would stay for the duration of the shooting.

Yet even as Monty, grinning, handed her into what he tagged "the best piece of getaway-car casting I ever saw," a messenger boy drove up and delivered to Elizabeth a small jeweler's package.

As the car sped through the soft, blue Kentucky twilight, Elizabeth tore the package open. A card fell out. "This is for weekdays," it read. "Can't get your engagement ring to you before Sunday."

Even Monty gasped at the size and splendor of the pearl and gold ring. "Take the month off, Bess Mae," Monty said. "That must be equal to your month's pay."

"More," said Elizabeth, gazing at the jewel rapturously.

The studio had gone to great pains to conceal where she

115

was to live in Danville. They had chosen a charming small house, far back from the road, hidden behind a lovely garden and great trees.

Yet even as the dusty old sedan pulled up before it, a young black maid came running down the path. "Oh, ma'am, New York is on the phone."

Elizabeth got out of the car so quickly she barely heard Monty saying, with irony, "I have a house, too, a proper distance away from you, and Dmytrik has a house a proper distance from me. I'll call you for dinner later."

As she raced through the door, she saw bouquets massed everywhere in the tiny sitting room. Through an open door into an old-fashioned bedroom she saw further bouquets, the scent of them heavy and beguiling on the air.

It was, of course, Mike Todd on the wire.

"Oh, Mike, dear, dear Mike, I'm out of breath. I just this instant got here and..."

"I know. I timed it like that. Called Hollywood to see when you left. Called Louisville to find out when your plane got permission to land. Figured out the driving time to Danville. I didn't want you there one second before you talked to me."

"Mike, I—I don't know what to say to you. You overwhelm me. I've got your pearl ring on now. It's the most beautiful ring I ever saw. It's the most beautiful ring any girl ever had. Oh, Mike, and here's this house packed with flowers and I know, without looking, they have come from you and oh, darling..."

"Are you going to bust out crying because I love ya? If you do, you'll never have a dry eye the rest of your life. Listen to me, kid, everything about you is real and rare. But do you know the craziest thing? You yourself don't know it, the woman there is in you, the actress. God help you, you're an artist, and I never met a happy actress yet, let alone one who is a happy artist. So that's what I've got to do for you, you hear me? I gotta let you be that artist, and I gotta show you how to be happy at the same time."

That first night in Danville Mike Todd talked to Elizabeth with such verbal extravagance for two straight hours. It was the greatest flattery imaginable, and an approach no man had ever made to her. Besides its obvious appeal to her ego, it was also an appeal to her mind and latent ambition.

She listened half-mesmerized, as she had to previous calls in Hollywood when he had talked to her in the same vein. Part of Todd's subtlety was that he never mentioned her

116

beauty. But in Danville, along with the daily gifts, the scores of wires, and the masses of flowers continually arriving, he also set up another pattern.

He said to her finally that first night, "Hey, it's time for you to eat. Don't eat alone. Go with Clift or Dmytrik. Eating alone is torture. Go right now. I'll call you back at your bedtime."

She did go to dinner with Monty, though she was so bemused she did not know where they went, or what she ate. As she returned to the little house the phone was ringing again. She and Mike talked another two hours before he said, "Shut-eye time for you. You've got a seven A.M. call tomorrow morning."

"How do you know that? How did you know when I came in to catch this call?"

"I found out. And tomorrow I'll know what time you break for lunch, and I'll call you then, and I'll know when you wrap up the day's work, and I'll call you then. Nothing's to interfere with your giving your greatest performance, kid, not even me loving ya."

Elizabeth soon figured that Mike was calling some assistant on the film each day to keep track of her time schedule, but she was both touched and flattered when she discovered he had also called the Coast and had a script of *Raintree County* sent to him so that he could also know exactly what scenes she was doing.

Thus he telephoned her every morning, to wake her, and every night, to wish her good-night, and in between, sometimes a dozen times during the day just to talk to her. They discussed her scenes. They discussed his production. They discussed anything from the weather to badminton. She learned not to be startled if, in the same twenty-four hours, his calls would come from London, and then from Paris, and sometimes the last would find him back in New York again. She asked him one day, "How much is your phone bill?"

"By the month. A couple of thousand, but this month I'm putting over the biggest project of my life—project Liz—so I expect it to triple that."

He was too smart always to talk to her about herself. Elizabeth came to realize also that he was too extroverted to brood about himself, but loved to have her share his projects, his enthusiasm. He told her about his conferences with Victor Young, the composer who was scoring *Around the World in 80 Days*. He put David Niven on the wire to her when they

117

were conferring in London, David being the lead in *Around the World in 80 Days*. He had Cantinflas, his Mexican star, speak to her when they were together in Mexico. Another time Mike told Elizabeth all the intricacies of leasing his Todd-A-O process to the theaters, a process he had bought when his enemies froze him out of Cinerama, the first wide-screen process.

There she was, working hard in a tiny Kentucky town, in the humid July weather, but Mike Todd, over long distance, brought to her a life of affable abundance from a dozen levels. The engagement ring he had sent her was a twenty-nine-carat diamond worth ninety-two thousand dollars. She wore that on her third finger, left hand; the pearl ring, worth nearly thirty thousand dollars, on her right hand. Casually one day he sent her a wide, gold bracelet with a string of diamonds threaded through it. Then he sent her great diamond ear-rings. And with every phone call he brought her more and more into the vivid world of his multitudinous activities.

"Over those five weeks of phone calls," Elizabeth said later, "Mike Todd and I came really to know one another. I had never in all my life talked as I did with him. There was nothing we did not discuss—ourselves, Broadway, Hollywood, food, people, travel, our likes and dislikes, sex, everything. Mike thought he was hard, but as I listened to him, I knew that I had never met anyone with such integrity, honesty, and feeling."

Mike phrased it in slang. "Liz digs me," he said. "She digs me deep. It's chemistry. That's why she's gotta marry me. She's the realest dame that ever was."

Hour by hour they fell more and more in love. They grew so in love that Elizabeth discovered she even dared disagree with him. That was a new source of freedom to her, she who had been forced to obey so many orders since childhood. One night during one of their calls she became so exasperated that she shouted, "I hate you, Mike, I hate you!" and slammed down the phone.

It rang immediately. "How can you hate me when I'm so lovable?" Mike asked.

They often talked until two in the morning, and once when they got on the subject of religion, they talked all night. Mike told her his feelings about his Jewish faith, and Elizabeth was suddenly aware of how indebted she was to Stanley Donen for the insight he had given her. She told him how she had

118

studied Catholicism for Nicky's sake but still had not found faith.

So engrossed were she and Mike in their religious discussion that Elizabeth was startled at hearing a knock on her bedroom door. "Hold it, darling," she said, "till I find out why the maid is waking me in the middle of the night."

It was then that she noticed the sunlight streaming into her room. She began to laugh. "Mike, darling, the car is here to take me to location. It's a good thing I'm playing a mad scene today, because the circles under my eyes may get me praised for realistic acting."

Mike called her twice that day on location to see how she was holding up.

"I'm wonderful," she said. "Who needs sleep when somebody like you loves them?"

"Just the same, you need a rest. Have they mentioned a layoff to you over Labor Day? It's this weekend, you know."

"Mike, nobody has layoffs on location."

"Oops, pardon me. I'll call you back at your dinner time."

For the first time since she had known him, she felt emptied out as he hung up on his call. When finally she filmed the last shot of the day, she was so tired she cringed as she saw the production manager coming toward her. She did not want to talk to anyone. She simply wanted to get back to the little house, wait to hear Mike's voice again.

"We just got a message from the Coast, Miss Taylor," the production manager said. "They have rearranged our shooting schedule. It gives you two weeks off beginning tomorrow morning. The studio said you want to go to New York. Is that right? If so, I have reservations for you out of here on tomorrow's first flight east. Okay?"

In that instant, her energy was back. In that instant, she felt her blood blazing. Mike had done this. How, she did not know, but he had done it. She would see him, be alone with him, have time for love, would know love again after so long without it.

She managed to keep her face blank. "Yes, thank you, that's fine. Send a car to pick me up in the morning, will you please?"

It was she who called Mike first that night. "Mike, you wizard, how did you arrange it?"

"I lost a couple of games of gin to the right people."

"No—really how?"

"That's how."

"Oh, Mike, two weeks. Mike, you'll meet me at the airport?"

"I'm there already."

"Oh, Mike. I love you so."

"I love you more. I'll show ya how much more. Now go to sleep till tomorrow, baby."

She was the first person out of the plane door the next afternoon in New York, but Mike was already halfway up the steps to her. His arms were around her, and she was not conscious of anything more at that moment.

The other disembarking passengers struggled past them. Photographers crawled around them. Microphones were held close to them.

Mike said, his arms still around her, "There's a chartered plane waiting for us just a couple of steps away."

"Is there? What for?"

"For Atlantic City."

"Are you and I going to Atlantic City?"

"Yep. The girl I love once told me she was happiest by the sea, and the Atlantic is the nearest sea I could hire in a hurry."

"Oh, Mike, how beautifully crazy you are."

"Shall we go now?"

"If you say so. If you say no, we won't."

"Will you always be this obedient?"

She giggled. "I doubt it."

"I doubt it, too. Come on, Obedient, shake your tail."

Atlantic City over Labor Day weekend was crowded and tawdry, and Elizabeth loved every moment of it. She loved the scent of cheap food frying in the boardwalk lunchrooms. She loved the sharp, salt air of the Atlantic. She loved the crowds. She loved the noise. She loved the garish hotel. And she loved Mike Todd, adored Mike Todd.

On Sunday morning she and Mike saw, by the New York papers, that their conduct at La Guardia airport had been in bad taste. "That does it," said Mike. "You've sullied my reputation. Now you gotta make me respectable. Wait here a minute, kid."

He was gone for more than half an hour. When he returned, he held out a battered jeweler's box to her. "It's the best I could find," he said, "and you know I get nothing but the best for the dame I love."

The box held a very old-fashioned wedding ring that obviously had been pawned. It was in heavy gold, scratched with years of wearing, and set in it were garnets so small as to be practically invisible. It couldn't possibly have cost more than twenty dollars.

"Oh, Mike, this ring has been loved for years and years."

"Like I'll love you."

"Darling, I can't wear it with any other ring. It's too— too—well—sincere." She took off his ninety-two-thousand-dollar diamond, his thirty-thousand-dollar pearl. She stretched out her bare left hand. "Now," she said.

He held her close in his arms as he put it on her third finger. "With this ring I marry you, deal doll, till I get to do it legally."

The tears splashed down her face. "Mike, I'm warning you. After you do marry me, I'll be like Ruth in the Bible. Whither thou goest, there I go with you, Buster."

He leaned over and kissed her. "Till death do us part." He didn't know he was making a prophecy.

Their holiday was quickly over.

"Tuesday after Labor Day, that's when New York begins," Mike told Elizabeth. "Me, I gotta get back to work. On the other hand, you've still got nearly two weeks of big, fat leisure. Would you wanta...?"

She mimicked him. "Yes. I wanta. I wanta, wanta."

"It won't be one long laugh, kid. I'll be in conferences all day and maybe all night. In them I'm no lily. What will you do with yourself all the time?"

"Sit in your office and learn you by heart. Or maybe stay in the hotel and dream about you all day long."

"A beautiful dame like you would be happy doing that?"

"This dame would."

She sat in his offices and began to know him. The air was dreadful with cigar smoke. The language was frequently dreadful, too. She wasn't really listening, though. She felt relaxed, spineless as an amoeba.

He seldom spoke to her during those days as she sat, surrounded by men, absorbed and waiting, but time and again his eyes flashed to hers and they needed no words. Unselfconsciously he would rush across the room, kiss her, then rush back to his desk, not losing a moment of the discussions around him. She saw that he did everything at top speed and with clarity. She saw how necessary friends and sentiment were to him. He was forever calling Eddie Fisher long distance in Hollywood. He had a score of New York buddies he called every day, and other pals in London, Rome, and Paris. Sometimes the conferences continued till midnight or later. Sandwiches, washed down with coffee or Cokes, would be hastily eaten instead of dinner. Mike never drank anything alcoholic. Nevertheless, on such evenings, he always remembered to order champagne for her.

On the days when business took him away, she stayed in her hotel, doing nothing whatsoever, just waiting for his calls. Even on those days he would usually manage to clear an hour for her, and then it was his delight to take her shopping. He bought her furs. He bought her gowns, and more jewels. One day he trotted her into a most expensive milliner's, and when the wand-thin milliner brought out fifty hats from which she could choose, she stared at them, bewildered. After all, she was California-raised and not accustomed to wearing hats. "Oh, wrap up the whole fifty of them and send them to her hotel," Mike commanded.

Mike wrapped her in luxury, whether it was the best table at the best restaurant, the best seats at the hit plays, or the best diamonds at the best jewelers. "For you, kid, I deliver the tinsel under the tinsel," Mike said. She laughed, not knowing quite how to explain to him that what thrilled her more than his gifts was that wherever she went with him in New York, it was he who commanded the attention. She was not Elizabeth Taylor with a new date. He was Mike Todd with a new girl.

As the euphoric two weeks spun by, she pushed back into her mind the fact that she had to return to the Coast on Sunday, *Raintree County* having wound up shooting in Kentucky.

Early that final Sunday morning Mike called for her with a chauffeured limousine. They were swiftly driven north from New York to a pretty village called Croton, near the Hudson River.

"You got any idea why we're up here?" asked Mike.

"Nope. It's pretty, though, sort of like Italy."

"Aren't you curious as to why we're here?"

"Nope, not as long as you stay with me. I am a silly, trusting young girl."

"Oh, no you're not. You've just become a grandmother, and I am taking you to meet your grandson."

"Mike Todd, you really do think of the most original things. Do I really have a grandson?"

"Yes. He's four months old. His name is Cyrus and you are

about to meet him, his mother, and his father, too. His father is related to me. He's my son."

"Oh, Mike, you softie. You dear, adorable softie. Tell the man to drive faster. I'm aging by the minute."

Elizabeth liked young Mike at sight. She liked his wife, and she adored tiny Cyrus. The junior Todds' home was simple and warm, radiant with family love. That Sunday, Elizabeth saw the Mike Todd that show business did not know, the doting grandfather.

The sun was setting when they headed back to New York. She was to go straight to the airport.

Mike settled down beside her in the limousine with a sigh of content. "I hadda be sure the baby approved of you," he said. "And he did. So now you gotta marry me, see?"

She was combing her hair. She stopped to put on fresh lipstick, too, before she turned to answer Mike.

He was sound asleep. Elizabeth shifted so that she could rest Mike's head in her lap without rousing him.

Looking down at him, she knew the gift of love that she could give him. She'd bear him a child. She had been warned, after Chris's birth, that she would risk her life if she became pregnant again.

But Mike Todd was worth risking her life for.

She did not wake him until they reached the airport. They walked out hand in hand to the flight line. She stood on the steps to the plane as she kissed him farewell.

He said, "Three weeks till you come back for the opening of my picture—I guess I can bear it. The minute you hit home tomorrow morning, you'll hear the phone ringing, and that will be me."

"I know, bless you. Darling, darling Mike."

She ran up the plane steps, and slipped into a window seat and waved until airborne. She was wrapped in a brand-new dream. She would get pregnant just as soon as they got married, and this time she'd hope for a little girl. This dream was much more real to her than the three final weeks of shooting on *Raintree County*.

The dream rather than a plane seemed to carry her back to New York the day after the film was finished, the day before *Around the World in 80 Days* was due to open.

This time the reporters were alerted, and they beat even Mike Todd up the plane steps to query her. "How do you feel about Mike Todd?" they asked.

She looked over their shoulders, into Mike's eyes. "I'm passionately in love with him," she said.

The opening of *Around the World in 80 Days* was a triumph. That night, when Mike Todd became the king of both Broadway and Hollywood with his very first movie, Elizabeth did not wait for the press to question her. She couldn't stop talking. "I've never known such a wonderful moment! I died a thousand deaths waiting to see how the audience would react. But now..." She drew an ecstatic breath. "What is so important to a woman as sharing success with your man?"

That night, she and Mike were surrounded by a crowd of pals, well-wishers, hangers-on, celebrities, characters, and charmers. The sun was high in the sky before anyone gave a thought to going to bed. They read the rave reviews in the morning papers. They ate scrambled eggs at Reuben's for breakfast. They went for a carriage ride around Central Park. Neither of them had sense enough to be tired.

Elizabeth knew just what she was going to do. She would return immediately to Hollywood, pick up young Mike and Chris, go to Reno and establish residence, and then within six weeks she'd be Mrs. Mike Todd.

But the next day a characteristic, strange shadow fell on her happiness. She was running across her hotel room to greet Mike, when her legs buckled. She screamed and pitched forward on her face, writhing with pain. Quickly the house doctor was there, putting her under sedation. Almost immediately other doctors were there, and she was in an ambulance. She was in a hospital, but by then the sedation worked, and she did not know that she was in surgery for nearly seven hours, while three disintegrated discs were cut away from her spine and new bone was grafted in their place.

She woke very late the following day and saw Mike sitting there, beside her, anxious and unshaved. Obviously he had never left her. Then she saw her parents in a corner of the room. They must have been sent for, she realized. She was too weak to cry. Mike leaned over and kissed her. "Go back to sleep, little dame," he said.

She did not wake for another twenty-four hours. Mike was still there, all alone, still unshaved. "Tell me, tell me," she whispered. He told her. He told her the whole thing.

"I'll never walk again," she said, weeping.

Mike scowled. "You damn' well will. The only thing the matter with you is a lack of faith in yourself. I'm going to make you get over that. People can be defeated only if they think they are."

"Mike, listen. Everything's wrong with me. I've had colitis. I've had heart trouble. I had that time when I nearly went blind, and I'm always getting colds or flu or something. All my life I've been going in and out of hospitals. I'm just not well most of the time. You mustn't think of marrying me."

"I won't think of anything else. Now you listen to me, little dame. You have to believe, not in something or somebody outside of you, not in me, not in your mother, not in anyone but you. You've got to believe in yourself."

"Oh, Mike, for you I'll try."

"Then you'll walk again."

But she didn't walk, not that week, not that month. She was surrounded by love, Mike's love, her parents' love, her public's love expressed in thousands of letters and wires and cards. She was given the finest medical and nursing care. But she remained paralyzed. Was it psychosomatic, as some of the press stated? Was it Elizabeth's reaction to stress? Or was it truly a birth injury as some of the medical men insisted?

Whatever it was, by the beginning of the second month Elizabeth, still immobile, knew she was steadily growing more depressed. A sense of melancholy duty pressed upon her. She asked her parents not to visit her on one particular evening. Then she called Mike and told him how low she was, and that she could barely endure the moments until he could reach her.

He was there beside her almost immediately, but presently she was quarreling with him. Then she was taunting him, then shouting at him, and he was responding in kind. Their faces were scarlet with anger when she yelled out, "I hate you, Mike, I do hate you! Get out of here! I never want to see you again, and I wouldn't marry you if you were the last man on earth!"

Mike knocked over a chair, he sprang across the room so quickly. He began shouting with laughter. "Oh, my God, you ham!" he said. "Now I know you'll win an Academy Award one day, for you sure had me winging. Only where did you get that corny dialogue? Now you listen to me, you broad. If I don't see you on your feet tomorrow, I'll whale the tar out of you, you understand?"

She did manage to stand up the next day. The next week she could walk a little. Three weeks later she left the hospital.

By that time she couldn't wait to get her freedom in Reno.

Mike talked to his lawyers. Elizabeth cabled Mike Wilding in London. Would he stand by to meet her in Mexico, please? It was only a matter of hours to get a divorce in Mexico. Or so they thought.

She went back to California, almost literally in Mike Todd's arms. He carried her on and off the plane.

Eddie Fisher and his wife Debbie Reynolds were there, among a mob of others to welcome them. Later Debbie said, "Mike adored Elizabeth. I had known him before he met her, and I never heard him make a fuss over a woman, but he just sweet-talked Elizabeth all the time. He was crazy about her boys. He was always telling her and everyone else what a great mother she was, and how beautiful she was, and how intelligent. She'd laugh and she'd say, 'Oh, come off it, Mike.' But she loved every word of it because he didn't just say it, the way other people do. He bought her clothes and he gave her jewels fit for a princess and he treated her like one. He made Elizabeth feel more beautiful than she is—if that's possible."

More than anyone knew, except Elizabeth and MGM, he helped her career, too. That was because MGM was aware that the finished *Raintree County* was not quite right. It represented a large investment. It was based on a best-selling novel, and it had been magnificently produced and directed. Yet in its previews it had not received satisfactory reactions.

"Let me have a look at it," said Mike Todd. He sat through a screening, he the master showman whose *Around the World in 80 Days* was doing fantastic business.

"This picture is too damned long," said Mike. "Sure, there's miles of local color and tons of subtlety, and who needs that? Actually the picture has just one asset, and I am not saying it because I am in love with this little broad. But you cut it to where it's almost all Liz, and you don't need to preview it to see what happens. I can tell you right now. The picture will be a hit, and Liz will get an Academy nomination."

Which was what did happen—but later, and tragically.

However, to Elizabeth, in January, 1957, the least important thing in life was what might happen to any picture. Mike had a battery of lawyers working on her divorce. They had set their wedding date for February 3 in Acapulco. "That's Atlantic City with a Spanish accent and a bigger ocean," Mike said, "the ocean for you and the jazz for me."

Mike couldn't even get married without showmanship. He had their union planned to the last lavish detail. Cantinflas,

Mexico's most popular personality and Mike's star in *Around the World in 80 Days*, was to act as host to the wedding party. There would be two ceremonies, first the civil ceremony, to be followed by a Jewish service.

Eddie Fisher was to be Mike's best man; his wife, Debbie Reynolds, and Mara Reagan Taylor, Howard Taylor's wife, would be Elizabeth's attendants. They, with Elizabeth's parents and Mr. and Mrs. Mike Todd, Jr., would be the only people invited to the actual ceremony, but later there was to be a party for hundreds.

Debonairly Mike Wilding arrived in Mexico on the Monday preceding the wedding. Just as debonairly Elizabeth and Mike Todd, with Cantinflas, met him. So did a mob of reporters.

"Gentlemen," said Mike Wilding, attacking before they got the chance, "I came here for one reason only—to sign my divorce papers. It is my divorce, too, you know."

"What about a chance of a reconciliation between you and Miss Taylor?"

"Good God, no!" said Mr. Wilding, smiling at his about-to-be-ex and her intended.

She, in her turn, smiled at both men. "Why don't you two men go take a swim while I take a nap? It's a long, hot drive to Acapulco."

"Great idea," said Mike Todd.

"Righto," said Mike Wilding.

In Acapulco, however, lazy, tourist Acapulco, ambition raised a surprising head. Arriving there, the two Mikes with their lady discovered an ambitious judge had their papers. Mexican elections were coming up, and the judge suddenly announced in headlines that he was against quickie divorces for rich movie stars.

Mike Wilding retired to his hotel to think that one over.

Mike Todd got on long distance. He called Mexico City lawyers. He called his Hollywood lawyers and then his New York lawyers. Next he called lawyers in Cuernavaca, another Mexican resort community. They all said to relax, they would call back. That was Monday. They didn't call back.

Tuesday Mike called them all again, adding a couple of lawyers in Chicago and one in Madrid, who might have influence in Mexico. They said they'd call back, too.

Nothing happened. Nothing happened on Wednesday, either, except that Mike called more lawyers, and that guests for the wedding began coming in on every plane, train, and yacht. The mayor of Acapulco was standing by to officiate at the civil ceremony. Fifty minions of Mike's were hustling about trying to find a rabbi in Catholic Mexico. They failed.

Thursday came. The flowers for the wedding were coming in by the truckload, including some fifteen thousand white gladioli that Mike had flown in to carpet the lawn of the estate where the wedding was to be held. The twenty-five cases of champagne Mike had ordered arrived, together with the cracked crabs, baby lobsters, caviar, and smoked turkeys for the buffet supper.

By Thursday afternoon Mike was in such a rage that if the entire Mexican government had fallen no one would have been surprised. But just before sunset the word came through. The divorce of Wilding vs. Wilding had been granted in Mexico City.

Welkin, as the saying goes, certainly rang from that point onward. Everything began going wonderfully right and wonderfully wrong. Mike got a cable that an automobile he had ordered for Elizabeth in London was now ready for delivery.

"The little dame will be quite pleased with it," Mike told one of the wedding guests. "It's quite a crate. It has a bar in it, and a place where you can cook up a meal."

"Will that make Elizabeth happy?"

"There's no such thing as a happy actress," the bridegroom said. "But I think I know a girl who's going to be a happy housewife. However, just in case she doesn't like cooking on her automobile stove, I bought her a yacht, too."

He really had. He had also bought her a ninety-thousand-dollar diamond bracelet as her wedding present.

The great Saturday dawned, and Mike had all his pals at work—Eddie Fisher, Cantinflas, Elizabeth's brother Howard, and Mike junior. They were rounding up containers for the flowers. They were checking on the fireworks that were to be displayed that night. They were conferring with the caterers about the placement of the tables. And then Mike senior nearly blew a gasket.

There was his own son putting pink and red flowers on their table. "Any fool knows a marriage cloth should be covered only with white flowers!" he yelled.

That was the way it went all day, crazy and beautiful. Said Elizabeth's father as he watched Mario Lepotogui, the mayor

128

of Acapulco, performing the civil ceremony, "Mike's the kind of a man Elizabeth needs. He'll lay down the law to her."

Said her mother, "You're so right, dear."

Then exactly at the moment that the Mayor pronounced them man and wife, the air conditioning broke down. "Couldn't stand the heat we're generating," said the bridegroom. "Let's just cut the wedding cake, and then we'll move the whole wedding party outdoors."

He kissed his bride and grinned at Eddie Fisher, standing beside them, waiting to kiss the bride, too.

"See," said Mike. "Liz finally made it. She's been trying to hook me all along, and now she's finally done it. I'll bet she's the happiest girl in the world tonight."

Elizabeth refused to go along with his clowning. "You are right, dearest Mike," she said, solemn as a beautiful, small owl. "I am the happiest, luckiest girl in the world."

Outside on a great terrace lighted by torches, two orchestras began alternating rhythms, one Mexican, one pure jazz. Against the starry sky at that instant the fireworks burst into light, spelling out the letters "MT" and "ETT" in entwined hearts.

When the orchestras paused, a group of wonderful native dancers took over. When they stopped for breath, Eddie Fisher sang love songs to the beautiful bride and his best friend, and people ate and drank. All except the host, that is. The bride, exquisite in the pale lavender chiffon gown Helen Rose had designed for her, sipped a single glass of champagne. She refused to admit, even to herself, how tired she was.

Her dad noticed it, though. He slipped over to her and suggested to her that she leave the party. She smiled tenderly at him as she refused. "I won't go till the last guest goes," she said. "This is the most wonderful night of my whole life."

Thus dawn was streaking the sky before Mike could lift her into his white Thunderbird and drive her to the seaside estate where they were to spend their honeymoon. The place was entirely surrounded by Mexican troops to ensure their privacy. There was no sound there, save the pounding of the waves and the singing of the birds, and no person except the servants. They stayed for one blessed week before the outside world began intruding on them again.

The Academy Awards were coming up, and *Around the World in 80 Days* had been nominated. The Cannes Film

Festival was coming up in France, and *Around the World* was in the running there, also. They made plans to attend both.

Through Mike's eyes Elizabeth began to see the other side of the film business, the side of financing, and producing, and talent grabbing, and sometimes double-crossing; the side of competition, excitement, inspiration, and originality all in one glorious jumble.

She came to know, through Mike Todd, both how unimportant and how vastly important a star could be. But this was only the smallest part of her education. He taught her joy, that wonderful combination of body and intellect and emotion all blended for giving and receiving pleasure.

Actually, for all her joy, she was still not well. Her spine was still bothering her, but she willed herself to rise above its pain.

Mike always seemed to move at a full gallop. Mike was always good-humored. Mike had an eternal zest for life. "You always look up," she said, "and you make everyone look with you."

"I look up to you on that gorgeous pedestal," he said.

It was in Palm Springs that they got their finest news: they were going to become parents. It was in Hollywood three weeks later that they got the second finest: Mike had won the Academy Award.

When his name was called out before that jury of his peers in Hollywood and before the millions watching on TV, he leapt from his seat and started running down the aisle toward the stage. Then he stopped. He rushed back and kissed his wife passionately.

Then he went toward the stage again, but this time with something like dignity. When he went backstage, however, and saw Elizabeth and the photographers waiting for him, he wouldn't be photographed without her. He held her in a bear hug. "It wouldn't be fair not to let the world in on the greatest love story of all time," he said.

And actually their marriage was just that. Mike loved New York. Elizabeth loved California. So they had a penthouse in New York and an estate in Beverly Hills. They also had a house in Connecticut, for weekends, and another in Palm Springs. Elizabeth had her little boys with her, and Mike was a wonderful father to them. Mike didn't like cats, but Elizabeth did, so they had two cats, plus several dogs, plus a duck. Mike said, "Liz is probably the only girl in the world who ever flew to New York holding a duck in her lap."

They had a yacht and cars by the half dozens, wherever they were, and when they were on the Riviera for the film festival, they rented the sumptuous Villa Fiorentina on the Mediterranean. In Rome they had a villa, in Paris a town house, but in Moscow they had to put up with a hotel. Mike actually hoped that in Moscow he might get to know the people. He loved all people, and he thought maybe he could get the Russians, just average Russians, to understand an average American like himself. Except, of course, that no-body could have been less average than he was, American or otherwise, but he was too genuinely modest to realize that.

The Todds even had a private plane, *The Lucky Liz*. Mike furnished it with foam-rubber couches, a buffet bar, deep-pile carpets, gold toilet articles, marked "His" and "Liz," and a tremendous double bed.

They lived it up, every minute, everywhere. They even had fun when they fought. They staged a tremendous row once in the London airport, when Mike wanted to fly to Paris and Liz didn't. They staged another, later, in Seattle when they flew in from Hong Kong. But it was a merry, beautiful Elizabeth who said then to the reporters, "We have more fun fighting than most people do making love."

Mike Todd drew back, registering shock. "Please, darling," he said, "there are Boy Scouts present."

Mike gave Elizabeth a present every Saturday because they had been married on a Saturday. And those presents were no mere trifles. In Paris at an auction of some of the Aly Khan paintings, Elizabeth spied a Degas and two smaller paintings she admired. Mike immediately wrote the thirty-thousand-dollar check for them. Another time, in Rome, she saw a diamond tiara in Bulgari's window. "Ah, it's the little things you like," said Mike, "little rubies, little emeralds, little diamonds." He bought the tiara for her, and before she ever wore it in public she wore it in private for him, just the tiara and her most seductive smile.

Her third pregnancy, however, was giving Elizabeth a hard time, and Mike drove her doctors crazy phoning them twenty times a day about her symptoms. She expected the baby about the first of November, but early in the summer she was already very uncomfortable. Nevertheless, she insisted upon accompanying Mike wherever he went, and quite successfully hid her discomfort from him.

The night of the London opening of his film, Mike gave a party for two thousand people. It really was a party. Duchesses rubbed elbows with commoners. Sixteen bands played continuously.

That night, pride in her man so filled Elizabeth that she could rise above her pain. She stood regally by Mike's side until the party ended at dawn in a London downpour. Mike put his arms around her and grinned as he said, "You never know, kid. Something about this party may sneak into the papers, and no matter what happens, I've now heard everything. There was a guy here who they tell me is a relative of a former Prime Minister. Well, just as he was leaving, he came up to me and complained about the free raincoat I gave him, like I gave everybody else. He said his didn't fit."

The date of that party was July 3. The Todds then returned to America and settled down at the Connecticut estate to avoid the midsummer Manhattan heat. On July 27, Elizabeth, badly frightened, felt labor pains. Mike called an ambulance, and with state troopers clearing the way, she was rushed to the Harkness Pavilion. It was a very haggard Mike Todd who came out, hours later, to speak to the press. "If she can possibly hold out till August 15, then the baby will be six months along," he said. "I'm staying right by her bedside, right till then."

Elizabeth fought, fought the pain, fought the calendar, but she couldn't quite make it until August 15. They took her into surgery and on August 6, by Cæsarean section, her tiny daughter was born.

The baby did not breathe. Nine doctors surrounded her, and minute after minute they kept her alive by mouth resuscitation. She weighed only four pounds, but she did have stamina from both sides of her family. After fifteen minutes she began to breathe for herself but the doctors didn't let her out of her hospital incubator for a month.

Her proud father told the papers, "Liz and I are grateful that we got what we wanted most. It was a miracle, thanks to the medical genius of the lineup assembled by Dr. Dana Atchley."

"Is she beautiful like her mother?" he was asked.

"Beautiful? Why compared to Liza, her mother looks like Frankenstein."

That afternoon Mike cabled Paris to have the most expensive baby dress procurable sent over to him. Liza was still in the hospital incubator when it was delivered, and Elizabeth did not upset the proud father by mentioning that modern babies, male or female, wear little save diapers for their first six months.

On Liza's first day at home, when she was exactly one month old, they bedecked her in her Paris frock. Little Mike and Chris were delighted with this extraordinary toy, particularly since their mother had told them Liza was just for them, their own baby. Big Mike was in such a state of dazed infatuation that he could barely leave the nursery for the first week or two. He was lost in the wonder of this little daughter, younger than his grandchildren.

If he was a little overboard in his infatuation, there was an excuse. On the day he and Elizabeth had gone to the hospital to bring Liza home, the obstetrician had had a brief talk with them. Quietly but explicitly he explained that Mrs. Todd could never bear another child.

Neither of the Todds had spoken. Their hands reached out and clasped each other's. Elizabeth closed her eyes. Mike, quite simply, leaned over and kissed her. For several moments after that they did not move. Then Elizabeth opened her eyes and smiled into Mike's. They each drew a long breath and stood up.

Without words they understood that neither of them was going to carp because their heaven did not have a solid gold fence around it.

On the contrary, that one small sorrow seemed to heighten the ecstasy of their special summer. The little boys flourished. Liza flourished. Her nurse was excellent. So were all their help. Elizabeth recovered her strength more quickly than she had after the birth of either of her sons. Her back troubled her less, and even she, who took her beauty so impersonally, could see that it had increased, and she was glad for Mike's sake.

Around the World in 80 Days was playing only in three spots in the United States, and it was continually sold out. The great capitals of the world, from Rome to Hong Kong, from Copenhagen to Melbourne were all clamoring for it. Having done all the advance traveling on it before Liza's birth, Mike refused to open it anywhere until Elizabeth was strong enough to go to the premières with him.

Some of this stubbornness was because he had experienced one opening alone. With the film a smash in New York and Los Angeles, United Artists, its releasing company, wanted to run it in the Middle West, too. Elizabeth was too pregnant to

133

risk flying. Mike was urged to make a personal appearance to jazz up the première. United Artists arranged his plane schedule so that he would be away only overnight.

It was the first night since their marriage that Mike and Elizabeth had been separated. "It is as though you had been gone for a month," Elizabeth sobbed in his arms when he arrived back at noon the next day.

Mike covered her face, her neck with kisses. "Without you I feel like half a pair of scissors. I promise you. Show business will never separate us again, never." Then he laughed. "I tell you, little dame, I don't know where I'm going to spend all the money that movie is bringing in, anyhow."

She raised her big eyes. "Darling, let your little loving wife help you with that big mean nasty problem," she purred.

Waiting for Liz's recovery, Mike began planning a production of Cervantes' *Don Quixote* to be made in Spain. He told his Broadway pals, "Every s.o.b. in Hollywood wants to play the Don, now that they know Liz is going to play Dulcinea. Well, I've got news for that crowd: They won't be in my picture. Funny thing about Liz. Even when she was a kid, she made like a woman in pictures. Now she'll have her chance to be a real actress because she'll play an unattractive woman. Cervantes had a line about Dulcinea. He wrote, 'I wonder what he sees in her?' That's a line I've used all my life about every other broad but Liz, and I never knew till now I stole it from Cervantes."

In actuality Mike's going into his office was mostly shadow boxing. He seldom could tear himself away from his home before eleven. He never stayed in town after four thirty, and in between he either telephoned Elizabeth or she phoned him. Besides there wasn't a thing to linger in town for. He had given up gambling. He had given up his big, black cigars because Elizabeth hated the smell of them.

"You're looking at the new Todd," he told his buddies.

Elizabeth grinned when he made that remark to her. "Dear New Todd, I'm sorry to tell you you're not looking at the new Taylor," she said. "You see, there just isn't any Taylor, new or old. There's only Elizabeth Todd, that lucky, lucky dame who is Mike Todd's wife."

The truth was that she was completely his wife in that halcyon year of 1956. Elizabeth Taylor, the movie star, had no part of her awareness.

Her picture *Giant* opened, and she received terrific notices. Warner's tried, with every inducement, to get her to attend some of its premières, but since she had merely been lent to them by MGM, they could not force her. So she ignored *Giant* to stay at home with her husband. When her friend Helen Rose came through New York, Elizabeth told her, "I'm changing to the woman I must be for Mike. I must retire. I have all I want—a home, a husband, a real family. I don't say I'll never act again, but I will act only for Mike."

She was growing, mentally, every day. All her shyness vanished as she and Mike talked and talked. Mike said things like, "I don't think it serves any purpose to analyze everything you do. It makes you a self-conscious person, and you tend to take yourself too seriously. What you have to learn is to accept gracefully the things you can't do anything about. See? Am I boring you?"

"No. I love you, and I refuse to defend myself against it."

"See? You've learned your lesson already. You're accepting gracefully something you can't do anything about."

Early in September she was finally able to go with Mike to other openings of his picture. They arranged never to stay anywhere more than a week, whether the theater was in India, Australia, Japan, or Alaska.

Everywhere the film was a hit. Every place they entered—hotel dining rooms, nightclubs, or private parties, the musicians at sight of them struck up the title song *Around the World in 80 Days*.

Mike never hired a mere suite for them, or one mere car to take them about. He took several suites all joined together, as he did in Honolulu's most opulent hostelry. In Sidney, Australia, he hired a hotel's whole floor. There, innocently, Elizabeth murmured something about the furnishings being a bit dusty.

That was enough. Mike had everything taken away, and in a matter of hours brand-new hangings were up, new carpets were down, and new chairs, tables, and TV sets were installed. In what was to serve as their sleeping quarters, a bed so big that it took every inch of space, was installed.

Wearing her magnificent gowns, bedecked with her jewels, Elizabeth Todd was evolving. On those trips there was never a waking moment that Mike wasn't in a crowd. The big publicity machine surrounded him with people—people with talent, people with money, and people with political influence and titles.

But he never pulled rank, and he went out of his way to be nice to the least important person. His natural gift was that he did not think of anyone as small. Still he was not a flatterer. He felt the equal of anyone, since everyone was equal to him.

Elizabeth was delighted, within herself, to stay in the background, to give him the spotlight, the center stage.

Hong Kong, particularly, enchanted them, with its mixture of races, its bedlam of noise, its smell of the sea, its tawdry vice contrasted to the solidity of its great banks and industry. "Let's buy a house here, and bring the kids for a look-see at the Orient," Mike said to her one morning.

They were breakfasting out-of-doors at that moment, in a luxurious, tree-shaded spot that overlooked the harbor where the sampans anchor. Elizabeth instantly saw what had caught Mike's eye. Off one of the shabbiest sampans a little family—stern father, round, smiling mother, and three small children—had disembarked and were moving in their direction. Like the Todd family there were two small boys and one tiny girl.

Elizabeth was all in white, a white sharkskin dress and white slippers with four-inch heels. She had a fine, dark tan, and her violet eyes were radiant. As she smiled at the little family, they stopped, transfixed. All except the tiny girl. She ran straight to Elizabeth, while her frightened mother hissed at her, trying to stop her.

But Elizabeth held the child close, while Mike corralled the two small boys. He hunted around in his pockets for Hong Kong dollars. To his annoyance he found none, while the parents, their faces blushing, kept apologizing for their children.

Mike signaled a waiter. "What are they saying?" he demanded.

"The old people sorry, say children think the beautiful lady is a goddess."

"Tell them she is. Tell them she brings great good fortune."

Elizabeth laughed. "Mike, the children would like all these silly jams and jellies on this table, and we haven't even opened them. And here, give the little girl this scarf of mine." Elizabeth pulled off the scarf that she had around her head.

Mike swept the table clean. The children squealed happily. The old Chinese father went into a huddle with his smiling wife, then with the waiter.

"Man says he invite beautiful goddess lissy and nice gentlemans to see sampan for thank you, perhaps?" said the waiter.

"Oh, Mike, let's go. Can we? We've never done anything

like that. Mike, this is where these children were probably born..."

"...and where they'll probably die, too. Could be the old man was born on the same sampan. You really want to go?"

"Yes, very much, unless you don't want to."

"Goddess, after you."

It was a pathetic old wreck of a sampan, its sail so patched that nothing of the original cloth remained. Its decks were rotting and the miserable holes beneath, where the little family lived, were dark and dreadful. Yet, there it was, a way of life that had existed, unchanged, for many thousands of years, and there was that Chinese family, visibly united by love, and trying to repay generosity with the only gift they had, a new sight for American tourists.

Mike said to his wife as they walked back toward their hotel, "It's fantastic, the instinct of animals and kids. They just come to you, automatically."

"Do they, I hope? Michael, will that be those children's inheritance when their parents die, that old sampan?"

"If it holds together that long, which I doubt."

"Oh, Mike, when I think of our Liza, and little Mike and Chris..."

They were standing then in front of their hotel. He kissed her.

"Will you be all right for a minute? I just want to run over to the theater and check the box office."

An hour passed. She was just beginning to worry when she heard his step and as he came in, he was grinning.

"Tell Mother. What magic have you been up to, Michael Todd?"

He laughed. "Did you ever try to buy a brand-new sampan and have it delivered? Kid, until you do, you haven't lived. I did it though. It will be delivered smack on the water about an hour after we take off tomorrow. Can you imagine that family when they get it? I had a photograph of you sent along with it, and whenever you get mean to me, I'll think of that family burning joss to their goddess, the violet-eyed Elizabeth. So learn to behave, will you?"

Back in New York, *Around the World in 80 Days* was about to celebrate its first year on Broadway, and Mike, the show-man, couldn't quite resist that.

He decided to have a party for 2,200 people, one that would outdo his original party for the film in London. He flew in guests from every section of the United States and quartered them in the most lavish New York hotels. He hired scores of bands and Madison Square Garden for them to play in, elephants with Sir Cedric Hardwicke to ride them, a birthday cake as big as an apartment house which Elizabeth would cut, and champagne enough to fill a good-sized lake.

The party turned out to be the most spectacular flop ever staged. There were gate crashers by the hundreds who drank up all the champagne, and more gate crashers by the thousands who ate up most of the food and threw what they didn't care for on the cement floors. The invited guests could not get through the disorderly throngs. Women's lovely gowns were stained. Too many men spilled liquor over too many dinner jackets. When Elizabeth tried to cut the cake, its layers lost their moorings and fell all over her feet.

Mike Todd got publicity all right the next morning—publicity and ridicule. He took it, laughing. Elizabeth took it, too, laughing beside him.

Mentally, however, she secretly shifted gears. MGM had sent her the script of a Tennessee Williams play, *Cat on a Hot Tin Roof*. She had been intending to try to get Mike to buy her out of her contract.

Yet she knew, by Mike's very concentration on her winning the Academy Award for *Raintree County*, that after the flop of his New York party, he had to have a "win." He was taking big expensive ads for her in all the movie trade papers. He was discussing the reasons why she must win the Oscar every time he encountered a newspaperman.

Elizabeth, herself, kept quiet. She didn't believe she could win, and actually she did not care. Still, if Mike wanted her to win, she would try.

Slyly she showed him the script of *Cat on a Hot Tin Roof*. She saw the excitement on his face as he finished the screenplay.

"Liz, this a great script. It will be a great picture. You oughta win for *Raintree*. But in case you don't, you havta win with this one. This part of Maggie the Cat . . ."

So he wanted her to make the film, did he?

"Mike, darling, they want to start shooting right away."

"No problem. I'll call the Coast, get us a house. You want to fly out tomorrow? Hanley can get us the reservations, hire some servants, all that. Be good for the kids, too. Sunshine, new playmates. And me, I'll take an office right there on the

138

MGM lot. Then I can keep two eyes on you and one on *Don Quixote....*"

Yes, it was what he wanted. She'd make the picture.

Two days later Elizabeth was back on the MGM lot for preliminary discussions with Richard Brooks, who was to direct the film.

Later, Richard Brooks said, "When Elizabeth walked in that first day on *Cat*, she was the most beautiful shock to me. I had not seen her since we had made *The Last Time I Saw Paris*. She had been a bewildered girl then, but there in February of 1957 she looked so well. She looked so completely happy. I told her that, and she said, 'I am happy. I am so happy with Mike I think we will stay happy all the rest of our lives.'

"Mike Todd was the dominant personality. She could relax. The men she had known before Todd had become absorbed by her. They lost their personalities; they became emotionally emasculated. Now Elizabeth was happy because she had found the emotional stability which being loved had given her."

The house the Todds had rented, long distance, was a fairly gloomy old pile, up behind the Beverly Hills Hotel, but the gardens were walled and great for the children. It was convenient to MGM. "And besides," said Elizabeth, as she vetoed his suggestion of either moving or completely refurnishing, "we'll be back in Connecticut again in three months."

So they stayed put and Mike told his pals, "I'm so happy I get scared. I get damned scared it can't last. You know, I've chased lots of things in my life, including happiness, and I finally caught it when I caught Liz. But at heart I'm a gambler, and that means I've got a good respect for the law of averages. I'm scared because the law of averages is being a little too good for me. It might change."

Then he grinned. "What the hell am I talking about, will you tell me?"

He really wasn't doing any work there in his office at MGM, but he wanted to be as close to Liz as he could. He didn't interfere. He went very politely to Dick Brooks and asked if it was all right if he came and watched the dailies, those quick run-throughs of a day's scenes.

Brooks agreed immediately, but even at that, Mike never came on the set until he knew the day's shooting was over.

Then he would go to the projection room with Liz, and holding her hand, he'd watch the day's action.

Essentially *Cat on a Hot Tin Roof* was a somber drama, the story of a beautiful young wife, unloved because of her husband's impotence, and of a dominant old man dying of cancer, the father of the girl's husband. Paul Newman was the husband and Burl Ives the father.

From the first day, Elizabeth was brilliant in her role, or as Richard Brooks says, "When we actually started working on the picture, I realized how much Elizabeth had grown. She had a new confidence in herself. She was freer to express herself as an actress. She was poised and not on trial any more."

What Mike said, looking at the dailies, was, "What I'm trying to achieve for this dame with ballyhoo, the award for *Raintree*, she'll get for *Cat* without anybody raising a hand."

The ebullient Todds didn't give a second thought to the fact that the Monday start of *Cat on a Hot Tin Roof* led off what was to be a particularly crowded ten days for them. The plan was for Elizabeth to get in four and a half days' work, ending Friday at noon. Brooks had promised to clear her scenes so that she and Mike could then take off in *The Lucky Liz* for New York. That Saturday, March 22, Mike was being feted by the Friars Club as Showman of the Year. On Sunday they would fly back to be ready for Elizabeth's work on Monday, but, much more importantly, for the Academy Award ceremonies the next Wednesday.

The picture's shooting would have to shut down, as far as she was concerned, by Wednesday. This Mike insisted upon. She must have hours for her hairdressing, her makeup, her grooming for the movie industry's most important night. Mike was pleased to be receiving a plaque from the Friars, but Elizabeth's winning the Oscar was much more important. He masterminded every detail from her publicity to her petticoats.

Originally Helen Rose had submitted a batch of designs, and the MGM wardrobe department sat ready to whip up the gown of Elizabeth's choice. The styles were all very chic, and Elizabeth could have been persuaded to wear any one of them. But Mike, the master showman, balked.

"What my little broad wears Academy night can't be just a dress," he explained to Helen. "It's too big an occasion. For her, for Hollywood. What she's wearing has to make news, like that time Dietrich walked on stage at the Academy in what looked like a plain black velvet get-up, remember? Then she moved, and there she was, visible from toe to hip. But I don't want that kind of jazz on Liz. It's a crazy thing about her—you can hang her with jewels, you can get her into a wild hat or fifty thousand dollars' worth of sables. Any other dame would look vulgar. She, somehow, stays a lady, don't ask me how.

"So how do we startle them and yet keep her ladylike quality? It sure as hell is no news that she's the most beautiful dame in the world. So we gotta go beyond that to make a headline. So how's this? Can you make her a dress for a goddess, take her out of this world?"

"Can I? Look." Helen's drawing pencil moved quickly across a block of paper. She drew the body of Aphrodite with the face of Elizabeth Taylor. "I'll take pure white silk jersey, Mike, like this, see, no trimming, just drapes and folds of that flawlessly simple material. And Liz will look like a goddess, the Greek love goddess. How about that?"

Mike Todd gave a quick snort of pleasure and stabbed the sketch where the draped lines indicated the slim waistline. "Welcome to my club. We're both geniuses," he said. "Now let Daddy give you another lesson. Right here, to highlight how my dame curves in, I'll provide some trimming. You know what I'll get? I'm going to get the biggest damned hunk of diamond I can find in this village, and I'll have it made into a pin. I'm gonta ride herd on that Guilaroff and get him to do her hair classic, straight back from that face of hers, with just a little knot on the nape of her neck—because, if you wanta know one of the simpler ways of taking a man's mind off his work, all you gotta do is show him the nape of a woman's neck."

Mike found the diamond for the pin within two days. It weighed twenty carats. The jeweler was smart. He also showed Mike two other diamonds of ten carats each. "These would frame Mrs. Todd's face ideally," he said. So Mike had them made into earrings.

Elizabeth, blissful with it all, left the gown at the studio for finishing touches, but she took her diamonds home.

It rains in March in California, a cold, mean rain. Also, as every studio head knows, there is virtually no star who at the beginning of a picture does not have some manifestation of first-day nerves, the movie actor's equivalent of stage fright.

Elizabeth, on the first day's shooting of *Cat*, felt chilly all day long, but blamed it on the rain. Tuesday she was headachy all day. By Thursday she had a cold and no mistake. Her eyes were running. Her nose was running, and by evening so was her temperature.

Friday morning her temperature was 102. She kept taking it at half-hour intervals, but it did not go down. As the afternoon advanced she began to feel gloomier than the weather, which was at its most desolate, the rain falling in tropical sheets, the winds howling.

Mike, the while, was getting hourly bulletins from his chief pilot, Bill Venner. The report was that the storm was largely local. From all appearances it would be easy to fly up and over it.

"No matter what, you're not going," Mike told Elizabeth.

"Darling, of course I'm going—for your dinner, to see you become Showman of the Year? Of course I shall. I've only got sniffles."

"And a temperature of 102. You're not going."

"Mike, dear, I can't stand it if you go alone."

"Who says I'm going alone? I want to talk to Joe Mankiewicz about directing *Don Quixote*. I'll talk to him on this trip."

Joe Mankiewicz, the distinguished director, later was to direct Elizabeth in *Suddenly, Last Summer*.

"Take me," Elizabeth begged as Mike hung up on the call. "I'm prettier than Joe."

"No, Kirk Douglas is," said Mike. "I'll get him."

"It's too wet," said Kirk Douglas. "Don't you know it's pouring out?"

"Oh, come on," Mike wheedled. "*The Lucky Liz* is a good, safe plane. I wouldn't let it crash. Besides the plane is covered with three million bucks' worth of insurance and that would cover you, too. How else would you ever rate three mil? Come on. You're a big boy, and I will see that you have a big time in a big town."

Douglas still refused.

Elizabeth threw her arms around her husband as he hung up on that call. "Don't go," she pleaded. "Either stay or take me. I don't want us to be apart even for a minute. I don't want you traveling with anybody else in our plane."

Mike kissed her. "Sweetheart, you know I gotta go. I can't let the Friars down now. But look. I won't even wait for Sunday. I'll fly right back tomorrow night, the moment the dinner is over. Why don't you let all the kids bunk in with you tonight? That'll keep you from being lonely till Sunday, and I swear nothing will ever part us again."

She knew there was a point beyond which he would not yield. She loved that quality in him, so she gave in. She got up that afternoon, put on the long velvet tea gown he loved, and kissed him good-bye.

By then Mike had corralled for the trip Art Cohn, his good friend and biographer, and Dick Hanley, his secretary. It was just getting dark when they converged on the Burbank airport, together with Bill Venner, the pilot, and Tom Barclay, the copilot. Just as they were about to take off, Mike changed his mind about Hanley's going.

"Go back to the little broad," he said. "She might need you."

As soon as Hanley left, the pilots got their clearance. Venner gunned the plane. Mike called Elizabeth on his air-to-ground phone.

"We're off, beautiful," he said. "Get a good sleep now. I love ya."

Disconsolately she hung up the phone. The wind still howled. The rain still poured. She still sniffled. She decided against bringing the children into her bedroom, fearing they might catch her cold. She went into Liza's nursery and discovered she was already asleep; tears came to Elizabeth's eyes as she looked down at that tiny face, so much like Mike's and yet so much her own.

The little boys were awake. "Tell us a story, Mommy." She plopped into little Mike's bed, pulled them both up close on either side of her. She told them an up-to-date version of Little Goody Two Shoes, only goody Goody turned out to be a boy. "Now you two go to sleep," she commanded, turning off their bedroom light.

She came back into her bedroom, got into the big double bed, and waited for Mike's call. Later, with a start, she woke and realized it was two in the morning. Was it possible that she had slept so soundly she had not heard the phone? She turned on the TV, which only sputtered at her. She looked about for something to read, but nothing held her. She was too restless. She rolled over onto the other side of the bed and kissed the pillow, but that only made her more lonely. She rolled back to her own side again and finally fell into an uneasy doze.

She woke just before daylight. The rain was still beating down. She dialed Dick Hanley. "Dick, this an awful hour to wake you, but has Mike called you?"

"No. Didn't he call you?"

"I don't think so. I was asleep. But if he didn't get me, wouldn't he have called you?"

"Not necessarily. Probably he and Art have been talking their heads off. Art's got two chapters to go on the book, you know, the ones about you—and you know Mike when he gets talking about you."

"I suppose you're right. I suppose the moment I hang up, the phone will ring and it will be Mike."

"Sure it will be. Relax."

"I will. Dick, about where would they be now?"

"I guess over Kansas or Indiana or such."

That was a bad guess, unfortunately. New Mexico was where the four men were, a mere five flying hours away. They were all dead.

Hanley received the news immediately after Elizabeth hung up. The phone rang under his hand. Hollywood's Associated Press reporter, Jim Bacon, was on the line, and he relayed the news that had just been flashed to him from the AP office in New Mexico.

The Lucky Liz had ridden out of the California storm and into a new one over the badlands of the Zuñi Indian country beyond Albuquerque. The pilots had radioed back for permission to climb. Presently they reported that *The Lucky Liz* was at thirteen thousand feet.

Moments later people living in those sparsely settled hills saw what they thought was a flash of lightning. That was followed by a great thudding sound. Then the darkness closed in again, and the silence.

Daylight revealed the plane, smashed to bits, and the four bodies.

Mike Todd's law of averages had worked. His luck had run out. His final act of love had been saving Elizabeth's life.

Yet possibly thereby he did not serve her.

Elizabeth with her co-star, Lassie. (CULVER PICTURES)

Mickey Rooney cuts Elizabeth's hair
to help her masquerade as a jockey
in *National Velvet* (CULVER PICTURES)

Two budding authors:
Elizabeth reads
Margaret O'Brien's *Memoirs*,
while Margaret seems
fascinated with Elizabeth's
story about her pet chipmunk,
Nibbles and Me.
(CULVER PICTURES)

On-screen and off-, Elizabeth fell in love with
Montgomery Clift when they co-starred in
A Place in the Sun.   (CULVER PICTURES)

Elizabeth wins an affectionate smile from co-star Spencer Tracy during a break in the filming of *Father of the Bride.*
(CULVER PICTURES)

Elizabeth as the real-life bride of hotel heir, Nicky Hilton. (UPI)

Jane Powell admires Elizabeth's gift at a baby shower.
Nicky had nothing in common with Elizabeth's
young MGM friends and refused to accompany her
to their parties—adding to the strains on their marriage.
(CULVER PICTURES)

Elizabeth and Nicky in a happy mood at a costume ball.
Shortly afterwards, their marriage broke up.
(CULVER PICTURES)

Elizabeth as Rebecca in *Ivanhoe*.
She hadn't wanted to go to London for the filming,
but there she rediscovered Michael Wilding,
who became her second husband.   (CULVER PICTURES)

Mr. and Mrs. Wilding
honeymooning in the Alps.
(WIDE WORLD PHOTOS)

Michael Wilding and
Elizabeth bring their seven-
month old firstborn,
Michael Howard Wilding,
to London for a holiday.
(WIDE WORLD PHOTOS)

Mike Todd takes a good look at his beautiful
bride at their 1957 wedding in Mexico. (UPI)

Mike, Elizabeth, and the famous tiara, at Cannes—
where his film, *Around the World in Eighty Days*
opened the 1957 film festival. (UPI)

Shattered by Mike's death,
Elizabeth was comforted by
his close friend, Eddie
Fisher. They were married
in 1959.   (UPI)

Elizabeth, Eddie and Liza Todd—
at four years old already a beauty.   (UPI)

Elizabeth in *Butterfield 8*,
the film she didn't want to
do—but which brought her
her first Academy Award.
(CULVER PICTURES)

Elizabeth, in *Cleopatra*,
comforting Rex Harrison as
Julius Caesar in an epileptic
seizure.   (UPI)

Elizabeth's children, (left to right) Michael Wilding,
Liza Todd and Christopher Wilding visit with her and
Richard Burton on the set of *Cleopatra*.   (WIDE WORLD PHOTOS)

A family night out: (left to right) Elizabeth,
Liza Todd, Richard Burton, Maria Burton, Michael
and Christopher Wilding.   (UPI)

(above) Britain's Princess Margaret chats with the Burtons at the world premiere of their film, *The Taming of the Shrew.* Sir Michael Redgrave looks on. (UPI)

(left) The famous Cartier-Burton diamond: 69.42 karats and $1,050,000. (UPI)

(below) *Who's Afraid of Virginia Woolf?* brought Elizabeth her second Oscar, but she was bitterly disappointed that Richard didn't win. (UPI)

Henry Wynberg was Elizabeth's
constant companion between her
marriages to Richard Burton. (UPI)

Elizabeth Taylor and John Warner announced
their engagement in Vienna, where she was filming
A Little Night Music. (UPI)

The Warners en route to Israel two days
after their wedding.
(WORLD WIDE PHOTOS)

Nancy Reagan and Elizabeth Warner applaud a speaker at
the Republican Convention which nominated
Ronald Reagan for President. (UPI)

The Warners host a country barbecue
for fellow Republicans at their
Middleburg, Virginia, farm. (UPI)

Elizabeth and John Warner
"down home" on the farm.
(UPI)

Princess Grace and Prince Ranier of Monaco
congratulate Elizabeth on her triumphant
Broadway debut in *The Little Foxes*. (UPI)

A radiant Elizabeth received the first humanitarian award
from the Damon Runyon-Walter Winchell Fund for
Cancer Research. With her here is Zev Bufman,
producer of *The Little Foxes*. (UPI)

Elizabeth Taylor as the wealthy widow, Helen Cassadine,
in five guest appearances on ABC-TV's daytime drama,
"General Hospital." A fan of the show, Elizabeth donated
her fee to charity.   (UPI)

CHAPTER NINETEEN

Richard Hanley, the perfect secretary, reacted with quick efficiency to the tragedy. He called Dr. Kennamer and arranged to meet him at once at the Todd house. Neither man had to break the news to the widow.

The moment Elizabeth saw them coming into her bedroom, she screamed. Rex Kennamer instantly gave her a powerful sedative, told her the details, explaining that Mike had died so quickly that he could not have suffered.

Elizabeth went on compulsively screaming. In the Sunday-morning quiet of that luxurious section of Beverly Hills, people next door were awakened, startled and frightened.

It was almost an hour before the drugs began to get hold and her screaming abated. She could not stay still. She paced up and down, threw herself on the bed, sprang up, paced once more. The words wailed out of her. "Oh, Mike, my darling, why didn't you let me go with you? I can't live without you, I can't, I can't. Mike, why couldn't I die with you? Oh, Mike, my Mike, my darling Mike."

Her little boys, outside in the hall, began to echo her screaming, without realizing what had happened. Outside, the news spread. The phones, Mike's beloved phones, with their dozens of different lines, began ringing everywhere in the house. The doorbells began ringing. Reporters drove up. Photographers arrived, and two climbed trees, hoping to catch a shot of the widow in her bedroom. Others invaded the garden at the back, angling for interior shots with tele-photo lenses.

Elizabeth, who had never been allowed to be alone in love, was not allowed to be alone in grief. Her parents arrived. Her brother, Howard, arrived. The crowd outside grew. Close friends came and had to be greeted. Telegrams and flowers came and had to be taken care of.

145

Richard Brooks was among the callers. Today he says, "When I got in to see Elizabeth, there was noise and confusion everywhere.

"Before I could say anything more than *hello*, she said, 'Have you come to talk about *Cat?*' I said, 'No, I just came to see you.' She said, 'Well, there have been others around here who seem very worried about it.' I said, 'I don't care if you never come back to work. You have to do what you think is right about it. I just came to see you.'

"She began talking about killing herself. People kept interrupting us. The funeral was to be the following Tuesday at the Waldheim Cemetery in Lake Zurich, northwest of Chicago. The people around her were making plans for her to fly there, planning her wardrobe and all that. After about a half hour, I could see that the drugs she'd taken were getting her close to incoherence. I stood up to go.

"That was when she said, 'Maybe I'll come back and finish the picture, but only because Mike would have wanted me to do it, because he thought I was good and really beginning to be an actress in the way I've always wanted to. Maybe I owe him that, but then I want to die, I want to die.'"

With Dick Hanley's aid that evening she slipped out, through a secret gate in the garden, and went to visit Dr. Max Nussbaum of Temple Israel in Hollywood. Dr. Nussbaum had been Mike's rabbi, and with him Elizabeth had often discussed being converted to Judaism.

Mike had thwarted her on that. He had told Dr. Nussbaum, "I don't want her to be converted until she is absolutely certain in her heart." Dr. Nussbaum completely agreed. But that night after Mike's death the rabbi gave her spiritual advice and the courage to face the funeral ceremony. Neither of them foresaw the horror she was to go through.

Only thirty people were supposed to be admitted to the private services for Mike Todd, planned for two o'clock. But while Elizabeth, her parents and her brother, Dr. Kennamer, Eddie Fisher, and Richard Hanley were flying to Chicago, a mob was gathering at the cemetery gates.

Ropes were up around the grave, and there were police. Over the grave was a tent with chairs inside for the mourners. Outside for about two hundred feet in each direction a carpet had been put down and white rose petals scattered over it.

The crowd kept growing. Word sped that Michael Wilding, with his new wife, had flown into Chicago from London. That brought a larger crowd. Mike Wilding, at the airport, said very quietly, "I am here in case I can help Liz." The crowd cheered and recruited new members.

Hastily the services were set back to noon. When the cortege came to the gates at twelve o'clock, it was nearly impossible to drive through the throng. Fans threw slips of paper through the car windows for autographs. Others yelled, "Hey, Liz, look this way," and snapped their cameras.

A group of gypsies appeared, with fiddles, tambourines, and guitars, and offered to play for the services. The police, fighting for control, had a rough time getting rid of them.

David Goldbogen, one of Mike's brothers, the first mourner to arrive, went inside the tent. Elizabeth's car was edging toward it when noisy arguments broke out. A cameraman was trying to crawl under one side of the canvas. The other cameramen immediately shouted to be allowed inside.

Finally the services began. Deathly white, withdrawn, Elizabeth Todd sat unmoving, ignoring the cameras, ignoring the whispers, ignoring everything. She did not bow her head for the prayers or seem to hear the chants. Even when young Mike moved beside the grave to speak of the dead, she did not lift her eyes. "My father was the greatest human being who ever lived," said Mike junior.

Only when they began lowering the casket into the ground, did she return to a dreadful awareness. She sprang up, threw herself on the casket, the black veil from her hat falling over her tragic face. She cried, "Oh, no, no, no! Mike, Mike, you cannot leave me here alone!"

Her father, her doctor, her brother held her back, but she could not stop weeping as the coffin was covered by clods of earth.

The camera addicts in the crowd thoroughly enjoyed it all. They shouted good-bye to all the mourners as they left the cemetery. They eagerly looked for but could not find Mike Wilding.

Lulled with another sedative, Elizabeth flew straight back to California on a chartered plane with the family group. It was very late in the evening when they returned to the dark house that was too still, with the scent of too many flowers in the air, and too cluttered with piles of telegrams, notes of condolence, letters of sympathy. The children were asleep. The mourners stayed until she fell asleep. Dr. Kennamer, carrying her to bed, said she would not wake till morning.

The next day was Wednesday, the day of the Academy

Awards. Helen Rose called early. "Elizabeth, about that white dress you meant to wear tonight..."

"Forget it." She did not say another word, but Helen had heard the tears in her voice.

Bill Lyon, from the MGM publicity department, the same Bill Lyon who had been her escort at her first kid party, went over to the Todd house that evening to be on hand just in case she might win for *Raintree County*.

"Only her brother, Howard, and his wife were there," Bill explained later, "and she was the most tragic figure. We all felt if we could get her at all interested in the Awards, it might help. We got her down into the living room of that huge house Mike had rented. She was wearing one of those magnificent house gowns Mike had liked to see her in. She had on no makeup and no jewelry except Mike's own wedding ring. That was the only thing that had been saved from the plane wreck, the ring of their marriage. We turned on the show, and one of the very first awards, a technical one, was to Todd-A-O. Well, all that did, of course, was to remind her of the year before, when Mike had won, when Mike had run back and kissed her.

"She just sat there with the tears running down her face. She didn't make a sound, but her tears continued. Finally as it was getting toward the top awards, she said, 'I am not going to win. Joanne Woodward is going to win. Nothing is going to go right for me now. Nothing will go right for me from now on, because Mike is gone.'

"Then the Award for the best actress came up and Joanne Woodward did win. Liz turned to me and said, 'Bill, order a corsage of white orchids right away. Have them sent to the Beverly Hilton before the Academy party, and Bill, tell the florist to have the card read: "Best wishes and congratulations." Have it signed, "Elizabeth and Mike Todd."'

"Then, she really broke down, and we had to carry her back upstairs."

Yes, it was dramatic, but because she was an actress and drama was her life blood, it was endurable, just as the funeral for all its horror had, for the same reason, been endurable. Elizabeth was able to endure the first week after Mike died, even if she could retain no solid food and slept only when drugged. The next two weeks were crowded with phone calls, telegrams, letters of condolence, tax men, lawyers.

The drama of it all, the duty, let her get through it. She had loved Mike so completely that she had barely wanted to see any of her old friends since her marriage. She had seen Mike's crowd, wherever they were. She had lived in Mike's world, had borne Mike's daughter, shared Mike's dream, his laughter, and his vitality, lived in his future, and loved him, loved him, loved him.

Now that was all gone. She had to stand alone, as she had never stood alone in her life, and because of the love Mike had taught her, she had to hold her head high.

The papers said that Mike Todd had left millions, but it was not true, as his lawyers soon pointed out. Mike had made money for the zest of conquest, and spent it for the thrill of pleasure.

"My husband was a showman, not an accountant," Elizabeth lashed out when one of the lawyers seemed a bit critical. "He wasn't a manufacturer. He was the theatrical genius who brought something new and vital to a tired movie industry."

She was assured of an income from *Around the World in 80 Days*, although the income would not endure long. Mike had been generous with his film, giving pieces of it to Mike junior, to members of his family, to Richard Hanley, his secretary. Besides there were a lot of partners to be paid off.

Mike had died partially owning several theaters that were still being altered for the Todd-A-O process to show his picture. He would have known how to manage all that, but no ordinary businessman would.

Grappling with such matters gave Elizabeth something to do during the days. Having her children, her parents, a few close friends around her, giving her love, receiving her love, filled up the evenings.

But then the hour would come when she had to go to bed—alone. Alone in the empty bed, she who had been twenty-six only the month before, and who had grown accustomed to the most ardent and continuous love. She would gulp down a sleeping pill and lie rigid until the pill took over. Whereupon the nightmares began. Night after night she had a nightmare of planes falling. Sometimes she would see Mike in the plane, the flames consuming him.

Often, waking from those nightmares, she would become so cold the whole bed would rattle from her shivering. "Control yourself, control yourself," she would whisper to give herself some sense of not being quite so alone. Only speaking aloud made her cry, because there was no answer. Some lucky nights she would fall back asleep and have her second dream, which was the one where she found Mike.

She would make a turning on a path in the country, or in a city street, and there was Mike, not dead, but giving her that wonderful smile. She would rush toward him, but just as she was about to reach him, something would intervene, an automobile or a strange animal. She would fight to get around the obstacle, but when she did, Mike would be gone again.

Many evenings she slipped out to consult Rabbi Nussbaum. He gave her books to study, the Torah with its laws and ideals, and histories of the Jewish people, including contemporary life in Israel. They were hard, dry reading, but she read them diligently. They brought Mike back to her a little.

Rabbi Nussbaum also pointed out that she had known as much love in her 414 days of marriage to Mike as many women know in an entire lifetime. He said, "You must live for that love, live for Mike's sake, and for your children and his children. It is your duty."

Except for seeing this spiritual adviser, Elizabeth Todd did not go out of her house those first two weeks. At the start of the third week she called Richard Brooks and asked whether she might come over. No, she wasn't coming back to work. She just wanted to see how *Cat* was going.

"We were doing one of the scenes where Burl Ives, as Big Daddy, first realizes he may be dying," Brooks said. "It was too late for me to change anything. I didn't know how such a scene would affect Elizabeth, but I decided the gamble was better than my turning her down. So I arranged for the set to be closed to all outsiders, and I told the cast she was arriving.

"I knew it would be hard on all of us. The crew was handpicked from a group she had worked with since her childhood. She loved them and they loved her.

"In the scene that day there were Paul Newman, Burl Ives, and Madeleine Sherwood. I told everybody that to ignore Elizabeth completely would be bad, but if we spoke to her about something that upset her, that would be bad, too.

"All we could do was play it by ear. We were shooting as she came in, after lunch, and we went right on, which wasn't easy. She was very pale, shockingly thin. But she didn't break down, and the actors didn't break up.

"She slipped into a chair. I kept thinking about Paul Newman being her leading man and how Paul Newman's wife had won the Academy Award away from her, but I certainly wasn't going to bring that up. When after a couple of scenes I saw her getting up to leave, I called out, 'Come over tomorrow if you feel like it.'

"As she reached the exit, she turned and said, 'If you would shoot just one small scene of mine tomorrow, I'll try to do it.'

"I kept it very unemotional. I took her script and marked off a scene. 'This one okay?'

"'Yes. Dick, please, can I come to work after lunch?'

"I knew it must be because of the sleeping pills that she asked that. 'See you at one thirty,' I said.

"She arrived, exactly on time, but without makeup. On a table in the center of the set there was a bowl with a big bunch of violets in it, and further upstage a vase of long-stemmed yellow roses. I hadn't known what to do about those flowers, whether it was wise or stupid to have them there. The violets were from the crew, who knew they were her favorite flowers, and the roses were from the cast. The whole outfit had wanted to make some gesture.

"She spotted the flowers the moment she came in and knew exactly what they signified. Then I saw the tears come into her eyes, and I could have shot everyone, myself included. She said, 'Thank you, thank you,' turned to go to the makeup department, and then faltered, and I knew she just couldn't go on. 'Have Hanley take you home,' I said. 'Your clothes aren't ready. You've lost so much weight Wardrobe is still altering them, but they'll be done tomorrow.'

"The next day she worked, on camera, for an hour. After that I never knew just what might happen. She always arrived at one thirty, made up. I always had a scene of hers ready to go, but some days she'd stop after one or two lines and would not be able to go on. Sometimes she would cry in that most painful way, silently, the tears just rolling down her face.

"Other times, under pressure of her role, and her own sorrow, she couldn't remember her lines—and she has always been letter perfect in her roles. But she did keep on coming until we'd got two weeks' work in the can.

"Now all that time, to protect her, I had been putting her in scenes where she didn't have to do much talking. But I saw as the days passed that she was literally getting weak from lack of solid food. There was a scene in *Cat* which was supposed to be a birthday dinner for Big Daddy, where everyone was gathered around eating ham and chicken. I arranged to put that scene in ahead of schedule.

"As the camera started that day, Elizabeth, as Maggie, began eating and she just couldn't stop. I had the scene done over and over, for some phony reason or other, and she

151

simply sat there, lost in her performance, and gorged herself.

"That was the beginning of her coming back to her real personality. There was a scene I had been dreading doing, and I now decided to risk it. She had no dialogue in it. It was all Judith Anderson's scene, with Judith, as Big Mamma, explaining about her realization that Big Daddy is about to die. She says, 'I guess things never turn out the way you dream they are going to turn out.'

"As Judith read the line, I had the camera shooting over her shoulder for a close-up of Elizabeth. I saw Elizabeth's eyes fill up. I signaled the camera to keep on going. She began to cry, and she kept right on crying. That was exactly what I wanted, but it was heartbreaking to watch, because it was real. Finally, while the camera was still grinding, Elizabeth simply walked off the set and shut herself in her trailer dressing room.

"I just went on, finished the scene, and we began lighting for the next one. When that was ready, I went over to her trailer and knocked. Elizabeth opened the door. 'I'll be all right,' she said. 'It was just when Judith said that things never turn out the way you think—well, I could only think of all my plans with Mike.'

"I knew then that her work was a catharsis for her. Still, as I saw her when we were through work, leaving for that big, silent house, I wondered what was to become of her."

She was wondering, too. When *Cat on a Hot Tin Roof* wound up shooting, MGM had nothing else ready for her.

She began seeing a great deal of Mike Todd junior. They talked on and on for hours about the man whom they both had loved. Young Mike wanted to follow in his father's footsteps, and if he could come up with projects starring his father's widow, what could be more effective?

Thus, toward the end of May in what had been Mike Todd's office at MGM, the new firm of Todd and Todd held a press conference. Young Mike, as president, announced that he and his partner, Elizabeth Todd, were shelving the very expensive *Don Quixote*. Instead he and Mrs. Todd were making a comedy, *Busman's Holiday*. He would produce, Mrs. Todd would star.

Mrs. Todd beamed at the reporters and photographers. They were the first casual acquaintances she had seen since widowhood. She discovered it was nice being out in the world again.

The script of *Busman's Holiday*, however, did not jell, and so Mike junior, once again using a pattern of his father's, bought into a film process. It was called, with clumsy humor, "Smell-o-Vision," and its uniqueness was that it shot out perfume over a theater as certain flowery scenes appeared on screen.

Young Mike decided to make a half-spoofing suspense film to go along with this. He called it *Scent of Mystery*. Would his beautiful stepmother partner invest in the enterprise with him? Would she do one scene in the film, please?

She would. She did invest, and she played a tiny scene in it. However, "Smell-o-Vision" was no Todd-A-O. The public threw up its nose at it, and Todd and Todd, stepmother and son, dropped a lot of money.

Summer came, and Elizabeth Todd, who had not been idle since she was eight, had nothing to plan for, no man to dream about. The Todd drama was over—except for her. The curtain had fallen on the great love story—except for her. Mike was her true love, forever, but he was gone.

When people tried being glibly sympathetic, she'd snap, "Don't hold out hopeless hope to me. There was only one Mike Todd."

Alone, she fought her melancholy, asked no pity. She faced the reality that her friends, the studio, even her devoted parents and her children had gone back to their own concerns.

Through many a sleepless midsummer night she paced about her house. The perfumes of the flowers in her garden wafted up to her, the night birds sang, and her stout blood ran hot through her veins.

She wasn't living a whole life that July and August. *Cat on a Hot Tin Roof* came out and was a hit, and her notices were the best she had ever received, but she cried as she read them, thinking of how much more they would have meant to Mike.

Lacking emotional expression, she tried being intellectual. She conscientiously studied the Jewish faith. She conscientiously made herself be a good and devoted parent to her children. But it wasn't enough. She was bored.

One night Nicky Hilton called and asked her out to dinner. She didn't go, and felt very virtuous—virtuous but lonely. The next day Arthur Loew, Jr., asked her to dinner. She accepted. Arthur, son of a movie pioneer, had been a friend of hers and Nicky's. Nobody would think anything of Arthur's dating her. He always dated glamour girls. Nothing ever came of it.

However, at dinner Arthur suggested that she come with her children to his Arizona ranch for a visit. His sister Jane was staying there with him. Elizabeth would be thoroughly chaperoned by her children and their nurses.

It was a diversion, packing up her youngsters, going into a new setting. Arthur was a fine host, Jane an excellent hostess. The ranch was beautiful. The children loved it. The visit was all very relaxed, and if Elizabeth had been fifty, she would have delighted in it. But she was twenty-six and restless with unused energy.

The lease on her house in Beverly Hills was about to run out. She had an empty apartment in New York and an empty country house in Connecticut. "I've done nothing about any of that since Mike died," she told Arthur. "If Liza were old enough to travel, I'd pack us all up, and go to the Riviera or some such place for a couple of weeks."

"Liz, why don't you? Leave the kids here, if you like. They're happy here. Jane is remaining here for a while. They could have their nurses stay with them, too, as long as you like. Go travel, Liz. It will do you good."

By simply having a man make up her mind, she felt more alert than she had for weeks. MGM came through, of course, got her reservations, followed her instructions to arrange a stopover in New York for a couple of days before she'd fly out for the south of France.

The New York papers photographed her arrival, announced where she was staying. Unable to endure the idea of staying at the apartment where, as Mrs. Mike Todd, she had known such happiness, she had checked into a hotel. Late in the afternoon Eddie Fisher called to welcome her to the big city.

"What are you doing here, Liz?"

"I'm on my way to the Riviera. Golly, it's good to hear your voice, Eddie. Why are *you* here?"

"I'm winding up a recording session. I'm here all by myself. It's lonely."

"Don't I know. Oh, Eddie, isn't it awful, being lonely?"

"Why don't we be lonely together? How about having dinner with me tonight?"

Elizabeth accepted, and that did it. That really did it. It was the first time she and Eddie Fisher had ever been out alone together. It was the first time they had met since Mike's funeral.

It did not occur to her to hide their meeting. It was a hot summer evening. Elizabeth wore a very simple—Paris simple—

black dinner dress, plain black satin pumps, and her smallest diamond earrings. Eddie took her to one of Manhattan's deluxe restaurants where the smart Broadway crowd gathers. Scores of acquaintances, old Broadway pals of Mike Todd's, reporters, the crowd from Tin Pan Alley, all of whom knew Eddie, welcomed them. As headwaiters bowed, and bus boys snapped to attention, it was for Elizabeth like being out with Mike again. She was back in the warm, rich, exciting atmosphere Mike had created everywhere.

And Eddie heightened that atmosphere the moment they were seated, by saying, "You want your usual soda?"

"My what?"

"Your champagne over ice cubes. You still go for that?"

She knew it was silly to be gratified by his remembering such a little thing about her tastes, but she loved it. He took over, just as Mike would have, and ordered her dinner for her. As she ate, she saw him watching her, his eyes admiring, as Mike's eyes would have been. She discovered she was full of talk, close, for the first time in months, even to laughter. They talked about Mike. They repeated Mike's jokes. They discussed his talent. They reminisced about Mike's wonderful taste, his positive genius.

"More wine, Elizabeth?"

"Down, boy, it must be getting late. It's been a lovely dinner, Eddie."

He moved a little closer to her on the banquette, and his hand clasped hers lightly. "You lost a husband, and I lost the best friend a man ever had."

Tears flooded her eyes. She could not immediately speak. Her voice shook when she said, "Mike was the greatest love I shall ever know. I shall never love anyone so much again."

His voice was muted. "I know that, Liz. I know that."

She freed her hand and became aware that they were the only couple left in the opulent dining room.

"The waiters want to go home, Eddie. You'd better take me back to my hotel. What time is it, anyway?"

"Say, can you believe it? It's one thirty."

She stared. It was the first time since Mike had died that time had moved swiftly.

They walked slowly to her hotel. Again his hand reached out and lightly clasped hers. She smiled at him gratefully as they stopped before her hotel. She felt more of a human being than she had for many weeks.

"'Night, Liz. Okay if I call you tomorrow?"

"Oh, please do, Eddie. Thank you so much for tonight. I've had such a good time."

As she entered her suite, high up over the city, the phone was ringing.

"Hey, Liz," Eddie said, "want to go up to Grossinger's with me tomorrow? . . . Grossinger's? That's where my genius was discovered, nine years ago. Thirty dollars a week, and I thought I was in the money. It's where Debbie and I were married, almost three years ago. Tomorrow Grossinger's is celebrating the completion of a swimming pool they've been trying to complete for the last six hundred years. I'm driving up with a couple of guys. Why don't you come along? It's beautiful, up in the Catskills, autumn leaves falling and all that. Jennie Grossinger, who runs the place, she'll flip for you. Say yes, huh?"

"Okay, great. What time?"

"We'll pick you up around four o'clock. Okay?"

"Yes. Thanks, Eddie. Eddie, thank you very much."

When they took off early that Saturday morning, they did not think of Milton Blackstone, Eddie's manager, and Danny Welkes, an old friend of Eddie's, as really being in the roles of chaperones. When Milton said he'd heard there were twenty reporters and photographers waiting for them at Grossinger's, they merely laughed.

They had gone through that publicity barrage so many times before, particularly at the wedding in Acapulco. They could easily go through it again.

"We'll get lost in the shuffle up there," Eddie said, "Jennie told me they expect at least fifteen hundred guests over Labor Day."

Elizabeth was still wearing black. She was wearing that day the simplest black sheath and only Mike's twenty-nine-carat diamond on her engagement finger. But she was immediately mobbed as they drew up at Grossinger's. People climbed on chairs to see her more closely. Children climbed on tables. And there were twenty photographers plus twenty reporters there, all snapping shots of her, all firing questions at her.

After that, she could barely move. Eddie, Blackstone, and Danny Welkes stayed on three sides of her always. When she tried to swim in the Grossinger pool, it became so crowded she couldn't take two consecutive strokes without being touched, without being almost mauled. When she and her three escorts walked along Grossinger's famous Lovers Lane, fifteen hundred other people walked down the lane with them, whispering and staring.

Saturday evening, when Eddie sang for the throng, Elizabeth sat at a ringside table with Milton and Danny and smiled at him. When he finished, they tried to dance together but immediately had to give it up.

Sunday and Monday Elizabeth was held captive by the throngs, and yet she knew these were the happiest days she had known since she lost Mike. As she and the three men headed back to Manhattan on Tuesday, she hated to see the holiday end, thinking of the emptiness ahead.

They were almost back in town when Eddie said, "Listen, why don't I dig us up a couple of friends and we'll go to the Harwyn Club tonight? There's never any mob there. The food is great. The wine is cold. The band is fine. Good idea?"

"Great idea," she said.

Eddie picked her up at eight that evening. With him were Rick Ingersoll, who was Debbie Reynolds's special publicity man at MGM, and the lovely blonde actress, Eva Marie Saint, with whom Elizabeth had worked on *Raintree County*. They all went to the Harwyn. Elizabeth still wore black and her simplest diamonds. Nobody did any hiding out, even if photographers soon surrounded the place.

Actually Eddie Fisher had been supposed to fly back home that night. Next morning Debbie Reynolds met the plane on which he was expected. What met her were the headlines and the photographs of her husband and Mike Todd's widow dancing merrily in New York together.

Now up until that morning of September 10, 1958, Eddie Fisher, aged twenty-eight, was on top of the world. He was the "Coca-Cola kid," star of the Eddie Fisher TV show, husband of cute little Debbie Reynolds, father of two chubby, cute kids. He had hit records going for him. He had personal-appearance tours and nightclub dates going for him. He had a recording contract with RCA that was due to pay him a million dollars before it ran out. When that time came, all signs indicated another contract would immediately be written. Let him croon something like "Oh, My Papa," and he melted a million hearts and for a half hour's work made a half a million dollars.

From the moment of his discovery he, a charming, curly-haired Jewish boy from Philadelphia, had done everything right. Eddie Cantor had originally recognized the sexy potential of his voice, and, hitting the teenage public at the correct wartime moment, Fisher became a recording star instantaneously.

Milton Blackstone moved in as manager, and Eddie did anything Blackstone told him. Blackstone was like a father to him. Next, the mighty Mike Todd became his good friend. Eddie turned Mike into his personal hero and tried to copy him in every way. Then Dean Martin became a pal, and Eddie listened to Dino's advice like a worshipful child.

That was Eddie's real gift, his instinctive ability to make powerful friends who were eager to aid him. Add his excellent, if largely untrained, baritone voice, add his natural obedience, his personal warmth, and you have the formula for his success.

He was simply being obedient when he met Debbie Reynolds. The idea came from the brain trust Blackstone had assembled behind the boy. Eddie made his Los Angeles debut on June 17, 1954. He was the hot shot with the teenage girls, and Debbie was a favorite of the teenagers in MGM musicals. That added up to teenage idol meets a teenage movie star the first time he encounters Hollywood.

Debbie wasn't the teenager she acted on screen and off. She was twenty-two, and she had never been kissed. At the same time Elizabeth Taylor, a few months her junior, was enjoying her second marriage, enjoying raising her two sons.

Debbie at twenty-two was cute enough to have been kissed, but she had been raised to yield to no man.

She was a natural leader, aggressive and smart. In school she led everything, won every contest. She was a whiz at sports and attended the Baptist church a couple of times a week. No one in the Los Angeles suburb of Burbank was surprised when she won a contest and got into the movies.

Her mother made all her clothes. At school she wore sweaters her mother knitted for her. On the necks of them were the letters N.N.

N.N. stood for *no necking*. She never once deviated from that command, not even when she got to Hollywood and became a star. At home she was still called Mary Frances, and she practically never had looked at any boy until the evening she went to the Cocoanut Grove with her father and mother, and looked adoringly at Eddie Fisher.

She had been told to look adoringly at Eddie Fisher, but she found she cottoned to the idea anyhow. And Eddie Fisher looked down on Debbie Reynolds flirtatiously as he had been ordered to. He sang his songs to her, as ordered. But he found it pleasant work. She was a cute girl. It was a cute gag they were involved in. He was then twenty-three.

Eddie Cantor was giving a party after the opening, for his protégé. Debbie Reynolds was invited, along with her parents. It was a great, glittering party, and Eddie Fisher barely left Debbie Reynolds's side. The photographers rose nobly to the bait, and the papers next morning ran rapturous columns about love at first sight.

Eddie was booked into the Cocoanut Grove for a couple of weeks. Practically every night of those two weeks Debbie, with her folks, was at ringside. Those evenings Eddie laughed, flirted with her, sang her love songs in his persuasive voice.

They were dating in the daytime, too. That is, when Eddie had a spare moment from his recording and Debbie had a day off. They were dating on the N.N. standard, of course. Debbie took Eddie to Burbank to meet her brother and her grandmother. On Sundays, clad in jeans, with her hair pulled back in pigtails, she let him see what a wow she was on the ball field. Oh, sure, there were cameramen and photographers present at these events, and the word *engagement* began to appear more and more in the columns.

Milton Blackstone, Eddie's manager, didn't want to have his boy get married. That would be bad box office. But Blackstone wasn't really worried. Their next stop was London. But in London Blackstone got a shock. No less than the Queen of England asked Eddie if it was true that he was going to marry that cute little Debbie Reynolds. Who would want to disillusion the Queen of England?

Yet some cads tried. There were some terrible press people who said the Reynolds family would never let Debbie marry Eddie, because of his faith. There were some others who announced that Eddie's sponsors would never let him marry on any terms.

What was a gallant boy to do then? He did the right thing. The moment he got back to America Eddie flew west, and announced his engagement to Debbie. Eddie Cantor gave another party. Four hundred guests that time, and Debbie told everyone she would be married in June. What date in June she didn't know. She didn't care, even if it was as late as the thirtieth, but to be married in June would make her lifelong dream come true. She said they would live in Hollywood after the wedding. In New York Eddie's sponsors howled. He had to broadcast from New York. He and his bride must live in New York. Debbie said they'd manage somehow to work things out. Eddie beamed and said, yes, they surely would. June was more than half a year away then.

The weeks flew by, and the fanfare continued. Every deed of theirs was headlined. Eddie sent Debbie a French poodle. The pooch made the whole world's press. Debbie tried to surprise Eddie by sending him a secondhand player piano for his birthday. The press heard of it and ruined her gag by telling the world.

One night on his show Eddie forgot the words of a song. "I must be in love," he said laughing—the audience loved it and the papers headlined it. One day on her set Debbie Reynolds blew a scene. "I know I'm in love," she said, and everybody on the set laughed, and the papers printed that, too.

Only the papers didn't stop there. One columnist asked, "Is this love or is this publicity?" Another told how Debbie was marrying Eddie for his money.

The young sweethearts ignored such carping and set the date for their wedding as June 17, a nice sentimental date, since it would be exactly a year since the day of their first meeting.

With the date fixed, Debbie, the little manager, went into high gear. She rented a house she thought would be ideal for her and Eddie. She started making out her guest list. She meant to ask 150 friends to the ceremony, but the list incredibly grew to 1,000.

Then Eddie called. His sponsors were insisting upon his staying in New York. Yes, yes, he adored her, but they must postpone their marriage until they worked out the details. Meanwhile he had to play London again. Why didn't she come over there, so they could clear up the whole situation?

Debbie and her mother went to England and sat backstage every night, waiting for Eddie. Mrs. Reynolds suggested that the children be married right then in some little English town. Eddie said nothing. Debbie refused.

When they all returned to America and her wedding date was pushed ahead again, Debbie went off to entertain our troops in Korea. Debbie lost weight. Her face showed strain, but she stuck.

Eddie certainly had lots of excuses for postponing their wedding date until September. His sponsors really were adamant about his having to broadcast from New York.

Eddie took Debbie as his wife finally on September 26, 1955. The place was Liberty, New York, Jennie Grossinger's place. They had only their attendants and their parents there,

Debbie's mother and dad and Eddie's father and mother, who were divorced. They were married at eight fifty in the evening—fifty minutes late because Eddie's mother got held up in traffic.

Debbie wore a white lace ballerina-length dress trimmed with white velvet and a white Juliet cap with a short veil. Her attendant was Jeannette Johnson, one of the girls she had gone to school with in Burbank. Jeannette gave Debbie an orchid-covered Bible to carry to her wedding, though Eddie was Jewish.

The press made it sound like the ending to a magazine serial, the Coca-Cola kid finally being married to the cute, good little movie star. Immediately they became Debbie and Eddie, the world's sweethearts. A couple of months later, when it was announced that Debbie was pregnant, they advanced to being the world's cutest new parents.

They cashed in on that world enthusiasm. They made a picture together, *Bundle of Joy*, not much of a picture, and Eddie proved to be not much of an actor. None of that mattered. The film was a hit.

When the baby came, they named her Carrie Frances, and Debbie announced that she'd like to have at least five children. Life was being adorable to them. Eddie's public hadn't deserted him. Debbie's public thought she was the living end. Eddie had to commute back and forth to New York for his show, but what of that? They really had everything.

On the surface, anyhow. But Eddie was a night person, a big-city boy. Debbie was a day person, a small town girl. He came alive at night, loved to go out on the town, and stay up till dawn. He was earning big money and he spent it in a big way. He gambled for high stakes.

Debbie was thrifty. She didn't like nightclubs. She didn't like gambling. She never procrastinated. She knew exactly what she wanted to do, just what she wanted to say about any subject, just where she wanted to go, and how to get there fastest.

Then Mike Todd came to town to make *Around the World in 80 Days*, and Eddie Fisher became his worshipful shadow. When Mike began courting Elizabeth Taylor, the Fishers found themselves part of an almost permanent foursome.

After the Fisher-Reynolds-Taylor scandal broke, there was a lot of nonsense printed about the former friendship of Debbie and Elizabeth. That friendship existed only in the minds of those reporters. Elizabeth and Debbie never were friends. During the Todd era they learned to tolerate one another as women do when their husbands are buddy-buddies.

But during the time of their foursome, everywhere that Debbie Fisher went, there was Elizabeth Todd, with her diamonds big as headlights, her Rolls-Royces, and her husband who gratified her every whim. Elizabeth Todd wore Paris gowns, exclusively designed for her. Hairdressers, make-up men, maids, tagged her everywhere. Elizabeth Todd had even looked beautiful and flawlessly groomed when pregnant. Debbie Fisher, carrying her second child, felt cumbersome in maternity smocks, many of which her mother made for her.

The Fishers had a mansion, originally Tudor in design, though Debbie had ordered decorators in to make it look cozy. Elizabeth Todd had several residences, each glorified with fine paintings, fabulous antiques.

Carrying her second baby, Debbie hoped for a boy, whom she'd name Kevin. He was a boy, but she named him Todd Emmanuel, at Eddie's request. Then the man for whom he was named died barely six weeks later.

Six months later, a mere three weeks before her third wedding anniversary, Debbie went to meet a plane on which she thought her husband was arriving. She met, instead, the news from New York about him and the widow Todd.

She reacted with spirit. "Why shouldn't Eddie go out with Elizabeth? We are all such close friends." She looked with amused scorn at the reporters. "My, how Mike Todd would laugh over this if he could hear you."

Only it ceased to be a laughing matter when Eddie didn't come home for a week. During that week Debbie was very courteous to the press. She came out of her big house that second day and gave them the best photograph of the year. She looked such an innocent, spunky little kid, wearing jeans and a shirt, with her hair pulled back in pigtails. She had on no jewels and barely a trace of lipstick. From the front of her shirt there dangled a bunch of baby-diaper pins.

That day Debbie told the press that she was quite shocked by the reports concerning her husband's continued meetings with their old family friend. The following day she said she was very, very much in love with her husband, but she might have to consult her attorney.

When Eddie did return, he said to the reporters clustered at the airport, "I am not in love with Liz and Liz is not in love with me." Debbie didn't meet him. He did not go home.

Instead he checked in at Joey Foreman's apartment. Seven hours passed before he drove out to his own house.

Elizabeth returned the following day. All she would say was that the rumors about her and Eddie were "garbage." (In 1962 she was to say the same thing about the first rumors concerning herself and Richard Burton.)

The press, racing madly to the Fisher home to check out that remark, discovered Debbie's press agents on the lawn, obligingly dishing out hamburgers and ice cream. As the press paused for refreshment, Eddie and Debbie scampered out of their back door and clambered over the garden wall. Eddie was wearing Capri pants, Debbie was again in jeans and a shirt with her hair in pigtails. They escaped in a car driven by one of her old school friends.

The next morning the Chester, Pennsylvania, *Times* was brought to the attention of Hollywood. It seemed Eddie Fisher was a columnist for that obscure publication. There, under his by-line, was Eddie saying, "I am willing to do anything to save my marriage. As for Liz and I being in love, it is utter nonsense."

Debbie called several editorial friends right then. "Don't blame Eddie for what's happened," she said. "I'm still in love with him. We never were happier than we've been in the last year. If it were not for Liz, it never could have happened."

Elizabeth remained silent until columnist Hedda Hopper got to her. Miss Hopper was the first member of the press she had ever met, way back in her childhood, and she had grown to regard her as almost a foster mother.

Miss Hopper, next morning, reported her as saying, "You know I don't go around breaking up marriages. Eddie's not in love with Debbie and he never has been. Only a year ago they were about to get a divorce but stopped when they found she was going to have another baby." When asked about the memory of Mike Todd, Miss Hopper printed Elizabeth's reply as, "Mike's dead and I'm alive."

Elizabeth protested later, saying: "She asked if I was aware of how much Mike was in love with me and I said, 'Oh, God, you know how much I loved Mike; I loved him more than my life. But Mike is dead now, and I'm alive, and the one person who would want me to try to live and be happy is Mike.'"

At the apex of the Fisher-Reynolds-Taylor triangle, she never once considered being politic. She probably could have had a little backstairs affair with Eddie, soon consummated, soon forgotten, and protected by her studio and friends, the world would not necessarily have been any the wiser. But though spoiled, she was basically honest.

During those weeks, she proved her honesty in another way. A news story came out calling Eddie Fisher "the love of Elizabeth Taylor's life." She could, by acting sad and subtle, have won sympathy for that. She wouldn't pretend. She called Louella Parsons and begged her to print for her a statement she was mailing her. Miss Parsons obliged. The statement said, "I deeply loved Mike Todd and will always cherish his memory as one of the most beautiful things in my life. I don't want anything to destroy that memory."

Confronted with such forthrightness, Eddie Fisher then stopped trying to be the soft-drink kid. Tired, haggard, he called a press conference. He said, "Debbie and I tried very hard to make our marriage work. We have been having problems for a long time. Debbie especially has done everything possible to make our marriage succeed.

"I alone accept full responsibility for its failure. Our marriage would have come to an end even if I had never known Elizabeth Taylor. The breakup was inevitable."

Debbie Reynolds said, "As God is my judge, I did not know he did not love me."

The storm of public indignation broke, and the irony was that this was one of the rare instances where it was the man who paid and paid and is still paying. Before public anger cooled, Eddie lost the whole edifice—his TV show, his home, his nightclub engagements, his wife, and the future income from his record contract, which was turned over to Debbie as part of his divorce settlement.

Debbie's career immediately took on new luster. Public sympathy was very much with her, and her picture price jumped to a hundred thousand dollars, about twice what it had been.

But the startling fact was that Elizabeth, cast into the role of "the other woman," saw her salary jump to five times that. *Cat on a Hot Tin Roof* had been doing excellent business, but when the Fisher story broke, it became box-office capacity everywhere.

This was despite a section of the public that turned on her with feline fury. She began receiving more than five thousand letters of vituperation and hate weekly. Groups of demonstrators, mostly women, organized to boycott her films. An important trade group, the Theatre Owners of America, took a public stand against her. Until that time she had been the strongest contender for their annual award because of her work in *Cat*. The Theatre Owners gave the award instead to Deborah Kerr. Their spokesman said, "To award Miss Taylor the honor at a time like this is out of the question." Apparently they didn't recall that Miss Kerr's very happy marriage had been broken up just a bit before that—and Miss Kerr had married the gentleman who had done the breaking.

Debbie Reynolds signed to make *It Started with a Kiss* with Glenn Ford for a hundred thousand dollars. Debbie said she was not sure she would get a divorce. Later she agreed to getting one in California, which would not become legal for a year.

Elizabeth Taylor signed to do *Suddenly, Last Summer* for a half a million dollars. So, there she was again, the girl who had everything. A great role to play, a great salary, a great love, and a great scandal.

By then Eddie was lyric about her. Out of his rapidly dwindling funds he bought her a bracelet of fifty diamonds as an engagement present. He said, "I know I am not the great love in Elizabeth's life, but she is the great love of mine." He was even more romantic when he talked to her personally. He told her, "I don't care that Mike is first in your love. I only care that you are with me. If I have you, I have everything."

She loved such talk. It was infinitely easy for her to look at this infatuated young man and know that she adored him. Also, with him she could have a full life, without having to renounce her eternal love of Mike Todd. She loved Eddie especially when he confessed to her that he had fallen in love with her when as a boy in Philadelphia he had seen her, the beautiful little girl of *National Velvet*. "I have never got over that crush," he said.

She had woven her spell again. Her ego was fed. She was adored. It was an ecstatic time.

Eddie called her constantly when he had to be away from her, just as Mike had. He didn't want her out of his sight any more than Mike had. He showered her with gifts. He helped her and the children move into a new house, the luxurious house in which Tyrone Power had lived when he was married to Linda Christian. He adored her children, missing his own. Her children adored him, missing Mike.

Yielding brought joy to her, joy to him. Elizabeth saw the happiness in his eyes when he discovered how dependent she was. "I'm a silly girl," she said, but she saw that he liked that, liked her having to have a man in her life doing the male things, looking after a woman, being the boss.

Until then everything about Eddie's life had made him the one to yield. Now he became dominant, and it made them both happy. It was well that they grew more and more in love, for they soon discovered they had few friends. The public reaction against them became so bitter they seldom went out. It became unsafe for them even to go for a drive along a public highway. Her Rolls-Royce or his sporty Dual-Ghia was recognized, and people blocked them in traffic and yelled insults at her. As for their friends, they seemed all to be occupied every night, busy going places, or at close range, busy looking in the other direction.

There were a few wonderful exceptions, such as Dean Martin. He called up columnists, pleading for a little kindness for Eddie Fisher. Dinah Shore made the same plea. Elizabeth's close friends at the studio, such as Helen Rose and Sidney Guilaroff, her hairdresser, and Dick Hanley, her secretary, Richard Brooks, Pan Berman, and her agent, Kurt Frings, stayed close to her. As for her parents, they never wavered in their constancy and devotion. In every way they proved that she was their adored child. There was, also, Eddie's Jewish mother back in Philadelphia. Debbie and Eddie's mother had never got along, but she and Elizabeth took a big shine to one another.

Nonetheless, on the whole, it was a bitterly lonely time for the lovers. They both loved bright lights, good food, laughter, and music, which they were then denied, so for those first months they had to create their own. Many evenings they turned on the hi-fi in Elizabeth's house and danced together. Because Eddie loved to see her dressed elaborately, evening after evening she would don her most extreme Paris gowns, put on all her jewels, and order food sent in from Chasen's. Then they would make believe they were at a great dinner somewhere, outside.

They grew more and more in love because of their very isolation. Perhaps Elizabeth never thought about Eddie's being the only young man in her life—except Nicky, who never had adored her. As the weeks went by, Eddie adored her without reservation. Once again, she was the goddess Mike had made her. And in her fashion she was still true to Mike. Everywhere in her house she had pictures of Mike Todd, and she never took off his wedding ring.

On March 3, 1959, while Hollywood was still snubbing her, she was converted to the Jewish faith at Temple Israel in Hollywood. Rabbi Nussbaum conducted the ritual, witnessed by her father and mother. All converts adopt a Jewish name at such a time. Elizabeth chose the Hebrew equivalent of her own name, which is Elisheba, meaning "dedicated to God." She wanted very much to live up to that.

Rabbi Nussbaum told the press: "She was a good pupil, and she has a good understanding of Jewish life and has read extensively in Jewish history. She is very intelligent."

Said Elizabeth, "This is something I've wanted to do for a long time. It has nothing to do with any future marriage plans."

This stirred up a new avalanche of letters from anti-Semites and a rumor, widely printed, that she was a patient at Menningers's mental clinic in Topeka, Kansas.

That particular report blasted off the last shred of Elizabeth's enforced calm. Seething with rage, she personally called all the papers. "This is a cruel and terrible thing to do," she said. "It is frightening to see a black headline insinuating that I am mentally disturbed. So I'm going out. I'm going with Eddie to Chasen's so that everyone can see me and know I am not a mental patient."

What the photographs of that evening showed was that she had put on weight, which in her was a sign of inward turmoil. What her friends saw were her nervous gestures and the circles under her eyes. But she carried herself more than ever like a goddess.

Having once gone out in public with Eddie, she kept it up. Academy Award night came, and she was a candidate for *Cat*. She went to the ceremonies with Eddie by her side and was, as usual, the most beautiful woman in the great crowd. She held herself so straight, so defiantly that she seemed six feet tall. She said levelly, "I won't win. There is too much sentiment against me." She was right. She lost.

Elizabeth was due shortly in England to begin *Suddenly, Last Summer*. Then to their surprise and delight Eddie got an engagement. It was in honky-tonk Las Vegas and at one of the lesser casinos, but it was work. It was his first chance at a comeback. Elizabeth, with her parents, took up residence at a nearby ranch, and the three Taylors were at ringside every night for Eddie's performance. He sang all his songs to Elizabeth.

Very nervous, wary, he came on to a very cool audience.

He particularly featured an old Cantor hit, "Whoopee," with its lyrics about another bride, another June, another sunny honeymoon. Then, as he said, "In response to a request from a young lady who shall remain nameless," he sang "To Love and Be Loved" and many another sentimental ditty.

Elizabeth never batted an eye about the bad taste of it, and the crowd laughed and loved it. After that his audiences grew, particularly since Elizabeth was always an added attraction. The public got so fond of Eddie that it cheered on the evening the news flashed that Debbie Reynolds had relented and would get a Nevada divorce.

Three hours after Debbie's Nevada decree was handed down, Elizabeth became Eddie's bride. The date was May 12, 1959. The setting was Temple Beth Shalom in Las Vegas. Rabbi Max Nussbaum and Rabbi Bernard Cohen officiated at the service. Francis Taylor, looking his most distinguished, walked with his daughter up the aisle of the Temple. Mike Todd, Jr., who had flown in from Spain, was Eddie's best man.

Solemnly, in English and Hebrew, the rabbis blessed their union and chanted prayers for their happiness. Elizabeth, followed by Eddie, sipped the sacred wine and exchanged wedding rings. Eddie kissed her and whispered, "Behold, Elisheba, thou art consecrated unto me by means of this ring according to the laws of Moses and Israel."

They looked at one another, tears in their eyes. They had suffered, but now it was all over. Now they looked forward to happiness.

That night they flew to New York. The following day they took off for Barcelona to honeymoon on a 110-foot yacht that Sam Spiegel, the producer of *Suddenly, Last Summer,* had provided. They were to sail from Barcelona to Cannes, where Elizabeth's children would meet them. During the week's interval they had a captain, a chef, a steward, a chambermaid, three sailors, three engineers, and a bilingual secretary to provide for their comfort.

The ship's larders were loaded with everything from champagne to salami. There were no phones, no photographers. The Italian secretary gave orders to the captain and crew to stay invisible, and flawless Mediterranean days and nights merged into a week of enchantment.

They went ashore at St. Tropez. They went ashore at Portofino. They ate French food. They ate Italian food. They bought souvenirs. Sometimes they were recognized, but more often not. They ended a flawless honeymoon in Cannes, picking up the children, flying to London.

Of course, there was the British press to meet them on arrival. Because she was happy, Elizabeth spoke without thinking. "We'll be on our honeymoon for thirty or forty years."

"Give or take a couple of years either way," said Eddie, humming "See a Pretty Girl" as he smiled at his bride.

Elizabeth said, "As soon as my present contracts run out, I'm quitting movies to be just a good wife and mother."

"I thought you said that eighteen months ago with Mr. Todd," said a reporter, and that was exactly the way he wrote it up the next day.

Sam Spiegel had hired a magnificent residence for them, "Crown House," just outside London. It was staffed with a housekeeper, a chef, a valet for Eddie, three gardeners, three housemaids, and a nanny for the children.

Elizabeth was excited about working again. Monty Clift was her leading man in *Suddenly, Last Summer.* Joe Mankiewicz was the director. If both men sensed the change in her, saw that her happiness was a strange compound, they did not speak of it to her.

Her role of a girl on the verge of a nervous breakdown was a difficult, demanding one. All through the shooting Monty had trouble remembering his lines, causing many retakes. But Elizabeth had always been so professional, so unusual in her ability to go effortlessly from scene to scene that Joe said teasingly to her, "Dear Elizabeth, you are the Grandma Moses of acting. What do you need a director for? Not for directing, surely. You're a primitive, that's all. In a scene, you simply *are* the person."

On the sidelines Eddie waited on her. Eddie fetched and carried. He was visibly more and more deeply in love. Still, he had no function. He drove Liz back and forth to the studio and in between stayed at "Crown House," singing and playing with the children.

Weekends he and Elizabeth often flew to Paris. She had always liked that—with Mike Wilding. In Paris Eddie bought her gowns as Mike Todd had. Elizabeth bought him wonderful, crazy things in Paris, too, like a Jaguar and a raincoat with a beaver-fur lining. Eddie said to Monty Clift, "Sometimes she's like a kid, no older than her own kids, rollicking around. Other times she turns very grand. But at all times, she's a woman with a capital W."

She was neither a Woman nor a child, however, during the last two days' shooting of *Suddenly, Last Summer*. She became then a very remarkable actress.

She did a twelve-page monologue in those two days, ending with her rolling on the floor, screaming with hysteria. It is considered a good day's work in a studio if two pages of script are done in one day's shooting. To do better than six in a day, as Elizabeth did, and in monologue, too, is superhuman.

For a whole week before she went into the monologue, she worked herself up to its emotional pitch. She knew it would demand every resource she possessed. She anticipated how drained she would be after it. Still the challenge excited her.

Mankiewicz was equally excited and challenged. When the day for the scene arrived, he excluded outsiders from the set. Secretly he told his cameraman that once Elizabeth got started on her hysterics, he was to let the camera roll without pause.

The mood of Tennessee Williams's play held her captive throughout the first day and into the second. At the start of the second day's shooting she was at highest pitch, yet held it, increased it, flamed with it. It was midafternoon when it finally was finished. The reserved British crew were cheering, even while most of them cried. Elizabeth herself could not stop crying. The scene was over, but her frantic sobs continued. When Eddie came in, calling for her, she still wept. With her head buried on his shoulder, she sobbed wildly all the way back to "Crown House."

Eddie kept saying soothingly, "Darling, darling, stop suffering. From what Mank tells me you've got the Academy cinched for sure on this one."

He was wrong, though.

With *Suddenly, Last Summer* finished, the Fisher entourage flew back to New York and confronted the problem of finding living quarters for their big household. Elizabeth loved the excitement of Manhattan even while she longed for the western sun. She yearned for a ranch where her children could have horses and pets. She could never ride again, because of her back operation, but mere proximity to horses gave her happiness.

She and Eddie had not been west since his separation from Debbie. Legally their Las Vegas marriage could be challenged in California if someone wanted to be troublesome.

In early autumn of 1959 they rented a big rambling house,

just outside New York, and also a tropical estate on the island of Jamaica. The latter Elizabeth called "Eddie's Eden." It was within easy flying distance, so that they two, quite alone, could go there for weekends.

They were still forced to be two against the world, and they were evolving a unique happiness. Elizabeth found solace in going to temple regularly. Eddie wasn't nearly as faithful to his religion as she was. She celebrated the Chanukah holidays with his mother. She often took small Liza to services with her, regarding her as a born Jew, because of Mike, and doubly so after Eddie adopted her. She did not try to influence her sons' religion, telling them that their father was Church of England and they must decide for themselves how they wished to worship when grown. Nonetheless she was very pleased when little Mike said, "Mommy, I want to go where you go."

She believed herself to be very tranquil and suburban as the winter advanced, but when Eddie received the word that the glittering Waldorf-Astoria was booking him, she knew that she had been deceiving herself. She had missed the crowds. She hungered for color and excitement.

On his opening night at the Waldorf Eddie went out before the sophisticated crowd and was more frightened than ever in his life. Elizabeth, radiantly beautiful, wand-thin, sat out front. She was perfectly aware that the audience was watching her as much as they were watching Eddie.

Yet with his first note she relaxed. His voice was better, his diction clearer than it ever had been. She sensed the audience reacting. Oh, certainly, there were drunks in the room, and some bores who came over and asked her for autographs, but it was still Eddie's evening. He was on for more than an hour and a half, and there were calls for encores and more encores. Backstage when it was over she fell rapturously into her husband's arms.

"Now I'm the one to sit and wait," she giggled. "And just you watch me. I shall be simply tremendous in my dear-little-woman role."

Yet her emotional barometer, or the effects of the New York winter, or both, brought on double pneumonia and a temperature of 105°.

The hospital was nearly an hour's taxi ride from the Waldorf. Eddie was doing two shows a night. Yet he made the trip after each show, an hour up, an hour back. Since he didn't finish the last show until two A.M., he never got to bed a second before five A.M. But he liked seeing dawn come up over the spires of Manhattan. To him it was a symbol of his new career rising, for he broke all records at the Waldorf. He was a "name" again.

This may have influenced Hollywood to send Mr. and Mrs. Fisher their first official invitation to come back. A luncheon was being given for Premier Khrushchev, and Hollywood wanted to show off its biggest names. In the same mail, the Desert Inn in Las Vegas invited Mr. Fisher for an engagement there.

"Let's go," said Eddie, "and if they throw us in jail for bigamy, okay. Even temporarily, the sunshine will do you good."

"Let's go and buy ourselves a house in Las Vegas," said his bride. "Everybody is welcome in Las Vegas."

Elizabeth Fisher, dressed by Dior, arrived at the Khrushchev luncheon. The setting, the Twentieth Century-Fox commissary, wasn't particularly glamorous, but there was at least twenty million dollars' worth of talent from Gary Cooper to Marilyn Monroe assembled.

Elizabeth was the last gasp in Paris *haute couture*. It was before the very short skirts had reached America, but the hem of her lavender wool dress barely reached her knees. By no accident the color exactly matched her eyes. She wore a large mink hat, and her only jewel was Mike Todd's great engagement ring. Her expression as she walked in was completely bland. With everyone staring at her and Eddie, she seemed not to see one single soul, especially Debbie Reynolds, nearby, wearing a very simple little black dress and a hat trimmed with small pink flowers.

The box-office queen was back—back in Hollywood. *Suddenly, Last Summer* was out, another smash hit, and Hollywood, with its respect for great acting, knew how superb she was. Thus, no sooner had Khrushchev left the room than scores of people rushed over to greet Mr. and Mrs. Fisher. Among them were many who had snubbed them the year before. Now they were extending dinner invitations.

Elizabeth of England could not have been more gracious than Elizabeth Taylor Hilton Wilding Todd Fisher at that moment. Everyone was so very kind. She was so sorry, but she and Eddie simply didn't have one moment free, not one.

The Fishers stayed in Hollywood long enough for her to have a conference with Pandro Berman out at MGM. He gave her the hateful word. She could not accept Walter Wanger's wild offer.

The Wanger offer was the most dazzling ever offered any actress, a flat one million dollars if she would make *Cleopatra*. Wanger at that time had only the idea of *Cleopatra*, but he recognized the Taylor power. Elizabeth wasn't sure she wanted to make the film, but Wanger kept building up his offer. He'd give her thirty-five hundred dollars a week for "living expenses." She would have cast approval, script approval, director approval. The works.

But Berman told her she could not accept that because her Metro contract was still valid. Before she would be free to make *Cleopatra*, she owed MGM a picture that would pay her her standard one hundred thousand dollars. The picture was called *Butterfield 8*.

The goddess rose up in wrath. Berman later grinned ruefully over the experience. "I think it was the money difference that upset her," he says. "Otherwise, with her sure dramatic instinct, she could have seen the Academy Award potential in the film we were offering. Instead she said it disgusted her. She demanded everything, and on some of the things I gave in to her. She insisted upon the picture being shot in New York. She insisted on Helen Rose's coming to New York to do her clothes. She demanded that some of her regular crew be sent to her. I agreed to all that.

"She didn't like the director we hired, Daniel Mann, who had a wonderful record behind him of having got Oscar-winning performances out of Susan Hayward and Shirley Booth. Elizabeth said we couldn't make her act and she would do a bad job, because she hated the character of Gloria. I told her I wasn't the least concerned with that threat. I said I was sure that her desire to be a pro and cooperate with other actors, and her sense of obligation to her public would keep her from doing any such thing.

"That was when she told me Eddie had been offered an Australian tour when he finished in Las Vegas, and she wanted him near her. So she demanded a role for him in the picture. I agreed to that.

"Eddie provided us with our most serious problem. He was nervous and afraid of doing the part. He was in a tough spot. We all knew that, but when we got going on *Butterfield 8*, there was trouble."

There was indeed. Elizabeth insisted upon working only

from noon until eight in the evening. She announced herself to the director by saying, "Nothing you can say will make me like this film, and nothing you can do will make me want to play it."

Mann, however, knowing temperament when he saw it, soon learned to handle her. When he wasn't entirely satisfied with a scene, he'd say, "Okay, that's it."

Elizabeth's own dramatic awareness would trap her. She'd retort, "Wait a minute. I think I can do it better."

But whenever Mann slipped and said, "Let's do so and so," she would look at him ironically and say, "Is this the way you want it? Is this what you mean?" and then she would burlesque the whole thing.

Nonetheless the artist in her bound her. She worked over her scenes. She worked over her lines. She had come, particularly through the two Tennessee Williams roles in *Cat on a Hot Tin Roof* and *Suddenly, Last Summer*, to have a sharpened appreciation of good writing. She improved the dialogue of Gloria in *Butterfield 8* and made the character much more convincing, a girl fighting for love and respectability.

Gradually she began to relax her antagonism. She showed it by ordering in magnificent lunches for everyone on the project in that old New York studio.

The night before Eddie was to do his big scene, she could not sleep for her anxiety. She called Danny Mann at two in the morning and said, "I want this to be good more than anything in the world, for Eddie's sake, but I feel so ill. I must be there, but I feel so ill."

She was there the next morning, however, and Eddie, wildly enthusiastic, that evening called Sara Taylor in Hollywood and said, "Oh, you don't know how wonderful your daughter is to work with. I've heard other people say that, but I didn't know how tremendous she was until I acted with her. Why, she even made me look good."

"Eddie was simply wonderful, Mother," said Elizabeth cutting in.

She exaggerated, and she must have known it. And she *was* vivid and wonderful as Gloria, and she must have known that, too. Still, she was too angry with MGM to admit it. She went back to California with Eddie and her children. One evening she and Eddie, together with her agent and his wife, were the only audience at a very private preview of *Butterfield 8* in a studio projection room. She was shocked to see that the big scene with Eddie had been cut out entirely. Angrily, she

174

began yelling at the screen. Later it was whispered around MGM that she had kicked both her slippers at the screen. Yet, she must have seen the truth of her performance, the truth of her own art.

For the moment, she was buoyed up over having been nominated for an Academy Award for *Suddenly, Last Summer.* It was her third nomination in three years, and she felt this time she had the lucky charm. The public-opinion polls all proclaimed her the winner.

She was so convinced she would win that she even told one newspaper pal, "I simply can't retire until I've won an Oscar."

Thinking of the Academy ceremonies, however, brought Mike Todd poignantly back to her thoughts. Then she had an inspiration. She called Helen Rose. "Have you still got that white Grecian gown Mike designed for me to wear the night I was up for *Raintree County?*"

"Of course I have, Elizabeth."

"Please get it out for me. I'm going to wear it to this year's Academy."

She had the diamonds Mike had bought her to go with that white dress, but she had never worn them. Now she got them out also.

"She came walking down into her living room that night," Helen Rose says, "and with her dark hair and her tan against all that white, she was the most beautiful sight I have ever seen."

The Academy of Motion Picure Arts & Sciences has a custom which for refined cruelty can scarcely be surpassed. There are five nominations in each category—Best Actor, Best Actress, Best Supporting Actor, Best Supporting Actress, and those twenty spotlighted people are supposed to be at the ceremonies in person. Each hopes to win, which means there must always be sixteen gallant losers.

The award for the best actress is the climax of the glamorous affair. The theater where it is held never has one vacant seat. On TV some fifteen million people look in. Along Hollywood Boulevard loudspeakers tell the people outside what is happening inside the theater.

During the April, 1960, ceremonies, the great moment came. The man from Price Waterhouse stepped out, handed out the envelope. The card was drawn, and the hush fell on the theater. Gary Cooper, making the presentation, called out, "The winner is Simone Signoret."

Elizabeth smiled brilliantly up into the flashbulbs that

exploded before her in that instant. She applauded wildly. She watched Simone Signoret, barely known in Hollywood, a tall woman nearing forty, a Frenchwoman born in Germany, appearing in *Room at the Top*, a British production, running up the aisle, running toward Elizabeth Taylor's dream.

She was quite sure that only she had heard Eddie's gasp, "God, no! Oh, no!" She wanted to lean over and kiss him, but she kept on smiling and applauding, smiling and applauding, feeling the eyes upon her.

Then and there she knew she would make *Cleopatra*. The hell with art. She would take the money. That million plus thirty-five hundred dollars a week for living expenses. With that she had everything any woman could ever want—with the annoying exception of an Academy Award. She had her children, she had her parents, and a small, deeply trusted group of friends. And Eddie, Eddie her dear love, whom she would have all her life.

CHAPTER TWENTY

With Eddie and her three children, Dick Hanley, and her hairdresser, Elizabeth arrived in London on September 8, 1960, to start *Cleopatra*.

It was very late at night, rainy, and cold. For such a distinguished group, however, the VIP lounge of the London airport was quickly opened. Champagne was immediately handed around to the Taylor party.

Elizabeth felt very blithe, downing her favorite drink. *Cleopatra* had a budget of five million dollars, and a fifth of that was going to her for salary. That certainly was a kick. No actress had ever before commanded such money. She hadn't yet studied the script, but she liked everything about Walter Wanger's production plans, particularly his subtlety in choosing to film it in the Todd-A-O process. That would bring her in some added pin money, besides the million bucks. Diamond-pin money.

Rouben Mamoulian, an efficient and talented man, had been signed as director, Peter Finch was to be Cæsar, with Stephen Boyd as Mark Antony.

The whole picture was to be finished in time to get everyone home for Christmas. Already every inch of space at London's three largest studios was occupied with the huge sets. Wanger had told her that not only the ancient cities of Alexandria and Cairo had been recreated, but that the mighty river Nile was dramatically flowing on Pinewood Studio's back lot. There Cleopatra's barge awaited her, Queen Elizabeth of Hollywood.

Yes, it was all a kick, and being driven through the predawn London drizzle toward the house that had been rented for her, she was most content. Despite the crazy, unreal world in which she had grown up, she had finally worked out a normal life for herself. She was just like a regular girl, with a husband and three children. Eddie wasn't as dynamic as Mike Todd, and it was a rotten shame that she couldn't bear him a child, but they did have a marriage, a solid marriage, and she deeply loved him.

Besides in two months, give or take a week, she'd have a whole beautiful million dollars, after which she would blow the whole acting racket and settle down to being just a quiet, domestic woman, Mrs. Edwin Fisher.

The cars stopped, she and Eddie in the first one, Dick and the children in the one following. She looked at the house chosen for her. "I hate it," she said.

"We don't want this," Eddie declared. He was holding her hand. He was always holding her hand. "What do you want to do, darling?"

"Let's go back to the Dorchester, shall we, even if it's only for the night? I love the Dorchester."

She had always loved the Dorchester. There she had come as a tiny girl with her parents. There Mike Wilding had courted her. There she had stayed with Mike Todd. And there, that night in September, 1960, the whole Fisher group was installed, just as the dawn streaked the sky. The suite they took was so big that it wouldn't stop, and naturally none of them asked the price of it. That was Wanger's problem. Still Eddie and the children and Dick all agreed with Elizabeth that it was infinitely more sensible for them to be quartered there than in a house, coping with servant problems, for a mere two months' residence.

The plan for the next morning was to shoot the scene of her entering Cleopatra's barge. Only it was still raining the next day, and very chilly. It was still raining and chillier the third day and the fourth. You couldn't shoot the queen of Egypt floating about in a drizzle.

On the fifth day Mamoulian abandoned the schedule and shifted to the scene where Cleopatra first meets Cæsar. That could be done inside on a sound stage.

Elizabeth was to be carried in, concealed in a rug. The rug would unwind, and she would tumble out, naked as a jay bird.

Wanger had assured her this was historically correct. That was the way Cleopatra had done it. Nudity had been her way of gaining Caesar's full attention.

"We can design some sort of leotard or bathing-suit thing

178

for you to wear if you insist," Wanger said, "but it would be awkward."

That had shaken her a bit, the idea of being naked there in a studio. She pondered. "No technicians up on the catwalk, Walter, staring down at me?"

"No, no, of course not. Black screens up around the whole set. Just you, Finch, the cameraman, Mamoulian."

"And I can tumble so fast that really . . ."

"Oh, sure. Your maid can unwrap you just as you go into the carpet, wrap you up the moment you whiz past that camera. Okay?"

"Yes, I guess so. Only don't let my mother or even Eddie hear about this until it's over."

She knew that before the film was over, all her physical attributes would be played up, but this was different. Mamoulian did six takes of the scene before he was satisfied, and along about the fourth one, she stole an upward glance at Peter Finch and grinned, rolling over fast so that her back was to the camera. As Maria, her maid, came forward and wrapped her up in her dressing gown, she hurried past Finch, looked at the carpet, and with a wry smile said, "It's the only way to travel."

To her annoyance when she woke the next morning, eager to get back to the studio, she found she had sniffles and a headache. "I guess it's chillier than I knew, being on the carpet," she said laughingly to Eddie. Eddie frowned as he touched her. "I think you've got a fever. I'm going to call a doctor."

She did have a fever, and the doctor ordered her to stay in bed. By the next morning she had developed pneumonia and was very ill. Even with expert care, nursing, and tremendous doses of antibiotics, it was two weeks before she was up and around again.

Mamoulian had done what scenes he could with Finch and Boyd in the interval, but since Elizabeth was in almost every foot of the action, the picture had closed down for three days, waiting for her.

She went back to work, and Eddie, assured she was fully recovered, flew to Hollywood to discuss a very flattering offer from Warner Brothers to be a producer.

Elizabeth hated to have him away from her. With her shrewd movie mind she knew that part of the deal was bound to be that she would star in some of Eddie's pictures. Still she

179

was willing to do that if it would help him. But within an hour of his leaving she was as restless as she always was when she didn't have a man around. During the week Eddie was in Hollywood, they ran up fantastic telephone tolls, calling one another three and four times a day. Eddie was jubilant. Warner Brothers had okayed his producing *Anna Karenina*. "Garbo did it in silents," said Eddie enthusiastically. "Vivien Leigh did it in sound, but wait till the public sees you as Anna. I told Jack Warner you'd play it the moment you finish *Cleopatra*. Is that all right?"

"It's perfect. Will you get back here by Saturday at the latest? I can't wait one moment longer."

"I'll be there, and you'd better wait. I'm a big movie producer now, remember."

To her annoyance she was running another fever that Saturday when she met his plane. She wanted to go to the theater with Eddie and prowl the London supper clubs later. Instead all she could do was to kiss her husband passionately and be put to bed, with a doctor and a nurse standing by.

Before dawn the next morning she awakened in such pain she screamed aloud. Specialists were called again. Once more she was rushed to a hospital. Several days later her illness was diagnosed as meningism. To cure it, she had to have several teeth out. Once again the picture had to close down waiting for her.

That made the insurance companies, headed by Lloyds of London, rise up angrily. They had, only the summer before, lost several millions because of the death of Tyrone Power while making *Solomon and Sheba*. Now they saw Elizabeth Taylor as a hazard that threatened to cost them several more millions. They refused to pay on Twentieth Century-Fox's policy with them unless she was taken out of the picture and Marilyn Monroe put in her place.

Walter Wanger balked. He would wait for Elizabeth Taylor no matter how long it took. He locked up *Cleopatra* for an indefinite time. Wanger, Mamoulian, Stephen Boyd, and the whole Fisher household flew back to the warmth of California.

That layoff gave the picture's three most important people an uncomfortable perspective on the film they had been making. As Elizabeth recuperated in Palm Springs, she, Wanger, and Mamoulian found themselves in accord: the script was really just another costume picture with stock characters and stilted dialogue.

They decided they would get a rewrite while waiting. Poor Twentieth Century-Fox, with half a million already gone and only twelve minutes of film to show for it, put a score of top screenwriters to work at once.

It was mid-January of 1961 before Elizabeth was declared well again. Wanger assembled his company once more and returned to London with a partially rewritten script. The promise was that new scenes would be airmailed over constantly. Then Mamoulian balked. Reading the new script, he asked to be let out of the whole project. Elizabeth said if he left, she would leave, too. She soon discovered she could do nothing of the sort. Twentieth pointed out they had a contract with her and would hold her to it. But they did let Mamoulian go. Then everything began coming unglued.

Peter Finch, originally signed for two months, had signed another deal for a play to begin in January. So, he picked up four months' salary and was gone.

The three studios that had rented all their space to the film had other rentals for January and February. *Cleopatra* must find new stages.

In the midst of this Wanger brought Elizabeth one piece of good news. He had signed Joe Mankiewicz as the new director, not only because of his great talent, but also because he and Elizabeth had worked together so vividly on *Suddenly, Last Summer*. Things began to look up. Rex Harrison was signed to play Cæsar. Mankiewicz arrived and announced he was rewriting the whole thing. Elizabeth, seeing some of the scenes he had already done, asked for her childhood friend Roddy McDowall for the role of Octavius. He was in New York in *Camelot*, but so what? It was merely a matter of buying him out of the show.

Buying Roddy out of *Camelot* gave someone the inspiration of raiding *Camelot* again and getting Richard Burton for the role of Mark Antony.

"Fine actor," said Wanger to Elizabeth. "You know him, don't you?"

They smiled at one another slyly. "Oh, sure I know him. I met him at Stewart Granger's."

Wanger and Elizabeth laughed together. Everybody knew about the infatuation Jean Simmons, Stewart Granger's wife, had for Richard Burton when they had been making *The Robe*. Hollywood had been amused and touched by Stewart Granger's jealousy during that time, and the way he had haunted the set of *The Robe*.

And before and after Jean Simmons there had been many others in Burton's life. Lauren Bacall had called him "wicked, wicked Richard." Little Dawn Adams, just before she married an Italian prince, had said of him, "Dick is a good actor on screen but much better off." Olivia de Havilland, who had been the star of *My Cousin Rachel*, his first American picture, had a great crush on him. Susan Strasberg's parents had grabbed her from his arms, weeping. Claire Bloom was said to have had her heart broken by him, as supposedly had young Roberta Haynes and seventeen-year-old Diane McBain when they met on *Ice Palace*.

The fascinating part of the Burton legend was that he never seemed to choose actresses who equaled him in .importance and all these infatuated females knew he was a married man who intended to stay married.

Wanger looked at Elizabeth admiringly. "You are unique, you know. I've never heard of your giving a second glance, off camera, that is, to any guy in your films."

They received the word that Richard Burton, for the payment of fifty thousand dollars to the *Camelot* company, could be had, but not before late spring.

"We'll go ahead with the scenes between you and Harrison," Mank told Elizabeth. "I'm shifting all the filming to Rome starting March 1, except the scenes on the Nile. There we'll be radical. We'll shoot it on the Nile."

Elizabeth giggled, remembering how the Egyptians had banned her films because she had once bought a hundred thousand dollars' worth of Israel bonds. "I shall thoroughly enjoy being the first Jewish queen of Egypt," she said. "Meanwhile come to my birthday party, which Edwin Jack Fisher is giving me on February twenty-seventh. I'm aging, Joe. I shall be twenty-eight."

"Let me quote what Shakespeare said about Cleo and pretend I made it up about you: 'Age cannot wither her, nor custom stale her infinite variety...'"

"Thank you, sir, you may come to dinner."

The whole company was invited to the party, but on February 26 Elizabeth came down with another cold. She was angry and exasperated as her temperature began soaring. Her tendency toward tachycardia made her heart race, which is dangerous with a high fever.

What made her become ill again then? Was it nerves? Was it her need for drama, and if it was, why did she need drama? Was she actually bored, without being aware of it?

Whatever it was, a virus or a neurosis, Dr. Carl Goldman, a great London specialist, was called in. He rushed her into the London Clinic, and within minutes he called in nine other medical men, among them Lord Evans, the Queen's physician.

By the next morning she had lobar pneumonia of the staphylococcus type, and because she had been given antibiotics during her recent pneumonias, they proved ineffective in her newest emergency. To complicate matters, she was still anemic from her attack of meningism.

By nightfall the word sped around the world that she was dying. And she was. Everything that advanced medical science could do for her was being done, but there was small hope of her survival. At the end of her second day a tracheotomy was performed on her throat, and a tube inserted to her lungs to help her breathe. Soon, however, she was barely able to gasp. She was fed via another tube through her nose. Beneath her breastbone there was inserted still another tube, which led to an electric device, also to help her breathing. By the third day the veins in her arms broke down, so that the antibiotics had to be given to her intravenously through her legs. By the fourth day she was developing phlebitis, which meant that presently those veins could not be used. When it was discovered that a needed antibiotic was not in London, Milton Blackstone procured it in New York and flew over with it.

She grew steadily worse, hour by hour. Her fever hit 108, a nearly unendurable point. She gasped, she struggled, she fought to breathe. She went in and out of comas.

Haggard, at her bedside, Eddie and her parents watched her tortured face, her clenched hands. They saw her lips moving, but her voice was too weak for them to understand her words. Later she told *Look's* fine reporter, Jack Hamilton: "When I was unconscious and dying, I felt I touched God. I had no time to pray. I just cried, "Oh, God, oh, God, help me!" I screamed to God, and He heard me."

She lived. She lived because she simply would not die. Outside in the streets around the London Clinic the people massed, hundreds strong and silent, and prayed for her. At the end of the fourth day the weary but triumphant Dr. Goldman told the press corps: "Out of every hundred who have Miss Taylor's type of pneumonia, rarely do two survive.

183

On four occasions Miss Taylor was as near to death as she could be. Her courage and willpower pulled her through."

It wasn't until March 28 that she was strong enough to leave the Clinic. Rex Kennamer flew over from Hollywood to make the homeward journey beside her. Once again the crowds gathered in the streets, but now they were cheering her. She was very pale, very thin, and entirely wrapped in mink as they pushed her out in a wheel chair, but her face was joyous.

The crowd rushed forward, out of police control. She was knocked from the wheelchair and fell, helpless, half under the waiting limousine. But she merely laughed, though weakly, and waited to be picked up. The police got through, rescued her, propped her up carefully inside the limousine as Dr. Kennamer sprang in on one side of her and Eddie on the other. As the car began to inch forward she called out in response to the crowd's cheers, "I always recover, and now I shall live to be a hundred and ten."

The doctors shook their heads with amazement. They said she wouldn't be able to work for another year or walk for another month. They underestimated her. Three weeks later she crept up the aisle at the Academy Award ceremonies to accept the Oscar for her performance in *Butterfield 8*, the picture which she and most of the critics the world around had despised.

She was blissfully happy, but she was not deceived. She had attained her greatest ambition, but she knew how little it now meant. Without Eddie's assistance she would not have been able to get to the stage. Under the long skirt of her evening gown her left leg was so swollen she was wearing a size-seven shoe on that foot, while her right foot wore its normal size four. On the stage Burt Lancaster, that year's top male winner, had to steady her while she whispered "Thank you" into the microphone.

She knew that she had won, not only for her three performances previous to *Butterfield 8* but because of the drama of her triumph in the London Clinic. The votes cast for her had been cast emotionally. But she was too happy to care. Mike Todd was not there to share her happiness, but she was no longer bitter about that either.

She was alive, and if life had turned out to be ironic, giving her an artistic award for reasons that had nothing to do with art, it did not matter. Her bout with death had taught her that merely to be alive was the highest privilege. She smiled at the great applauding audience there in the theater and beamed at the greater watching audience on TV. She knew how completely she intended to live every moment of her life from then on.

She began it that very evening. Dr. Kennamer and Eddie murmured that she ought to go directly home after the Academy ceremonies. It was ten in the evening in California. She grinned mockingly at them. "Now hear this, boys. I'm going to the Academy party."

She got her way, of course. The traffic boiled up so that it was nearly eleven before she and her group could reach the Beverly Hilton—but reach it she did. The photographers swarmed around her as Eddie and Rex Kennamer helped her to her table. Mike Todd, Jr., and his wife were with her, and her old friend Pat Newcomb. They all told her she could stay one hour, no more.

"All right," she said, beaming. She tried to eat, but she couldn't, for there were never less than fifty photographers surrounding her, asking her to turn this way, please, that way, please, just one more, please. There were never less than another fifty people trying to get through to her—other stars, directors, writers, friends, all offering congratulations.

She sat holding Eddie's hand, smiling, smiling, as she sipped the most expensive champagne in the world. It was too much effort to talk. It was too much effort to walk, and neither mattered at all. She was sitting on top of the world that night, and she had no intention of sitting anywhere else ever.

Her victory over death had changed her more than even she knew. She loved everything that summer—Eddie, her children, her parents, her friends, sunlight and warmth, and food, and the scent of flowers.

Outwardly those closest to her found her simpler and sweeter, but actually hers was a deceptive sweetness and simplicity. She did everything and nothing. Sometimes she would buzz through a riot of shopping and partying, and other times she would lie silently out in her garden, watching the play of sunlight on the trees, the flight of birds. She was constantly singing. She read voluminously as she never had before, everything from novels to biographies to gossip columns to volumes on religion. She went to temple faithfully.

She wore her two wedding rings constantly, Eddie's on her left hand, Mike's on her right, and she wanted to be with Eddie every moment. When he had a brief engagement in Las Vegas, she went with him.

She answered every letter of the thousands she had received during her illness. She understood the difference between such letters and the denunciatory ones she had received during the time when Eddie had left Debbie. She understood the reaction of the public, the love and the hate, as part of human nature, and she did not fight it. It was the stuff of life and therefore beautiful.

She spent hours sitting in the sun, squatting beside her children, drawing with them. Young Mike drew planes and ships. Chris was dreamier, a sketcher of trees and flowers. Liza's blobs only Liza, looking up with eyes so like her mommy's, could explain. The pets, five dogs, four cats, were always with her and the children.

She did unlikely things. In midsummer, still recuperating, she spoke before a Los Angeles Medical Fund dinner. Around her was a most distinguished audience. Seated next to her was Robert Kennedy, the Attorney General of the United States.

Elizabeth stood, still very frail but radiant, and said quietly, "It may seem a little odd that an actress should be called upon to speak at an occasion like this. I feel very deeply about the purpose of this occasion. Therefore, I hope I will be pardoned if what I have to say is perhaps more serious than might be expected of me—perhaps even rather personal, because also I have had more than a passing acquaintance with death. Too close. Close enough to know what death is like—and that is far too close.

"Throughout those many critical hours in the operating theater of the London Clinic, wanting to live was so strong within me—so overpowering—so all consuming—that I remember it, strangely perhaps, as an incredible and agonizing pain. As if every nerve, every muscle, my whole physical being, was being strained to the point of torture—by this insistence upon life—to the last ounce of my strength, to the last gasp of my breath.

"But then gradually and inevitably and finally, that last ounce of strength was drawn.

"I remember I had focused desperately on the light hanging directly above me. It had become something I needed almost fanatically to continue to see—that light had become my vision of life, itself. But yet slowly, as if its source of power were my own fading strength and inability to breathe, it faded and dimmed—ironically enough, like a well-done theatrical effect—to blackness.

"I have never known, nor do I think there can be, a greater loneliness.

"Then it happened. When I say 'then,' I do not know how long, or when, it was. I can only recall my awareness of it. First, there was an awareness of the hands. Pushing, pulling, pressing, lifting—large, rough hands and smaller, gentler ones—incessantly, insistently manipulating my body as if to force it to respond—in some way, in any way, even as a reaction to discomfort or pain. I bless all those hands for the beating they gave me.

"And then—the voices. From a great distance at first, so far away they seemed to me forgotten voices I had once heard, and which now I seemed to remember. But ever so slowly they grew louder. And like the hands, some were gentle and some were harsh—some pleaded with me, some shouted—they cajoled and commanded me—I was to do what they said, somehow I was to bring myself to do what they demanded of me—to cough, to move, to breathe—to live.

"I didn't know whose hands reached out to me through that terrible blackness—and whose voices answered the thousand cries for help within me which I thought went unheard—but there they were, and they were life. Those hands would not stop, and those voices would not be silent until I answered them. I did. How? I don't know of anyone who could tell you—or me.

"I coughed. I moved. I breathed. And I looked. That hanging lamp—that most beautiful light my world has ever known—began faintly to glow again, to shine again.

"I looked up at the faces. I could not remember seeing them ever before. The doctors, nurses, therapists—I cannot give you their professional titles—of the London Clinic. It was their hands which had pulled me, and their voices which had called me back to life.

"It was only later that I learned how many of those men and women had remained with me continuously. It was only later that I learned of the nurse who had collapsed from exhaustion. That my anesthetist, Dr. Middleton Price, had

187

literally not left my side since being called to the Dorchester Hotel more than three days before.

"Yes, ladies and gentlemen, I think I can speak to you with some authority—perhaps not about the scientific equipment and economic problems of a hospital, but about the humanity within it. It is a particular and rare kind—a dedicated humanity. One hesitates to use phrases like 'dedicated humanity.' It offers opportunity for the cynical, and I've heard them say, 'So what? It's their job. So they're doing their job.'

"That may be quite true. But of all of us here who work at a job—in an office, studio, a factory, or home—how many live so intimately with life and death? No, the heartbeat of a hospital, just as that of a church, a synagogue, or a mosque, is neither time-clocked nor alarm-clocked. It is the beat of dedicated human hearts, of all faiths, races, and nationalities.

"I can say only that whatever gods each of us or any of us may thank, for whatever blessings we have—let us be properly thankful to them that hospitals have come into being, and let us pray that all humanity will be similarly blessed."

She meant every word of it. Nothing could upset her then—big things such as racial prejudice or little things of no significance. She grew accustomed to Eddie's always having to have a mob around him. That seemed to go with the musical temperament, but she didn't mind it. There were always ten or twelve for dinner, so what? She soon shut out the beat of records always playing in her house, mostly Eddie's.

She did not realize, as her health steadily returned, that some of this easy tolerance of hers was because she was making a commitment such as she had never experienced before, a commitment to the role of Cleopatra.

Until then she had always approached her roles with the utmost casualness. A quick study, she would read her part, and then she was ready to go on. But with *Cleopatra* she was in daily huddles with Mankiewicz and Wanger. Joe read scenes to her, sometimes within an hour of his having written them, and she was fascinated to see Cleopatra emerge, a beautiful woman defeated by love.

"You must play her in a feline way," Joe said. "Not a leopard, not even a cat, but a leopard kitten, soft but dangerous." The end was tragedy, but that excited her. She had never played tragedy, but under Joe's direction she felt that she could.

Wanger quickened her interest by showing her the costume sketches, the sketches for the new sets. He brought her a rough recording of the music for the sound track. He even showed her the new budget that would let him spend a fresh ten million dollars. All of it thrilled her.

Thus, long before she returned to Rome, late in September, 1961, Elizabeth was thinking about a love so great that it would make death seem bearable. Only occasionally did her true personality break through her dream, and at such moments she knew she needed to get back to work for the mere money of it. Eddie made large sums when he worked, but his engagements were infrequent, and he was as extravagant by nature as she was. She had fantastic bills from her illness still to pay. She had three children to support, an expensive way of living to maintain.

Wanger and Joe were at the plane to meet her as, with Eddie and Dick and the children, she landed in a pouring rain in sunny Italy. Nevertheless she wanted to go immediately to Cine Città, the big studio out in Rome's suburbs, to see the sets and her costumes. Eddie and the others went directly to the villa that had been rented for them on the ancient Appian Way.

"Before you see anything else, you must see 'Casa Taylor,'" Wanger said as they drove in through the studio gates.

"What's that?"

"It's this," said Joe, as they pulled up beside a small building surrounded by flower beds.

The entire building was her dressing room. Besides the very special dressing room, she had a private bath, a private kitchen, a dining room, a massage room, and an office and dressing room for Eddie.

Elizabeth stood on tiptoe and lightly kissed her two escorts. "This is quite different from that lean-to I had at MGM when Lassie was my leading man," she said.

"Even there we have made improvements," Joe said. "Now you have sexy Rexy and Richard, the Iron-Hearted."

"They're here already?"

"Yes, Sexy Rexy with a new wife, Richard with the one he's had since nineteen forty-nine. Plus their two children. All of you have villas fairly near one another. The first thing we shoot tomorrow is the council-chamber scene with all three of you."

189

The next day, while working, Elizabeth was to discover that Richard Burton had another companion with him, Pat Tunder, a twenty-year-old beauty from the Copacabana in New York, and that leggy Miss Tunder had a small role in *Cleopatra*.

CHAPTER TWENTY-ONE

The Fisher villa on the Appian Way had seven bedrooms, almost no baths, a staff of seventeen servants to run it, and what the Italians call *sale di rappresentazione*, or "representation rooms," which meant several huge, drafty, marble-floored rooms for receptions. The chief "representation" had no draperies at the windows, and Elizabeth, who got a decorator in to re-cover some chairs and couches, was later to wish she had ordered hangings, too.

That was after the Burton scandal broke, when the *paparazzi*, those demon photographers of Rome, equipped their cameras with telephoto lenses and took shots of her inside the house. Originally, however, with the villa set behind high walls in the middle of acres of gardens, she had no idea she would need such privacy.

Actually she was thinking of nothing but *Cleopatra*. She was not even depressed when she woke the morning she was to go to work and discovered the rain was still falling. As it was to turn out, it would be the worst fall and winter Rome had known in twenty years.

Elizabeth discovered how well Wanger was looking after her, however, when the studio car came for her. It was a heated Rolls-Royce.

She had made up at the villa and put on her costume for the council scene. Thus she came to the sound stage at Cine Città wrapped virtually from head to toe in her blackest mink coat. A dazed young Italian pulled open the door to the stage, and she walked regally through.

She had to walk no more than a hundred yards from the stage door to the center of the huge, beautiful set, but every two feet of that distance a small electric heater radiated warmth. She did not indicate that she even saw them, but they were evidence that she could control this great production by one sneeze.

She did not indicate that she saw Rex Harrison stand up at one side of the set, a smile of greeting on his face. Her eyes did not even flick in the direction of Richard Burton, slowly rising from his chair at the other side of the stage. As for Pat Tunder, who was sitting close to the camera, Elizabeth walked straight by her as though she were nonexistent.

She was making an entrance, and well she knew it. That was the way she wanted it for *Cleopatra*. Behind her, Eddie, Dick, the hairdresser, the dresser, the coffee maid, and the sewing woman tagged at a respectful distance.

Joe Mankiewicz ambled over to her, moving gracefully despite his bulk. Her back by then was to everyone else, so that she could wink at him. He kissed her hand in burlesque deference. "Ready, Madam Queen?"

She bowed with an equally burlesqued deference. "I was born ready, dear sir." She dropped off her mink coat and left it to her maid to see that it didn't hit the stage floor. She saw Joe suck in his breath, and she was quite sure all the other men on that stage were doing the same, for a great deal of her was revealed in her Cleopatra outfit and all of it most artfully. She swung in Harrison's direction to dazzle him and give him a cordial greeting, and then, as though it were an afterthought, she turned toward Burton.

The night before she had heard a story that was all over Rome—the story of the bet he had made that he could make her fall in love with him.

"Hello, Dickie," she said. She remembered that he hated to be called Dickie.

"Hello, Liz," he said, and she almost laughed, wondering whether he remembered she didn't like being called Liz. It was crazy, though, what a beautiful speaking voice he had for such an ugly man. He looked her up and down. "I understand I shall be seeing more of you. They let me look at all your costume sketches." He moved closer to her and lowered his voice confidentially. "You're too fat," he murmured in a tone that made it sound like a caress.

She was speechless. Rage burned through her. "Lights!" yelled Joe Mankiewicz at that instant. "Take your places, please. Let's run through it."

She moved across the stage, finding her marks by the simple method of going where the heat of the lights was hottest. This was one of her technical tricks, allowing her to move about without ever looking down to see that she was standing in the correct camera range.

She had no lines with Burton in the scene. She had merely to sit across the set from him, with Harrison between them, and glance at him occasionally. She did not relax until after the third take when Joe said, "Vanish, Richard. That's all for you. Elizabeth and Rex, stand by."

She moved, her head held high, toward "Casa Taylor" to wait there until the next scene was lighted. She did not look back to say good-bye to Burton. It would be two months before they would play another scene together, two months during which she would lose fifteen pounds.

Joe was shooting in sequence because, incredibly, he was writing the script at night, filming his scenes the next day. Yet they were masterly. In two months Elizabeth and Harrison did almost half the production, portraying the bittersweet love story of a girl queen and an aging warrior, a true story of people who had once lived and loved.

Elizabeth, the romantic, felt lost in another age, another time. Elizabeth, the technician, however, discovered during the very first morning that Harrison intended to have every inch of film due him, and as many more as he could steal from her.

She responded to such an unspoken challenge, and they developed a lively respect for one another as they maneuvered for advantage. Late afternoons when they sat with Mank, watching the dailies, they would smile warily at one another, delighted with the results they were achieving.

Nevertheless, it was work, tiring, depleting work, and it began to wear on Elizabeth to come home nights and usually find Eddie with a gang around him. He had acquired a new personal press agent in Rome, and a new accompanist, and a new voice teacher. Along the Via Veneto, particularly in that section called "the beach," there were always groups of ex-Hollywooders eager to be acquired.

Many nights ten to twenty people sat down for dinner at the "Villa Papa." She had nothing against any of those people, except that she was basically not a crowd person. When she came back from the studio, emotionally spent, she wanted either to relax or be made love to, ideally both. But there would be Eddie, smoking his big cigars straight through dinner, and playing his own records, over and over again, many times the same record for hours on end.

Occasionally she revolted and snapped, "What is this, a

home for displaced Americans?" More often she simply smiled lazily and drank an Italian *vino rosso*, which she had discovered and adored. Presently her wry sense of amusement would begin to function and she saw Eddie's followers as not too different from the whole new pack of pets she had acquired in Rome. She had been given a St. Bernard that was almost as big as a small pony and that tiny Liza often did ride. She also had a collie and three terriers as well as two Siamese kittens.

She had ordered white woolly rugs put down on all the marble floors of "Villa Papa," so that she and the children could tumble comfortably about on them, playing with the pets.

One night in a spirit of merriment she idly took off a diamond bracelet and gave it to one of the Siamese to play with. Suddenly Eddie was yelling. Since he practically never lifted his voice at her, she looked up, startled, and then realized that the bracelet was one he had given her. "Oh, darling," she said, "how can a kitten scratch a diamond, for heaven's sakes?" She quickly put the bracelet back on, but he was very hurt and angry.

That evening, she fell asleep promising herself that she would make everything up to him the moment *Cleopatra* was finished.

She was tremendously touched that weekend when Eddie told her of his yearning to have a child "by us." He knew this was not possible, but his dream persisted. "Much as I love them, your children aren't my children," he said. "My own children are now Debbie's, even if she has been very generous about my seeing them." He drew a deep sigh. "If only you and I could have a child . . ."

Inspiration came to her.

"Eddie, do you remember about Maria Schell telling us she had something to do with an orphanage in Munich? She tries to get homes for children that are handicapped. How about our going up there this weekend and asking her about it? Then we could have a new baby in this villa, our baby."

Eddie was delighted with the idea, and neither of them saw the least inconsistency in this proxy parenthood. Maria Schell found them a chubby one-year-old girl, who had a malformed hip. The baby was doomed to be a cripple for life, unless she was given the most expert care, which would eventually include several expensive operations.

They adopted the baby on the fifteenth of January, 1962, and named her for Maria. She was supposed to be the bond that would bind them together forever. But a month before that Richard Burton had come back into the picture, and the passionate love scenes of *Cleopatra* were going on. Not only on the set but in Burton's dressing room and Elizabeth's lush, private dressing villa and in heated Cadillacs and heated Rolls-Royces and in the gardens of the "Villa Papa."

As Richard Burton crowed to his buddies in the company, "I saw her fall in love with me when I told her she was too fat."

The girl, Pat Tunder, had vanished. She was, as Wanger and Mankiewicz had said, a very nice girl. She was also infatuated. When Burton was on the set, there was Pat, planted in a chair as close to camera range as she could get it.

Presently, without a word being said, it became a duel of chairs to see whether Miss Taylor's chair or Miss Tunder's occupied the best position. One day Miss Tunder maneuvered so that she sat smack in front of Miss Taylor, blocking off her view. The next day one of the nicest ladies connected with the management of *Cleopatra* was driving Pat to the airport, seeing her off to America.

What Mrs. Richard Burton thought of all this no one knew. Richard said of his wife, "She is my security." When they began *Cleopatra*, the Burtons with the two Burton children, Kate, aged four, and Jessica, eighteen months, moved into a villa smaller than "Villa Papa" but very near it.

When the headlines first broke about her husband and Elizabeth, Sybil Burton probably was not at all surprised. She had outlasted her husband's other romances ever since she married him in 1949.

As Welsh as he, born, like him, in a small Welsh village, where motherless Richard was raised in poverty, Sybil was what is called "posh Welsh," meaning well-to-do. She and Richard met and almost immediately wed, when they both were doing their first movie, *The Last Days of Dolwyn*.

Sybil gave up her career then, and over the years came to understand her husband very well. Prematurely gray, gay and witty, she loved him completely and seemed to believe, as he did, that no woman could resist him.

Her attitude toward his flirtation with Elizabeth at the beginning was no different than it had been with all the others. She took the attitude of the Chinese monkeys, who resolutely see no evil, hear no evil, and definitely speak no evil.

Men reacted to Burton's personality, too. Many admired

him tremendously. Others were antagonized. Close friends said, "Dick can't stand it if he comes into a room and doesn't completely dominate it. If there is even a dog there, he'll stop everything until the dog is fawning all over him. As for women, he'll stop at nothing until he has them drooling."

Sir John Gielgud, the ruler of London's theatrical circles, calls Burton "That horribly rough fellow."

And he was rough in many ways, this Richard Jenkins of Pontrhydyfen, Wales, turned by his own ambition into London's Richard Burton of the great speaking voice. He was too barrel-chested to look his height of five feet eleven. He never was able to become a gourmet, his favorite dish being French fries between two slices of bread. But he was brilliant enough as a young man to win a scholarship to Oxford and to graduate with high honors. Brilliant he was, in the Royal Air Force during the war and brilliant too when he was persuading a woman that romance was the only important thing in the world, no matter how temporary.

Yet, oddly, he never quite made it career-wise until *Cleopatra*. While frequently acclaimed on the London stage, he still had not attained the stature of Sir John Gielgud, Sir Laurence Olivier, Sir Alec Guinness or several others. He had been expected to blaze at noon with *My Cousin Rachel*, his first Hollywood film, but it failed with the public. *Prince of Players* was awful. *The Robe* was a hit, but that was because it was the first film shown in Cinerama. *Ice Palace* was a dud, and *Alexander the Great* was a monumental flop. Even in the TV series based on the life of Winston Churchill, in which Burton was the great statesman's voice, he did not click.

Thus when he went into *Cleopatra* late in 1961, he had everything at stake. He was thirty-seven years old, and he had no more time to waste.

He played the council scene, that first scene of *Cleopatra*, with Elizabeth in early October, and then was sent away with what movies call "the second unit" to do battle scenes. "Second unit" means scenes with hundreds of extras, much action, and usually only one principal player in them.

Finally he returned to Cine Città to play Joe Mankiewicz's beautifully written love scenes between Cleopatra and Mark Antony, her new love after Cæsar's death.

It was a miserable day when Burton strode in, resplendent in Antony's costume. The rain was pouring torrentially. To protect Elizabeth's health the giant arc lights had been left burning all night long on the set purely to give heat, and the

196

small heaters were spotted wherever they could be kept out of camera range.

The company had reason to be nervous about Elizabeth. The week previous she had suffered a slight cold, but recovered. Then she had bruised her left leg, still sensitive from her antibiotic shots. She had insisted upon working, however, and Mankiewicz contrived to do her scenes entirely in close-up so she could sit in a wheel chair while performing.

She had, while working with Harrison, grown more and more queenly both on screen and off, and she began her first love scene with Burton with the same austerity of manner. But now Cleopatra's mood was more intense. The actor playing opposite her was fiery, demanding. Elizabeth was in and out of Richard Burton's arms, murmuring the passionate lines Joe had written so masterfully, hearing equally passionate lines whispered to her in a most persuasive voice. She had to look long and lovingly into the eyes of a dominant male.

They shot the scene four times, but by the fourth take the queenly star had lost track of all mundane things. She and Richard Burton stood face to face, mouth to mouth, silent, unmoving, until Joe said, "Would you two mind if I say *cut*? Does it interest you that it is time for lunch?"

She returned to reality and smiled at her director. "Oh, I'm so hungry," she said. She turned in the direction of the exit, her maid, dresser, and hairdresser immediately moving to follow her.

Richard Burton turned away, also, and began gathering a bunch of cronies together. Richard swept them all up as he said, "Let's all have a drink and eat in my dressing room." Then, just as Elizabeth reached the stage door, he raised his voice and called, "Liz, come join us. We'll have some laughs."

She faced about, and anyone could have seen that she intended to refuse. Burton, however, was grinning at her. "Come on, Pudgy," he coaxed. "It will be fun."

Pudgy! She had dropped many pounds since she had last seen him. Pudgy! She simply couldn't openly resent that. She laughed. "Why, thank you, Grandpa," she said. "I accept."

His dressing room was much too small to accommodate so many people, but that did make for fun. There was a small divan against one wall, and Elizabeth plopped down on it. Richard mixed drinks.

"Everybody's bottoms up!" he shouted, and downed his drink. Then he said in an exaggerated stage whisper, to one of

197

the crew, "I always fall in love with my leading ladies, you know, but I may escape this time. She's so homely."

Burton waited until the laughter died down, Elizabeth's the loudest, and then he went on conversationally, "Do you know I am getting two hundred fifty thousand dollars for playing Mark Antony? It's a fact. Of course, the girl's getting more."

Yes, it was fun, and Elizabeth had not laughed for many weeks. They all had another drink and presently some food sent up from the café, such nondescript food that no one could possibly dislike it. It was nearly two hours before they were called back to work.

Elizabeth, returning from lunch, walked toward her usual thronelike position at one side of the set, her retainers closing in. But Burton, watching the tableau, called to her while the lights were being adjusted, "If you'd like to hear a story that must be whispered, come over here." That man was giving her orders again! Still, it was such fun to laugh again. She went over to him. He whispered to her. Her laughter echoed over the set.

The love scenes that afternoon were sensational. When the work was through for the day, Elizabeth said, "Now I suppose I ought to ask you for a drink in my dressing room, Richard?"

"If you do, I promise to drive you home afterward."

They did have the drink, and he did drive her home, a long, long way home through the violet twilight of the Eternal City. After that they lunched together almost daily, though usually in a crowd. After that their chairs were almost always side by side on the set and they whispered to one another continually and laughed constantly.

After that her whole mood changed. She smiled at her fellow workers and greeted them by name when she arrived in the morning. She called farewells to them when she left at night. She even came to work on Saturdays. At the end of each day's work she and Richard had a drink in her elaborate dressing room, or his, and always he drove her home, the long, long way home, while the bells of Rome rang and rang and the fountains splashed.

Now dinners at the "Villa Papa" ceased to be mere twosomes between Mr. and Mrs. Fisher, or large clumps of displaced Americans mostly in the music business. There in December, 1961, and early 1962 the dinner parties featured Mr. and Mrs. Richard Burton as guests of Mr. and Mrs. Edwin Fisher, with Mr. and Mrs. Kirk Douglas when they were in town, or Elizabeth's agent, Kurt Frings, and other such handsome people. And if after dinner the host played the piano loudly and sang his songs, or if the record player revolved one disc of his loudly time after time, who listened?

Now Elizabeth Fisher began to be seen in the nightclubs of Rome, always in large groups that almost always featured Mr. and Mrs. Richard Burton. There was a new sheen to her beauty, and her eyes were as bright as the tremendous diamonds she wore around her neck and in her hair and hanging from her earlobes and shining on her fingers. She had brought three hundred dresses with her to Rome, but those weren't enough really, and she had to telephone Paris to order more.

"Liz?" said Sybil Burton when queried at that time. "I adore her. She's an old friend."

The bland phase began then, with everyone acting as innocent as though they were all at a taffy pull. Sybil Burton would be in Rome, then suddenly be in London, then back in Rome again. Eddie Fisher began to do a lot of traveling, too. He bought the movie rights to a book, *The Gouffé Case*, and announced that he would produce it and star his wife. He and his wife bought a three-hundred-thousand-dollar chalet in Gstaad, Switzerland.

Richard Burton continued to be as adroit as the daring young man on the flying trapeze. There were several occasions when he lunched with Sybil, put her on the plane for London, and that night dined with Elizabeth. There were also the days when he lunched with Elizabeth, then flew to London to dine with Sybil and his children. On one of those trips he read the Bible all the way over and back.

When he went to Paris to do some added shots for *The Longest Day*, he met Sybil there. They dined at Maxim's and had a high old time along the boulevards before they gathered up their children and flew back, a happy family, to Rome. "Sybil is my wife, you know," Richard told the reporters the next day. One bold newspaperman asked whether he was planning to marry Elizabeth. "I am already married. That's all I have to say," he said.

But it wasn't. "I find my co-star very seductive," he added. "Off screen she's just a nice charming girl, but on screen she looks at you with those eyes and your blood churns." He did not add what all Rome knew, that on the night before he met Sybil in Paris he had brought Elizabeth back to her villa at four A.M.

Yes, indeed, it was all very bland, and the space in the newspapers was terrific.

Except that on February 18 Elizabeth, lunching with Walter Wanger, doubled up suddenly with pain. She had to be dispatched to a hospital by ambulance. The *Cleopatra* press agent announced she had an attack of food poisoning. Richard Hanley, very much the devoted secretary, said, "Food poisoning? Where did that idea come from? We've put her in the hospital for a complete rest." The Rome papers said it was an overdose of sleeping pills, a suicide attempt due to her desperate love of Richard Burton.

Eddie said, flying into Rome, "I've been in Portugal working out a TV deal." Then he smiled. "Being married to Elizabeth is being married to the most impossible woman in the world. You can only get away with it if you are in love the way we are."

Burton was very British, when the papers reached him. "Bloody rot," he said. But Elizabeth remained hospitalized. The headlines got more insinuating, so he finally issued a formal statement that said:

> For the past several days uncontrolled rumors have been growing about Elizabeth and myself. Statements attributed to me have been distorted out of proportion and a series of coincidences has lent plausibility to a situation which has become damaging to Elizabeth.
>
> Mr. Fisher, who has business interests of his own, merely went out of town to attend to them for a few days.
>
> My foster father, Phil Burton, has been quite ill in New York, and my wife, Sybil, flew there to be with him for a time since my schedule does not permit me to be there. He is very dear to both of us.
>
> Elizabeth and I have been close friends for over twelve years. I have known her since she was a child star and would certainly never do anything to hurt her personally or professionally.

Elizabeth recovered, and if she had continued to play her allotted smooth role in this stylish charade, all might have been serene. But she was not a Sybil Burton. She was not Maria Schell, her good friend, who moaned, "Why, oh, why can't Elizabeth lie just a little?"

She could not lie, she would not lie, even politely. She was the widow of Mike Todd, who had said to her, "Let's have red be red and black be black, even when it hurts. Let us live our whole lives to the absolute damned limit." She was Elizabeth Taylor, who in the London Clinic had fought death and won—won the glory of being alive, of living fully every second.

Morality? Rightly or wrongly, truth was her morality.

Thus, having fallen in love with Richard Burton, having, probably to her own chagrin, fallen as quickly and easily as the silliest little movie starlet or the leggiest New York chorus girl, she refused to hide it. She would not confirm or deny one single thing.

There were events, however, which the press for all its snooping did not learn. For instance, one morning a jeweler from the Via Veneto appeared on the set of *Cleopatra*. With him he brought a necklace of ancient scarabs, which could be authenticated as going back to the time of Cleopatra.

"Oh, how beautiful," Elizabeth gasped.

"You want them?" asked Burton.

"They are so wonderful."

"They're yours," said Burton, and he immediately dispatched his secretary to get the price of them, then and there. It was his first costly gift to her.

By the end of March, 1962, Eddie Fisher was in a hospital in New York. "Mr. Fisher is tired, overwrought, and in need of a sedative," his doctors said for publication. Milton Blackstone, queried about his star's private life, stoutly declared that there wasn't a thing wrong between Eddie and his wife. When Eddie was released from the hospital, he called a press conference. "I'll get Elizabeth on the phone and have her tell you guys personally that there's nothing wrong between us," said Eddie.

The call went through to Rome, loud and clear, but again Elizabeth would not lie. She was unavailable.

The storm of public disapproval then broke in full fury. In London, a member of Sybil Burton's family spoke for her: "Sybil has told us that all the talk about her husband and Elizabeth Taylor is a publicity stunt." In the Congress of the United States, Representative Iris Blitch introduced a bill to have Elizabeth and Richard Burton forever barred from entering the United States. In Rome, even the Vatican noticed them, thundered against them.

In film circles, particularly in London, one story was repeated and repeated. "It *is* publicity," said the gossips. "Burton hasn't made it on mere acting, so now he's going to make it on headlines."

Easter came. Pilgrims pour into the capital of Christendom from all over the world, and from Holy Thursday until the Tuesday after Easter all Rome closes down so that people may worship.

Cleopatra closed down, too, and all Rome sputtered when the *paparazzi* revealed that Hollywood's Cleopatra and London's Mark Antony were observing Easter alone together at Porto Santo Stefano, which overlooks the Tyrrhenian Sea. They had arrived in two cars, and there they were, in bathing clothes, stretched out in the sun.

At Santo Stefano, however, something visibly went wrong between them. Toward nightfall, Elizabeth was seen driving her car at tremendous speed back to Rome. Shortly thereafter she was in the hospital again, and again the whisper of the sleeping pills went around. Everyone connected with *Cleopatra* officially snorted, "Nonsense." Unofficially they regarded one another solemnly. The situation was getting out of hand.

Did Elizabeth have everything to lose and nothing to gain by such behavior? Yes. Did that deter her? No. Rather, it stirred up her defiance. For she was lost in love again, in love with a man with dominance in his voice, a man who was not her slave, a man who might still escape her. The basic female in her was embattled. Never before had she had such an adversary as Sybil Burton, nor such a challenge as Richard Burton.

Her filmed love scenes with him became more and more real, more and more underplayed. Burton often larked before and after them, but not Elizabeth. This was her passion, off the screen and on. This—at least for the time being—was her destiny.

Meanwhile, Burton loved to tease her. There was a night scene to be shot as the ending for the first half of *Cleopatra*. The set was a floating barge on a phony lake on the back lot of Cine Città. The barge was operated by a huge winch so that it could be made to disappear into the distance.

The evening was one of those occasions when everything went wrong. The mood of the scene was melancholy. When the lights of the set were right, the winch would not move the barge. When the winch began operating, a car would go by outside, its headlights ruining the take, or an airplane would fly overhead, ruining the sound, or someone would forget his lines.

Eventually they got the scene, all except one final glimpse

202

of Cleopatra, a tiny figure alone on the disappearing barge. Mankiewicz quickly caught the shot, then called out, "All right, home everybody."

Every light in the studio went out, and there was Elizabeth all by herself in the darkness. "Richard, Richard, Richard," she screamed, and then she tried to laugh at the joke when the lights blazed on again.

Mankiewicz also tried certain stratagems, including one that was entirely disciplinary on his part—and very sly, too. Because he was writing each night, it meant that even his stars got their lines fresh each morning, with small time to study them.

Elizabeth, however, had always been a very quick study. She would come in, walk around with the fresh pages of her scenes, have her makeup put on, and by the time she was on the set, she knew them perfectly. But on the day they were doing the banquet scene, she came in very fatigued. Joe knew that she had been out until nearly dawn with Burton. She kept fluffing her lines.

"Go home for the day," Joe said to her presently. "Go home and rest."

"How can I? It will upset your schedule."

"No it won't. I know a girl here in the studio who can read your lines off camera. Dick can do his lines as though you were here, and we'll splice you in later. Dick's are mostly reaction shots, anyway. Go on. Go home now."

She had been trained to be obedient to directors, and she didn't dare tangle with Joe. But she waited to see the girl he had standing by. She was very young and pretty. Elizabeth never fluffed one line in the entire script after that.

During this time, for her to go back to the "Villa Papa" was no relaxation. The *paparazzi* were always there, and things had reached a point where, except for Dick Hanley, there was no one in her household she dared trust. She dismissed a servant who promptly gave the press a story about how she walked about at home clad only in nightgowns, though beautiful ones, by Dior. She also had to deny rumors in the press about another servant who claimed to have a tape of intimate conversations between her and Burton. It was claimed that the tape was played at parties in Rome, London, and Hollywood, but if anyone has ever heard it, no one will admit it. This is typical of what they went through.

Ah, yes, they were in the headlines, Elizabeth and Richard.

The papers were full of them, and so were the magazines. In a million bars in every country in the world, in ten thousand nightclubs, they became the butt of dirty jokes.

Besides this, there were endless business rumors. The studio supposedly offered Richard Burton a bonus if he would remain in the picture. Certain it is that both were paid well for the extra work they had to do as the weeks and months went by and *Cleopatra* remained unfinished, at ever increasing cost to Twentieth Century-Fox. Elizabeth had long since earned her million and was laboring then for the tidy sum of $9,000 a day.

In Hollywood there was an untrue rumor that Michael Wilding was about to attempt to take his boys away from her. Wilding, the perfect gentleman, immediately said, "I have no plans to seek the custody of my sons. Elizabeth has been a good mother to them." From Germany came the flash that the German courts would take the baby Maria away from her, but actually, a few months later, they gave Elizabeth full custody. Sybil Burton could not be reached.

But at least the press had stopped worrying about Eddie Fisher. Back in America, Eddie's career was once more in full swing. Those singing lessons he had taken in Rome were paying off, and the headlines were paying off for him, too. On his opening night at the Tropicana in Las Vegas, he walked on stage to the tune of "Arrivederci Roma," which they could translate even in Vegas, and then said, "I haven't been here for two years. Since then, nothing much has happened."

In Vegas and Hollywood, Eddie was dating the newest and prettiest, like Ann-Margret and Juliet Prowse. By mid-June, Eddie was telling his great reporter-pal, Walter Winchell, "I'll file for a divorce so that Liz can counterfile and win on the grounds of mental cruelty." He said this would enable her to remain in Europe and he was doing it because their mutual lawyer, Louis Nizer, had said it was the only solution. When Winchell asked him what he thought of her having said, "I will never return to the United States. They all hate me and I hate them all," Eddie said, "It doesn't sound like Elizabeth. False friends are probably making up those statements." Then he added, "When you're in love, you do what the heart, not the head, dictates. She's in trouble, Walter. Please stop printing those jokes about her. I only ask you, please stop hurting her in the paper because I still love her."

The final day's shooting on *Cleopatra* came on July 11, 1962. Very fittingly, it ended with Elizabeth's death scene, and in it she was very thin, very tragic, very beautiful, and very much alone.

Cæsar was dead. So was Mark Antony, and the men who had portrayed them had returned to their homes and their wives. Better than twenty million dollars had been spent. If the picture still did not make a profit, the one held responsible would be Elizabeth Taylor.

Said Elizabeth, smiling just a little wanly that final day, to the *Cleopatra* company, "I am going to Switzerland where my parents are with my children." But there was no man waiting for her at home. The movers were at the "Villa Papa," filling seven vans with her children's toys, her objets d'art, and the pets. The St. Bernard required a special car all to himself.

Mr. and Mrs. Richard Burton were in Switzerland, too, with their children, and Mrs. Burton declared there was nothing wrong with her marriage.

Yet presently, as autumn approached, Richard Burton was in Paris. The stated reason was to do what are known as "loops" for *Cleopatra:* that is, certain corrections on the sound recordings of certain speeches. And there in Paris, as the chestnut trees turned gold, was Elizabeth, and her Paris address was the Lancaster Hotel, which was also Mr. Burton's address. They were among friends at the Lancaster, for residing there at the same time were Cary Grant, Audrey Hepburn, Marlene Dietrich, the Rex Harrisons, and Alec Guinness. There, too, was a mob of reporters and photographers keeping twenty-four-hour vigil. But Sybil Burton was not there.

Neither was Sybil Burton around in late November when Elizabeth and Richard arrived together in London to co-star in *The V.I.P.'s,* which Anatole de Grunwald was to produce. This made an intriguing situation, since Anatole de Grunwald had been the producer of *The Last Days of Dolwyn,* the film wherein Richard Burton met Sybil. In 1962 Mr. de Grunwald had happened to remember a fine script by Terence Rattigan which MGM had owned for some time but had been unable to cast. Two and two in the movie business can be made to add up to eight if all concerned are smart enough. Mr. de Grunwald was smart and so was Richard Burton.

Rattigan, one of England's best dramatists, was also a close friend of Richard Burton's. And so, on the seventh of December, 1962, Elizabeth Taylor and Richard Burton arrived in London—by train, because of the awful fogs.

She was at her most beautiful and slimmest that dismal

winter day. Framing her radiant face was a flattering white lynx hat, and a collar of the same white lynx was on her very chic black suit. There was a strong-arm squad of men present to brush off photographers and reporters, and she and Burton quickly departed from the railroad station in separate limousines. But they both ended up at the same hotel, the Dorchester—Elizabeth's Dorchester.

At the Dorchester she and Richard had wonderful suites on the same floor, and when they went down to the MGM studio at Elstree, their dressing rooms were close to each other. Elizabeth's was far and away the more elegant. De Grunwald had ordered partitions knocked down so that she had a very spacious three-room dressing-room suite. Burton's was just the regulation one any actor would get.

Elizabeth's salary was still twice as large as Burton's: one million dollars compared to his half million. However, that was not a new thrill for her. She had earned a million for *Cleopatra*, plus a piece of the gross. For Burton, however, the $500,000 he received for *The V.I.P.'s* was a new high.

Sybil Burton waited three weeks before she joined her husband in London. She rented a house in Hampstead and serenely told the press she was getting it ready for Christmas with Richard and five-year-old Kate and four-year-old Jessica. And sure enough, there was Richard home for Christmas and for many an evening thereafter.

Still he did not neglect Elizabeth. He seemed to have adjusted to her extravagant tastes. This time he did not give her mere scarabs, genuine though they might be. He gave her a beautiful emerald and diamond brooch with matching earrings, which fitted in very neatly with her other jewels, conservatively valued at $350,000. And during the Christmastide, which is the season to be jolly, as the carols say, he spent many evenings with her.

He began introducing her to his friends, such as Lord Devon, who was interested in launching a Welsh theater in London. He had her meet Lord Bute, who had given the land for the theater. He presented her to Terence Rattigan, the successful playwright who wrote *The V.I.P.'s*, and to Robert Bolt, the distinguished scenarist of *Lawrence of Arabia*.

This was entering the inner world of intellectual London, quite different from but as colorful as Mike Todd's world, entirely different from Eddie Fisher's world of nightclubs and music.

Thus, in the winter of 1963, Burton had to be declared president of the How to Eat Your Cake and Have It Too Club. There he was with two homes, two sets of children, two adoring ladies, the salary of a prince, and an apparently dazzling future.

Every day during the shooting of *The V.I.P.'s* he and Elizabeth lunched at a pub called The King's Arms near the MGM studios in Elstree. Elizabeth had originally discovered it in 1947 when she made *The Conspirators*. Burton hadn't known the place, but it was very much to his taste—a beer, bread, and cheese type, though he and Elizabeth always drank champagne, frequently augmented by brandy. Whenever other lunchers would ask for autographs, Elizabeth would grin and sign them "Taffy," which is what she called Burton—Taffy the Welshman. This was high, romantic defiance, and she loved it.

But she wasn't Welsh, and Sybil was, and there were some who openly objected. One January night Richard was attacked by a gang of men outside London's Paddington Station. One version of the story is that it was a group of Welshmen who fell upon Burton, but Elizabeth insists that it was done by London's young ruffians known as Teddy boys. And she ought to know, for the photographs taken that night show her looking at Richard with concern and tenderness, particularly at his battered, swollen eye.

Burton explained it rakishly. He said, "They rearranged my face a bit. It's a very dangerous face to have, the sort that makes some men want to punch it, especially if I happen to be looking in the direction of their women."

However, when Louella Parsons printed that he and Sybil had come to an arrangement by which he'd gain his freedom, both the Burtons quickly denied it. Scoffed Richard, "Louella is talking through her hat." Snapped Sybil, "It's absolutely ridiculous."

Whereupon, within a matter of weeks, in New York, Sybil did announce their separation. She said, however, there would be no divorce. In London, Richard confirmed this. He went even further. He said, "I love Liz, but marriage is out. Liz and I aren't made for marriage. She has not had much luck in her love life. Apart from Mike Todd and myself, of course, she hasn't known any real men."

Distinctly, Burton seemed to be trying to make it very clear that he was the one in the driver's seat. For he was simply a member of Elizabeth's entourage when they came on the set mornings. She would walk in, her back very straight, her head very high, and behind her would follow her two secretaries, her hairdresser, her wardrobe woman, her makeup artist, her Welsh Sealyham, also named Taffy, and sometimes her parents and her children.

Elizabeth, in her infatuation, aping all that Burton did, began to ape his language. But this again showed her talent for identification, particularly when she is in love. Burton said, in praise, "Her language can be as salty as a sailor's."

At last, in June of 1963, *Cleopatra* was released. The critics, both American and English, soon shattered Elizabeth's dream that this would be her great artistic triumph. She received instead her poorest notices ever. Burton won some praise but more censure. Nevertheless, the public flocked to it.

Rex Harrison won the accolades, he who had been the forgotten man in the advance publicity. Rex even had to threaten suit to get so much as his photograph included in the Burton-Taylor love posters for the film. So there may just have been a spark of witty revenge in the manner in which Rex and his talented new wife, Rachel Roberts, proceeded to take over the complete social sponsorship of Sybil Burton in New York and Hollywood.

When *The V.I.P.'s* was completed, Richard went into *Becket*. Devotedly, Elizabeth sat on the set of *Becket* daily and raved to the reporters about Burton.

"He speaks verse like prose, and his prose sounds like poetry," she eulogized. "The way he does poetry reminds me of a Van Gogh painting, colorful, bizarre, wild. Richard has a passion for the writer's word. My nicest present to him is a set of the hundreds of volumes of Everyman's Library, which I had bound in calf." The present had cost her ten thousand dollars.

Most men would have responded in kind to this flattery. Burton's reaction was to criticize Elizabeth publicly for her physical shortcomings. Average mortals, who did not even know her, regarded her as the beauty of the age. But Burton told London's *Daily Express*, "Elizabeth isn't particularly attractive physically. She has the shape of a Welsh village girl. Her legs are really quite stumpy. Her chest isn't anything extraordinary." Then he grumbled, "Richard Burton is now my epitaph, my cross, my title, my image. I have achieved a kind of diabolical fame. It has nothing to do with my talents as an actor. That counts for little now. I am the diabolically famous Richard Burton."

Asked how that reputation would affect his relationship with Elizabeth when they married, he said, "You can be certain that I shall be in the center of the stage. Elizabeth will be in the wings. Knitting."

Elizabeth merely laughed, and continued to do so when he went even further in *Playboy* magazine. There he said, "I can hardly describe her as the most beautiful creature I've ever seen. She is a pretty girl and she has wonderful eyes. But she has a double chin, an overdeveloped chest, and she's rather short in the leg."

Then he added, "I couldn't be unfaithful to my wife without feeling a profound sense of guilt."

"Physically or spiritually?"

"Neither."

This was so contrary to all the exploited passion of the *Cleopatra* publicity, so startling in view of the twin penthouses at the Dorchester, the pub-crawling at night, the social engagements, that Burton was asked for a fuller explanation. He gave it.

He claimed that he had moved "outside the accepted idea of monogamy without physically investing the other person with anything that makes me feel guilty, so that I remain inviolate, untouched. I am a terrible puritan, you see, despite my attempts to be anything else."

This remark fascinated those in the *Becket* company who had heard Elizabeth calling, as she sat on the set daily, "Come kiss me. It is fifteen minutes since the last one."

The day after *Playboy* hit London, Fergus Cashin, a press buddy of Burton's, sought him out. Rubbing his hands over his face, Burton said, "Don't tell me, love. They've been sending that story up to me all morning. Peter O'Toole (his *Becket* co-star) has been reading it to me, asking me what it means. Elizabeth has been on the phone.

"Did I say it? You know me. Of course I did. It was an interview that lasted six hours, tape recorder going the whole time, and refreshments. I dictated enough to make *Gone With the Wind* look like a slim volume of verse. Every time I talk to anybody, I've got to write my biography."

Elizabeth arrived at that point, with her children, and took over the interview. She smiled merrily and said, "I'm not mad with Richard. I love Richard. I'm going to marry him."

Burton held out a few weeks before he confirmed her

nuptial news. Still, when he finally did confirm it, he did it very positively. He told the same newspaper pal, Cashin, "I'm going to marry Elizabeth. No ifs. No buts. She wants to marry me. I want to marry her."

So the following day, when that story hit the headlines, he denied it. And Sybil, discovered in a New York bar, denied that her husband was going to get free at all. She said, "He's tied, hand and foot, like so much lend-lease. I'm not going to cut the leash, and when I get him back, he will be two million dollars richer."

With *Becket* finished, Burton packed up to fly from London to the small inaccessible Mexican resort of Puerto Vallarta, for *Night of the Iguana*. Elizabeth was not in the film. The three important feminine roles in it were to be portrayed by Deborah Kerr, Ava Gardner, and teenaged Sue Lyon.

The gossip columns of the world lit up like pinball machines over the possibilities implicit in such a trio faced by Richard Burton. He was sure to flirt with Ava Gardner, said the columns. He was sure to overwhelm Sue Lyon. Deborah Kerr? Well, her husband was with her at the location, and Miss Kerr has always been dignified and discreet.

Hollywood chuckled. The magazines frothed all over their covers. One proclaimed: "Liz Crawls Back to Eddie." Other publications implied a similar, humiliating fate for Miss Taylor.

The entourage at the Dorchester's twin penthouses began to break up. Elizabeth's parents were the first to leave for Hollywood. They took the Wilding boys and baby Maria with them. Next, the two secretaries departed for California. Finally Elizabeth, with Liza Todd and Burton, flew to Mexico. Behind her Elizabeth left stacks of manuscripts for films that had been submitted to her, masses of million-dollar offers to star in any story she desired, with or without Richard.

She had something infinitely more important than film stardom on her mind. It was the first journey she had taken since her childhood in which she was not the star, traveling with devoted secretaries, kowtowing studio officials, and tactful press agents to smooth out details.

Montreal was the first stop out of London. Such a mob of reporters, news cameramen, and just people crowded around her that she was separated from Richard. Holding Liza in her arms, she cried out fearfully, "Where's my husband? Where's my husband?"

Burton did not rush to comfort her. He snapped at an inquiring reporter, "*I* didn't say that," referring to their marital relationship. It did not anger her. At Toronto, the next stop, she beamed at the press and said, "I shall be Mrs. Burton in three months."

Sybil did shed Richard, despite all of her statements and all of his to the contrary. Then Elizabeth discovered she would have to submit to some skirmishing to get rid of Eddie. But in the interim she received such evidences of devotion as few women have ever known.

Michael Wilding was in Mexico too. Retired from acting, turned an agent, Mike had preceded Elizabeth to the tiny Mexican seaside town of Puerto Vallarta and the neighboring village of Mismaloya, where *Night of the Igauna* was to be shot. Both places are primitive, tropical, and very beautiful, and had within the last few seasons become artists' colonies. The original idea of the *Night of the Iguana* company had been that the cast of the film would live in Mismaloya and do the filming there and in Puerto Vallarta.

The Mexicans had grown accustomed to artists being highly informal about everything. They were prepared for movie stars such as Elizabeth Taylor and Richard Burton behaving unconventionally. Still, in their Catholic land it was confusing to have an ex-husband of a beautiful woman acting as emissary for her and the gentleman to whom she was not married.

Presently Mike had Casa Kimberly, the finest house in town, under lease to Mr. and Mrs. Hayman, which were the names under which Liz and Burton were traveling. Hayman is actually the name of Burton's manager. Situated among papaya and banana trees and coconut palms, Casa Kimberly had six bedrooms and six baths—a unique thing in Mexico—as well as living rooms. Mike saw to it that the Haymans' seventy-four pieces of luggage were unpacked and Liz's clothes hung up, first of all.

There was only one piece of mosquito netting in the house. Mike got enough to cover every bed in the place. He bought all the insect spray in the village, all the ice, and informed the real estate agent, who was also the village grocer, that he knew the first thing his ex-wife and her escort would want would be a cold drink. Then he oversaw the staff of servants and had all the deluxe canned goods from the grocery sent to Casa Kimberly, together with every egg in town. He proceeded to have a wire sent to Mexico City ordering more—more eggs, more canned goods, and particularly more liquor. Then, when Elizabeth and Burton arrived he remained a couple of days as their houseguest.

The Night of the Iguana began shooting, and nobody flirted with anybody. They were all strictly professional, doing their scenes as John Huston ordered. Miss Elizabeth Taylor, a visitor, sat quietly on the sidelines in Mismaloya, where most of the picture was being shot.

She was living up to what Burton had promised. She was in the wings and he was in the center of the stage. Only she wasn't knitting. She was waiting, waiting for him. And she was loving him with the open honesty that has always characterized her.

Sue Lyon's fiancé, in his very early twenties, came to Puerto Vallarta. Deborah Kerr and her husband, Peter Viertel, lived quietly in the house that they had rented. Ava Gardner went out with some of the men about the town.

Elizabeth waited, and she gave parties at which the whole company was entertained. She grew more and more tanned under the hot Mexican sun. She had slimmed down, way down, and wore outfits delectably in contrast to the actresses in the *Iguana* company, since their roles demanded that they look tawdry and tired.

Huston worked so expertly that he finished the production ahead of schedule. Then he and the company packed up and flew back to their respective homes, Switzerland for the Viertels, Madrid for Ava, Ireland for Huston, Hollywood for Sue Lyon and her fiancé. The tourists, who had flooded into Puerto Vallarta, left too. But not Elizabeth and Richard and little Liza Todd. They had bought Casa Kimberly.

Late in December in New York Sybil Burton got her divorce, together with a million and a half dollars. That was the first step.

January, 1964, arrived. This marked the start of the third year of the Burton-Taylor romance. In midmonth Elizabeth filed for a Mexican divorce from Eddie, charging desertion. Her wedding clothes were ready, made by a fabulous new designer she had discovered in the little town. The designer, Nelly Wouff, had flown back and forth to Mexico City to hunt out wonderful laces, fine brocades, lovely silks. The radiant bride-to-be expected to be married a few days after filing the divorce action.

Only Eddie, unexpectedly, proved difficult. It appeared he wasn't quite ready to oblige the young lady. First there was a corporation to be dissolved, the one he and Elizabeth had established when their love was new. It was called the MCL corporation. That stood for Michael-Christopher-Liza, Elizabeth's children. The idea had been that they would make beautiful movies together, with Eddie as producer, Elizabeth as star. Then, too, Eddie had adopted Liza and the baby Maria. Legally they were Liza and Maria Fisher.

It was a botherment. In the waiting interval, however, Elizabeth's loved ones responded. Her parents and all the children moved into Casa Kimberly, followed by her brother Howard and his wife and their five children.

Richard Burton, the man who had broken up her fourth marriage and was about to be the other half of her fifth, spent many an hour in the little *cantinas* of Puerto Vallarta. He could be found declaiming there, his superb speaking voice letting many-syllabled words trip lightly from his tongue. Whether his audience was made up of expatriated Americans or simple local people, he talked vividly of anything that occurred to him, from Welsh ballads to English politics, from Dylan Thomas to Shakespeare and Hamlet, which he was to play in New York in the spring.

Sometimes, when his listener was an American, he would mutter, "You understand I have to get out of the clutter of my house." Always he drank prodigiously.

Finally came spring and his Hamlet, and Elizabeth's divorce, and the wedding. . . .

CHAPTER TWENTY-TWO

Midway through the decade that lost us President John F. Kennedy to an assassin's rifle the age of Camelot was coming to an end. It was 1964. The world may not have understood the Taylor-Burton relationship or, for that matter, particularly cared. But they were good newsprint, and a media blitz of their goings-on served to titillate the general public into wanting to be in on the action. Whatever else, it would never be dull; not to mention that it would sell newspapers. The public would not be disappointed; they would get their money's worth for as long as it would amuse them to eavesdrop on the intimately private life of this last of the truly glamorous movie queens and her bohemian king. Breathlessly they waited to see who would win the battle in the final inning, expecting that that might happen at any time. On the surface Burton seemed stronger. Elizabeth, once again in love with a dominant male partner, at first seemed less forceful than usual, more submissive. But though she appeared to be leaning on Richard, she was actually holding him up.

Fascinated, the fans watched as they shifted roles. The highly accomplished actor and the movie star—or was it the teacher and the student; parent and child. Which was which?

Whatever the combination, the public became addicted; they couldn't get enough. Women wanted to be Elizabeth, but only when she was happy, rich, and healthy—not to mention slim and beautiful. Men wanted to be Richard, with all of the fantasied sex as the ultimate reward.

When they flew home from Mexico, they stepped into a frenetic world in Hollywood. Newsmen and fans nearly trampled them to death at Los Angeles airport, and there was a wild chase to the hotel. The three-ring circus of the decade was about to go into its final act. The clowns were brought in.

Eddie Fisher demanded a million dollars and a percentage of *Cleopatra* for the dissolution of their production company and losses on projected work, and for a fast divorce to allow his wife to marry the man she now loved. (It was granted—on the grounds of abandonment—on March 6, 1964, in Mexico. Elizabeth and Richard were in Toronto at the time.) After a five-day visit in Hollywood, Elizabeth and Richard Burton moved on. Burton was scheduled to start rehearsals for a production of *Hamlet* in Toronto on January 30, 1964.

On the 29th of January the couple, secretly booked as passengers Rosamund Sutherland and Walter Rule, boarded a Trans-Canada flight to Toronto. James Benton, their aide, followed on another plane with fifteen pieces of luggage and twelve dogs. Their arrival created a strong show of public disdain as they entered the lobby of the King Edward Hotel in Toronto. Teenage boys picketing the hotel carried placards: "Cleopatra lovers—drink not the wine of adultery."

And: "Elizabeth Taylor daughter of the flesh—she walks among your children."

The stones or morality were thrown from as high as the Ontario legislature. Elizabeth was visibly disturbed by this reception. Her violet eyes clouded over. Burton, seeing this, quickly turned to the young men as he rushed Elizabeth past, saying, "Well—you can't blame us. We've been trying to get married for two years now. It's not our fault."

Elizabeth stopped suddenly as she spotted three young girls, about thirteen years old, huddled in a corner by the reception desk. Her face lit up with a big smile as she went over to them, shook their hands, and said a few words, leaving them absolutely entranced. As the lobby elevator door closed she looked beyond the glowering faces and waved to the girls.

With Elizabeth at his side Burton rehearsed for his role as the prince of Denmark. Called upon to avenge his father's murderer, Burton, as Hamlet, was forced to face problems of duty, morality, and ethics—some of which may have been a little close to home. Elizabeth's effect on his performance was very apparent when, having avenged the ghost of his father, the prince's death scene brought the curtain down to thunderous applause. Her eyes were filled with tears of pride. How many of the audience were watching Shakespeare and how many were studying the husband-to-be of the fascinating Miss Taylor could not be determined.

On March 15, 1964, in a quiet Unitarian ceremony in

Montreal, Elizabeth, now thirty-two years old, became Mrs. Richard Burton. Burton, thirty-eight years old, was her fifth husband and she was his second wife. That night at the theater he stepped forward after the final curtain and tossed the audience a line from the play: "There will be no more marriages." (Burton never was one to pass up a cue.)

Delirious, the mob was for them. Throngs of fans waited for them as they left the theater. As the couple fought their way through, Elizabeth was thrown to her knees. She laughed good-naturedly when Richard brought her to her feet.

Monday, the 23rd of March, on their arrival in Boston to continue touring *Hamlet*, normally "proper" Bostonians swarmed toward them. The crowd at the airport pushed through doors, trampled police barricades, and raced out onto the runway, following the plane all the way into the hangar.

On their appearance, what seemed like hundreds of disembodied hands reached out tearing at their hair and clothing for souvenirs, and Elizabeth suffered back and arm injuries as a result of the crush. When they finally made it to the Sheraton Plaza Hotel, one thousand fans and curious spectators were waiting in ambush. Elizabeth was pulled in all directions at once; pulled and pushed, for at least five minutes, from one corner of the lobby to the other. People tugged at her arms and even crushed her face against the wall as she tried to free herself to reach her husband. She screamed his name. Richard, his face flushed with anger, battled through the mob to rescue her. Even the slightest jolt could cause her severe pain and aggravate the condition of her back. Tears streaked down her face. "I have encountered mobs all over the world but never anything to this extent," she said.

In her hotel suite she was treated by a doctor, given a sedative, and put to bed. On completion of the engagement for *Hamlet*, they left Boston for the Broadway opening.

Around this time they paid $14,400 to the immigration service of the Mexican Government to become permanent residents of that country. The street they lived on didn't even have a name—though everyone who lived there knew the street, the house, and its occupants. To outsiders who inquired, the taxi drivers would flash their teeth and nod and say, "Ah, Eleezabeth and Reechard...ah, *si señor*, we know...."

And, if they didn't "know," the barefoot street urchins

would direct you up the atrociously uneven cobbled roads to the back of the town and point to a narrow, yellow stone, arched bridge spanning the street. And there it was, the once secret hideout of the Burtons.

"This," Richard had said, "is as close to Paradise as we can get."

Elizabeth agreed, saying, "We'll never leave here. There's nowhere else in the world like it."

Towering above the street was a windowless, whitewashed wall about twenty feet high and part of the three-story home itself. Across the street, reached by the bridge, was a smaller house also owned by the Burtons. There was barbed wire along the rim of the wall and a massive wrought-iron gate at the entrance, and inside, out of the reach of children, were three conical bells. If you were not invited, or rang the bells during siesta, nothing would happen. The Burton guests would always arrive at the correct time—the cocktail hour— and send a note up via the Mexican maid. She would disappear, then return to unlock the gate, point the guest's way up two flights of pink stone steps, and vanish again. At the top, breathing hard, you would eventually locate the bar—and the Richard Burtons.

Richard would welcome you and make you a drink, and if you were all going out for dinner, Burton would explain that Elizabeth was upstairs getting ready: "She'll take about three hours. We're only going 'round the corner, but she treats everything like a premiere."

At the back of the living room, with its whitewashed walls and ironwood beams in the ceiling, was a large, square, open, paved courtyard with a small bedroom at each corner. On the top floor was the Burtons' bedroom, with a balcony where they would sunbathe in the nude. "The only place the photographers never could get at us," said Richard.

There was a pool across the bridge, in the house opposite. The "playhouse," as it was known, also had rooms for guests. Outside the open windows the sunsets turned the sky russet, pink, orange as the Mexican night closed in with its customary swiftness.

This was the place they would run to when the pace got too hot. They could live in complete isolation, with no telephone, no need for the Rolls-Royces and other expensive baubles, away from the martini-belt talk and the prying cameras; when they were there, everything had to wait.

217

In New York, during the run of *Hamlet,* Elizabeth arrived in a limousine in front of the Lunt-Fontanne Theatre at eleven-thirty each night. The police struggled to hold back the crowds, which were twelve deep, and she waved as she went to her husband's dressing room. Coming out with Richard, she would smile and wave again. With a disarming instinct, she helped to keep things under control.

"I have learned," she said, "that there's no deodorant like success.... All of a sudden, after the opening night of *Hamlet* in New York, everybody was beaming and sighing. People who hadn't spoken to us in two years were patting him on the back and giving me a kiss on the cheek."

Burton was to refer to *Hamlet* as "an unmitigated disaster that set a record," though he never elaborated on the comment. What he may have meant was that it did not elevate him to the heights of a Barrymore or an Olivier. Yet, with Elizabeth Taylor in the wings how could it fail to be a commercial success. His *Hamlet* on Broadway (136 straight performances) made more money than any other Shakespearean production in history. But was it Shakespeare, Burton, or Elizabeth the public came to see? Whatever or whoever, they got the whole package.

When Burton opened on Broadway in *The Lady's Not for Burning* in 1950, his star was barely blinking: he got one line in the *New York Times* review—"as a dazed but susceptible clerk, Richard Burton gives an amazingly sober performance." The real reviews went to the star, John Gielgud. Now his marriage to Elizabeth Taylor had brought him to the cover of *Life* magazine twice in one year, and a string of films were to follow. Elizabeth said, in one of the *Life* interviews, that she married Nicky Hilton for a rose-covered cottage; Michael Wilding for friendship; Mike Todd because he was the pursuing, dominating male; and Eddie Fisher because she thought he needed her.

As for Burton, she said, "He has jungle essence." But she was drawn to him the first time they met on the set of *Cleopatra* because he was so pathetic with a hangover. His hand trembled as he tried to drink a cup of coffee. When she helped him to bring it to his mouth, she was hooked. Elizabeth, who admires strength, seems to fall for her men's weaknesses. Discussing his sexiness she said, "It's not the way he combs his hair, not the things he wears, he doesn't think about having muscles. It's what he says and thinks.... My favorite time is when we're alone at night, and sometimes, for hours, we talk and giggle about—maybe books, world events, the children, when we first met, problems, daydreams, real dreams.

"Richard even loses his temper with enjoyment. It's really beautiful to watch. . . . It's rather like a small atom bomb going off—sparks fly, walls shake, floors reverberate."

They were the crowned heads of Manhattan that spring. When they walked into the Copacabana nightclub to their ringside table for Sammy Davis Jr.'s opening night, people gasped. Elizabeth was ravishingly beautiful with her new consort in tow. Looking down at them from a choice table on the balcony was Eddie Fisher with a party of twelve.

Their hotel suite was flooded with presents, invitations, and offers. Author-producer Carl Krueger sent them a joint contract for two million dollars for ninety days' work. His movie, to be filmed in Israel, was based on his novel *Son of the Star*. They declined the offer, but they did agree to appear for a fund-raising benefit for the American Musical and Dramatic Academy.

The once-only program, on Sunday, June 22, 1964, was called "World Enough and Time." It was a wide-ranging assortment of excerpts from prose and poetry and would be Elizabeth's first appearance in front of a live audience. Philip Burton, Richard's foster-father and alter ego, was to be moderator of the show. He had been asked to join the faculty of the school to provide training in drama, music, and dance. As expected, the $35- to $100-a-seat engagement was sold out. There were fifty police officers stationed at the 46th Street theater. The front row center orchestra seats were filled with well-known faces: Mayor John Lindsay and his wife Mary, Eunice Kennedy Shriver, Montgomery Clift, Carol Channing, Anita Loos, Emlyn Williams, and Beatrice Lillie (Lady Peel), to name but a few. In row C was producer Walter Wanger. He had, in effect, brought the cast of characters together in Rome that fatal summer. It changed the lives of Eddie Fisher, Sybil Burton, and the star-crossed lovers of that evening's performance, and affected countless others.

Philip Burton stepped forward, in black-tie, to introduce the program, in his deep, rich voice. His pupil, once the coal-miner's son, Master Jenkins, now joined him. The audience, while listening to them and probably comparing the sounds of their voices for similarities, kept watching the wings for the last of the family trio to appear. They had really come to see Miss Elizabeth Doolittle, who, after studying her lines with the high school drama coach, might turn into a fair "legitimate" lady. One wag whispered to another, "Well, let's see if she can do it." Then she appeared in a blue, off-the-shoulder, Grecian gown, her ears aglitter with sapphires and diamonds. Everyone received polite applause.

Richard began with Marvell's "To His Coy Mistress," then recited D. H. Lawrence, Welsh poet Davy Jones, then Alfred Tennyson, and William Shakespeare, winding up with the St. Crispin's Day speech from *Henry V*. It all sounded like King Arthur from his *Camelot*. The audience heard him but stared at her.

When she arose for her first piece of recitation, she was greeted with wild applause. "Now she'll make a mess of it," Richard mocked genially. Elizabeth, without a microphone, spoke in a sweet lyrical voice. In various dialects, accents, and humors she recited from the works of Elinor Wylie, Elizabeth Barrett Browning, Robert Frost, and Dorothy Parker. Although most of her readings were done with solemn intonations, she fluffed several bits of poetry and—embarrassed—giggled. However, she was quite distinguished, and about halfway through her performance Richard, who had been observing, said aloud, "I didn't know she was going to be this good."

During intermission, from her seat on one end of the aisle, Bea Lillie (Lady Peel) shouted to Carol Channing at the other, "If she doesn't get bad pretty soon, people are going to start leaving."

Repeating their entrances for Act II, Elizabeth now appeared in an off-the-shoulder, silky, white, Grecian gown, with stunning jeweled hair-ornaments laced through her high-piled coiffure, which had been changed for the new costume.

There were dialogues between the two from the second act of *The Lady's Not for Burning* and other classics. She did not have the elocutionized affectations of the Burtons—but she was simply enchanting. At the close of the performance, however, Elizabeth made a false start in reciting the 23rd Psalm. "So sorry," she said. "Let me begin again. I sure screwed that one up."

At the enthusiastic curtain calls she again giggled nervously as she held on to her husband's hand.

The next morning they read in the papers that Twentieth Century-Fox was suing them for $50 million dollars, holding them responsible for the disaster of *Cleopatra*, because of their scandalous and irresponsible conduct. *Cleopatra*, the last of the old-style spectaculars—astronomical costs, opulent sets, cast of thousands, elephants (and an elephantine overtime shooting schedule), overheated publicity, and a torrid offscreen affair between the stars—brought the entire mess down upon the studio empire. Had it been a success, Elizabeth Taylor probably would have been canonized by the studio for her "sins."

Producers rushed to cash in on the popular hysteria around the Burtons. They wanted them at any price. Actor-producer Stanley Baker wanted them for a film to be made in South Africa, but a vociferous women's campaign arose in South Africa to bar Elizabeth from working there—because of her highly publicized affair, which they judged as immoral.

MGM, which had profited $14 million worldwide from *The V.I.P.'s* their first picture after *Cleopatra*, was anxious to get the Burtons for another film. For the *V.I.P.'s*, Elizabeth received a million and Richard a half a million, both with twenty percent of the gross, for a total $2.8 million. MGM repeated the offer for *The Sandpiper*. They moved the Burtons, cinematically (and literally), out of the "VIP" lounge at the fogbound London airport and onto the beach at Big Sur in sunny California.

Burton accepted everything that came his way and Elizabeth seemed to follow. He said later, "It was difficult for a working actor who had known hard times to refuse work. I was still hungry as an actor and believed I had no limitations. It just wasn't in my nature to turn down offers, especially as they became so lucrative. But there is no doubt that many of the films I made were mediocre and my reputation suffered for it."

His reputation may have suffered, but not his bankbooks or his life-style. They chartered a DC 3 from Los Angeles to fly to Monterey, but because of fog, they were diverted to Salinas and made the twenty-mile trip from the airport to Monterey in an MGM motorcade. For their stay they were given a secluded Spanish-style mansion, built around an adobe, in the old section of the city.

A soupy fog swirled around the shooting location at Doud's Beach in Monterey County that September. Richard, bundled in a heavy red windbreaker, clapped his hands furiously.

"*Eeew*, me arthritis," he exclaimed. Elizabeth, wearing a filmy blue smock over a lavender bathing suit, was all goose pimples. Her friends, photographer Richard Avedon and her pal from *Lassie Come Home*, Roddy McDowall, were shooting stills of her, Avedon for *Life* magazine.

At lunch, Burton, who had just read Charlie Chaplin's biography, commented, "Chaplin was unquestionably the world's greatest comedian. But I wonder if he had any sense of humor." The Burtons did. They did their imitations of Rex Harrision, who had starred with them in *Cleopatra*. They laughed over a comment that Harrison's wife, Rachel Roberts, had made—she had looked Burton hard in the face and said, "I don't see talent...I see pockmarks." After Elizabeth excused herself from the table a reporter asked Burton to verify a magazine's calculation that he had racked up some fifteen thousand amatory conquests before his marriage to Miss Taylor. Burton reeled back, shock written all over his face. "Fifteen-thousand? How can they print such preposterous rubbish." His green eyes flashed. "Fifteen-hundred maybe...."

When *The Sandpiper* opened at Radio City Music Hall in New York, it proved to be another one of those mediocre films Burton would talk about later. It was a 24-karat fake. However the glitter mesmerized their fans. The voyeurs gladly lined up for the love scenes between Elizabeth and Richard. If Burton had sold out, he had sold out (and married) into superstardom. That year—1964—racking up performances in *Beckett*, *Night of the Iguana*, and *Hamlet*, he became Number One in the box-office ratings of the top ten. Elizabeth slid from her previous position—sixth place—right off the list (she was eleventh).

They were to make one really great picture together, *Who's Afraid of Virginia Woolf?*—the movie version of the stage hit. She would portray Martha, a fifty-two-year-old, slovenly, foul-mouthed, boozing, bitch of a neurotic to Richard's portrayal of her husband, George, a browbeaten college professor. Their casting for the roles was the talk of Hollywood. Elizabeth had won out over a dozen leading actresses, including the formidable Bette Davis, who swore she was born for the role, and the right age for it as well.

Taylor, twenty pounds heavier and wearing a salt-and-pepper wig, ripped the screen to shreds. As Martha, she proved to be the champ in the sadomasochistic marriage. Burton's outstanding support of her in his role sustained her characterization all the way.

Before their departure for Paris, for further film commitments, the Burtons were scheduled to recite poetry before fifteen thousand people in the Hollywood Bowl. She insisted they be introduced as Richard and Mrs. Burton. Earlier, she had wanted to change her name to Elizabeth Burton, but her agents fought her on this. Nevertheless, at a party for Julie Andrews, at the Beverly Wilshire Hotel, everyone to whom she was introduced as Elizabeth Taylor was told, "I'm Elizabeth Burton!" During a radio interview, introduced as Elizabeth Taylor, she shot back, "I am Elizabeth Burton!" She was the best unpaid public relations representative Richard could ever have had.

Christmas, 1964, in Paris—Richard surprised Elizabeth with a new full-length mink coat and a mink ski-jacket. Always visually very compelling she was in rare good health at that time. "The miracle of being well," she said, "has nothing to do with me. You can help yourself, but it has more to do with a state of peace, a state of happiness. Since I've known Richard, since we've been together, I've known no illness, and I'm sure that is deeply psychological. It's so profound a thought, I can't go into it in a couple of minutes. I believe that one's mental state of being is connected with one's physical state. I guess that I'm proof of the pudding."

Burton had to be in England to begin *The Spy Who Came in from the Cold* early in 1965, and in London, at the Lancaster Hotel, Elizabeth was questioned by reporters who wanted to know about the rumor that began October 26th in Paris. Why did she return her American passport to the U.S. consul there and sign papers?

"It's true I am trying to give up my American citizenship and become completely British. I want to become British more than anything else. Not that I love America less, but I love my husband more."

Elizabeth, a dual national, born in London of American parents, wanted to give up her American citizenship but objected to a phrase in the document saying she must abandon all fidelity to the United States. She told the consular official who visited her at the hotel that she felt that the U.S. had been good to her, and that she did not want to imply that this was not the case. The consul deleted the words, as she requested.

But in Washington the State Department took the position

that the words "abjure all allegiance and fidelity to the United States" are mandatory. Her oath to the U.S. was valid. According to newspaper reports at the time, she was notified by letter that she remained with dual citizenship. Under American civil law a citizen cannot exercise citizenship in two countries. Taylor countered that she elected to use the citizenship of her birth and her husband's birth. She had never given up British citizenship. In Washington, Robert J. McCloskey, State Department press officer, said she could go through with the renunciation anytime she wanted to—if she signed the prescribed form. She made it clear that she could not sign a statement with the words "abjure all allegiance and fidelity to the U.S." She would do nothing for the moment. Therefore her position stood as it was. Burton commented, "I think it was Dr. Johnson who said that patriotism is the last refuge of scoundrels."

Within the next few weeks Elizabeth was confronted with a series of mishaps. They began when she was in Dublin, where Burton was on location. A crowd of over three hundred had gathered outside the Gresham Hotel, waiting to see her leave. When she came out, she greeted them in her usual friendly manner and stepped into her limousine. Unbeknown to her driver a young boy, fifteen-year-old Noel Dempsey, had parked his bicycle in front of her limousine so as to catch a glimpse of her. As they drove off the driver failed to see the bicycle and it fell under the car. When she learned about it, she had a new one sent to the boy's home, with a lovely note of apology.

Shortly after that incident she was robbed of $75,000 worth of jewelry—the thieves carefully choosing the best. "The robbery made me very sad," said Elizabeth. "Some of the pieces belonged to my great grandmother."

Then, during the same period of time, while Elizabeth was being driven to the Ardmore studio to meet Richard, an old woman stepped in front of her car at Loughlinstown Road Junction. Mrs. Alice Maud Ryan, seventy-eight, was fatally injured. Witnesses testified at the inquest that she stepped onto the road in front of the oncoming Rolls-Royce. And this was followed by another terrible shock, this time much closer to home; Elizabeth's mother telephoned to tell her that her father, Francis Taylor, sixty-five, had suffered a cerebral hemorrhage at their Bel Air home in California.

Elizabeth boarded an aircraft for a direct polar-flight to Los Angeles, where her brother Howard was waiting for her on arrival. They rushed to Cedars of Lebanon Hospital to join their mother at their father's bedside. In order to appease the waiting newspapermen, she answered all their questions with, "What can I do, except pray?"

While Elizabeth was with the family during the crisis, Richard was looking for a house for them in Hampstead, England. They planned to settle down to a family life. Elizabeth had grown up in that area and Richard had spent his youth there. "We have lived for three years in hotels," he said, "and we are anxious to provide a real family atmosphere for Elizabeth's four children." Elizabeth, at thirty-four, was talking about retiring before she was forty.

"I have never been ambitious, and even after those marvelous reviews for *Who's Afraid of Virginia Woolf?* I am still going to retire fairly soon. I can't pinpoint the actual date, but it might be within the next two years. Richard is also planning to retire as an actor. I hope we both have the sense to leave graciously. At the moment we are enjoying a peak of success, but it's the law of gravity. The only way for us is down."

Her husband and children always came first, and she longed for a home.

When her father was out of danger she returned to London. Yet, something must have happened during her absence, or she had had time to reflect alone, but whatever it was, she was obviously disturbed on her return. She revealed some uncertainty about herself and Burton.

She talked about Burton as being a difficult husband; and she did not consider him necessarily the last man in her life.

"Sometimes it's not easy to be with Richard, especially when he becomes angry. Then I think he is capable of almost anything. Sometimes he drinks too much." And with her admirable frankness, she continued, "Now, I'm thirty-four years old. I have half my life behind me and my future must be for my children. Richard is very independent. I let him do what he wants. Sometimes he disappears for three days running—with friends, or he goes fishing." (Burton, having all the bait, must have had quite a catch, which was probably thrown back into the sea rather than brought home to fry.)

Did she still love him? "Naturally, even if he is a monster. He has such a strong personality that he is capable of making Elizabeth Taylor into Elizabeth Burton."

While having problems with her present husband, she was soon to have problems with her previous one. Eddie Fisher brought charges against her claiming that she would not let

225

him visit her daughter, eight-year-old Liza Todd Fisher, whom Fisher had legally adopted. Elizabeth, summoned to testify in Los Angeles on October 11, settled with him out of court. The last few months of 1965 were not the best for her.

Putting it all behind her, Elizabeth moved on into early 1966, which would add a new notch to her career. The Oxford University dramatic society announced her appearance with them. Elizabeth would appear, without salary, for a week starting February 7, in a new university production of Christopher Marlowe's sixteenth-century tragedy *Doctor Faustus*, with her husband Richard Burton. Taylor would play the role of Helen of Troy, whose fabulous beauty "launched a thousand ships," a minor nonspeaking role. Burton would be Dr. Faustus, the medieval scholar who sold his soul to the devil in return for kisses from Helen who "sucks the soul of my lips."

Burton, an Oxford alumnus, was thought of as only having had one other stage triumph—in the New York production of *Hamlet*. Professor Neville Coghill, who was to direct *Doctor Faustus*, had last directed Burton in Shakespeare's *Measure for Measure* twenty-one years before, when he was an undergraduate. Professor Coghill said that during his time at Oxford he had had only two men of genuis to teach, the poet W. H. Auden and Richard Burton.

Actor-writer Emlyn Williams, who reached the heights of stardom as a stage actor, described Burton as tremendously cultivated, knowing poems and whole books by heart. "He was incredibly well read and yet made light of it."

Having written a book and several essays, Burton's ambition was to become a professional writer. It was too bad that he couldn't find an interesting subject that would have inspired him to do so, for he was in greater awe of inspired writers than he was of inspired actors.

Burton must have had much to reflect on, particularly in the light of his present position, and projected plans for the future. Now, as a major name-attraction, he was helping to raise money to enlarge the theater. The couple would accept no salary and paid their own expenses. The students would pay the normal entrance fee of 10 shillings and 6 pence ($1.47).

For this performance Richard could be as verbose as he wished, and he might have been secretly pleased that his wife and co-star would be silent for a change. No matter, she garnered all of the attention. As usual the audience waited in virtually tangible anticipation for her entrance.

But the critics remained cool. Bernard Levin of the *Daily Mail* wrote: "Once upon a time Mr. Burton played *Hamlet* with as much promise as has been seen in England since the war. But that was a dozen years ago. It's wonderful what a regimen of rotten films will do."

Overall it was considered university drama at its worst. How did this affect the conquering hero? Well, the show sold out and tickets were blackmarketed. How did this affect his Helen of Troy?

"I was bitten. I felt so at home on stage. All at once something marvelous happened inside of me," she enthused. "I'm dying to do a play with Richard. I don't think I'd forgive myself if I didn't have a go. The little bit I did as Helen of Troy in Richard's *Doctor Faustus*—I wouldn't mind whether it's a comedy or a drama. But not a musical. Have you heard me sing? Of course I might be destroyed by the critics, but that is a chance I will take!" Sixteen years later she would take that chance—alone.

A few weeks later, on March 2, 1966, Elizabeth faced another tragedy within her immediate circle. Her chauffeur's son, seventeen-year-old Jean-Louis Sanz, died from a bullet wound in the head. The French police report said that he had been firing a pistol at targets in a shooting gallery. Whatever happened, the circumstances were not clarified. Elizabeth stood beside her chauffeur at the funeral and, swathed in a heavy mink coat and wearing a black-veiled turban around her head, she sat beside Gaston Sanz inside the chilly church of St. Vincent de Paul during the low mass. Her presence attracted a crowd of newsmen to the industrial suburb of Clichy, but the more than one hundred mourners hardly noted her presence.

At least ten bodyguards hovered nearby to shield her from photographers. Partway through the service she left with one of her secretaries to go to the sacristy, saying that she was not feeling well. Shortly afterwards she returned, and when the service was over, she offered her condolences to the other members of the family present. Then she joined them on a bus to Le Bouget airport for a flight to Biarritz, where young Sanz was to be buried. No matter how she felt, when she was needed she was there.

When the Burtons arrived in Italy in the spring of 1966, for a new movie, Elizabeth checked into a Rome clinic, but true to form, she was ready when it was time to return to work. The Burtons produced their next film together. Probably at Richard's persuasion it was *Taming of the Shrew;* Elizabeth was elevated to Shakespeare, attaining renaissance status alongside her scholarly husband. Competing with him in his own domain, she proved to be a strong artistic adversary. They even sang a renaissance roundelay together.

That summer in Rome, as they often did whenever they were there, they fell in love with the Eternal City. "My wife and I wouldn't mind spending the rest of our careers in Italy playing Shakespeare," Burton said. So they plunged right back into another classic, the movie version of *Doctor Faustus.*

It might also have been easier for Elizabeth to face Eddie Fisher's sudden charges of desertion from the distance of Italy. Fisher claimed that the Mexican divorce obtained by her in 1964 was invalid. He called her a bigamist. Elizabeth laughed it off: "He's got to be joking."

Fiercely loyal to those she loved, she signed to do a film in Rome to get the self-destructive Montgomery Clift back to work as her co-star. The part, in *Reflections in a Golden Eye,* would help him professionally, and at the same time she could care for him personally. But it wasn't meant to be. Before filming could begin, Clift was found dead, at the age of forty-five, in his apartment in New York. Elizabeth was shattered.

"Hey now, Bessie Mae, you save those tears," he had told her, one day seventeen years ago, during the shooting of *A Place in the Sun.* Oh, how she had loved him once, her dear, lost Mr. Schwartzkopf.

On recollection, years later, she said, "One doesn't always fry the fish one wants to fry. Some of the men I really liked didn't like women."

Marlon Brando replaced Clift in the movie. That December the reports from Rome, where they were filming, were anything but dull. The "cold war" was on between Taylor and Brando. Secretly it was hoped that Elizabeth would somehow deflate the well-known Brando pomposity. They spoke to each other only on camera, and Brando also avoided Burton, who came on the set to watch his wife working. It was said that Elizabeth came to work late just to make Brando wait; though that would have been surprising, in view of all her years as a professional actress. While Brando remained aloof and silent, she chattered away cheerily in Italian with the crew between takes. Meanwhile Burton, not known to always pass up a show of temperament himself, sat grimly looking on—for reasons only he was aware of.

The Rome newspaper *Momento Sera* had a field day. Elizabeth responded to Brando's haughtiness by making it clear that he had the role only because her first choice— Monty Clift—had recently died. There was no danger of Elizabeth becoming enamored of her co-star this time.

When released, the picture was a total flop. Even so, every picture either Elizabeth or Richard made brought them at least another million dollars. They made a fortune. They spent a fortune. Elizabeth was used to it. Richard wasn't. They became tax exiles. That year (1966) she finally gave up her American citizenship and took British nationality exclusively. She must have signed the paper, together with all of its clauses and mandatory procedures. But as always she paid her way when, in 1972, the Internal Revenue Service, for what they classified as back taxes, collected their dues.

The glamorous globe-trotters began 1967 by jumping first from Rome to Paris, then to London, in February, for The Royal World Premiere of *The Taming of the Shrew*. It was all considered another colorful episode in the lives of Taylor and Burton, and the public, probably believing that the real Burtons were on show, enjoyed his taming of the shrewish Taylor on screen. The press found it a lot of fun: "The royal rowdies of filmdom may not have quite everything, but there's glitter in everything they've got." The Vatican's *L'Osservatore Romano* praised *Shrew* for its taste. This was the same paper that had once branded her a scarlet woman. And there were some who had called for her banishment from Rome. The Vatican newspaper had called her an unfit mother. Which somehow shows that, if you survive it, the next time around you could become a madonna.

On April 10, 1967, the Academy of Motion Picture Arts and Sciences gave Elizabeth her second Oscar for her portrayal in *Who's Afraid of Virginia Woolf?* She also swept up the New York Critics Circle Award and the Foreign Press Association honors. Burton, for the fourth time, failed to win an Oscar after being nominated for the same film. For all her glory, Elizabeth was distraught over his loss. It also upset her that director Mike Nichols lost.

On the French Riviera, where they were filming *The*

Comedians, the couple refused to speak to newsmen. They remained secluded in their luxurious Villa Fiorentia. Just before dawn in Nice, Elizabeth and Richard listened to the Oscar presentations by shortwave radio, while reporters kept vigil outside. The following day they emerged from the villa for about an hour. They sped away in a chauffeured limousine to a picturesque restaurant at nearby Antibes, ate quickly, and roared off again in the car as newsmen tried to ask them questions. Elizabeth was grim-faced. Burton looked less than happy too.

Unhappy as the Burtons were in Nice, in Sussex, England, there was a couple who couldn't have been happier: Paul Scofield, who won the best actor award over Burton, for his performance in *A Man for All Seasons*, was sharing a bottle of champagne with his actress wife, Joy Parker.

As a consolation they would average another $5 million from their share of the film. It isn't difficult to imagine that Elizabeth would have forfeited the money for the prize. The chance of receiving "his and hers" Oscars would never come again for the husband-and-wife acting team.

The Burtons wrapped up *The Comedians*, their seventh picture together—the picture they had been warned not to make because of the depiction of political life in Haiti—in 1967. Graham Greene's novel portrayed certain conditions in the Caribbean nation, and Greene himself, following publication of his book, had been threatened and didn't dare set foot in Haiti. Most of the film was produced in Dahomey, West Africa—without permission from the government. Threats were made against anyone who had anything to do with the film. Producer-director Peter Glenville received anonymous warnings, and they included Elizabeth and her husband. If the Burtons were not especially worried, it was because they had been threatened so many times before. "We get an average of three letters a week threatening the kidnapping of the children, and worse," Richard said. "In fact, we don't even see the details of most of them. Dick Hanley, our secretary, turns them over to the police. Would you believe it? We actually have a policeman assigned to watch each of the four kids, just to be sure."

After completing *The Comedians* and the film version of *Doctor Faustus*—with Burton as producer, director, and star, and with Elizabeth again as Helen of Troy—they were now free to work again for a major studio. Universal Pictures was betting over $5 million that the box office magic of Taylor and Burton could turn a two-time stage loser by Tennessee Williams into a movie winner.

On a rocky, arid, sun-drenched coast in Porto Conte, Sardinia, the Burtons, their close friend Noel Coward, and a supporting cast were laboring over an adaption of *The Milk Train Doesn't Stop Here Anymore*. In a part which had been "created" by Tallulah Bankhead on Broadway years before, Elizabeth was to play the dying Flore Goforth, widow of five of the richest men in the world. Burton had the part of a semi-artist, semi-poet, semi-conman, who had come to see the widow die. "I just play 'em, I don't analyze them, thank God," Burton said.

He almost did see "the widow die"—off camera. Elizabeth had just stepped out of her dressing room trailer when, only seconds later, it cut loose and plunged over a 150-foot embankment into the sea. The $28,000 trailer had slipped its brakes and safety blocks and wheeled over the heads of six crew members as it crashed its way down to the sea. Elizabeth had been very close to being carried away with it. One pauses to wonder what bad luck seems to pursue her and what good luck saves her, so often it seems, moments before death has its grip.

Most nights, around midnight, Noel Coward would gossip with Elizabeth over crystal brandy glasses on the moonlit terrace of the fragmented villa that served as the principal set, and which overlooked the Mediterranean Sea. They were usually waiting to shoot a scene.

Sitting in his dressing room at three A.M. one morning after four hours of waiting for his wife and Coward to finish their chat, Burton gave some thought to his stage career.

"I would like to do a play," he said to his visitor. "But—I really became an actor by accident, and so I don't miss it the way some of them would." He gestured toward the cove where his new 110-foot steam yacht rode at anchor—"Besides this kind of work pays very well, as you may have noticed." That was a modest remark, considering the Burtons' pay envelope for *Boom!*, as the film was to be retitled, was to become their standard one—$2 million dollars for the couple.

The yacht, he said, gave them luxurious mobility. "It's the first time I've been able to carry my books with me." (The perfect argument for yacht owning.) Also, when they wanted a change from sea travel, they could just as easily fly. Richard had given Elizabeth, as a gift, a million dollar De Haviland

Falcon ten-passenger jet plane, complete with kitchen, stereo equipment, movie projector and screen. By air, by sea, by land, the Burtons were apt to drop in at any time. At one Venetian jet-set gala Elizabeth, in a white gown showing lots of cleavage to display her jewels, completely stole the show away from Princess Grace of Monaco and the Onassis clan. She would willingly publicly display her bosom to a point of distraction, but she refused to do a nude scene in *Boom!* where she has to tell Burton, "My bedroom is full of treasures—including myself."

This was during the time when nude scenes were rampant on film—actors were asked to strip at any provocation. It was an awakening of sexual mores in which provocative allure was replaced with naked ennui.

"I think nude scenes in films are utterly absurd," said Elizabeth quite rightly.

The casting of Taylor as a world-weary, aging, despotic millionairess was one of several unorthodox moves. Sitting under the arc lights, sipping brandy with Coward, who played a "waspish witch" of the international set, she had never looked more full-blown and healthy. As for the role, Elizabeth said, "I should be twenty years older, Richard should be twenty years younger, and the 'witch' should be a woman instead of Noel Coward."

Coward, elegant, urbane, fastidious, and witty, at the age of sixty-eight, found that the Burtons were "old pros." This was the first time they had worked together, though they had been friends for many years. "They know exactly what they're doing every moment, and it's a pleasure to play with them. Not like this 'method' nonsense."

No matter what Coward, or anyone else involved in the film, thought about it, only Taylor evinced any true insight. Again, on screen she overpowered Burton. His performance with her looked washed out. He simply looked bored. This time they just seemed out of place together on the screen. *Boom!* bombed at the box office.

In the sixties had come a sexual revolution. The postwar movie audiences were largely under thirty, and the Taylor-Burton team was going out of style. They were slipping. The public had had just too much, and the new permissiveness had taken away much of their originality. Elizabeth fell to last place in the top ten box-office ratings in 1968, though publicly her strong fascination still held. In that, she was still number one. Madame Tussaud's Museum in London immortalized her in wax. She was now housed under the same roof with Jack the Ripper and Sir Winston Churchill, among countless other famous and infamous immortals.

At the close of 1967 Elizabeth went home alone for the holidays. She wanted to be with her family in California for Thanksgiving and Christmas. She went back to be with her father and mother, to some semblance of what she knew to be reality.

"People seem surprised to think I can still face up to reality. Only last week someone accused us of living in a fishbowl. But it isn't hard to come back to earth, to the things that matter," she said defensively. "I have my husband and my children and that's all I want." As for having everything: "I haven't had tomorrow. There are still people to meet, places to go, the funny and stupid and sad things that happen. We still enjoy them—that's why I like waking up in the morning."

Early in 1968 the Burtons were back in Rome. There were film commitments to "wake up in the morning" for, people to see, places to go—and days ahead of unexpected events.

While in Rome, through his agents in New York, Burton bought the 33.19-carat Krupp Diamond, at Parke Bernet Gallery (now Sotheby, Parke Bernet) on Madison Avenue, for $305,000. He made the front pages with the purchase, while, elsewhere, Elizabeth was paying thousands for full-page ads in *Variety*, *The New York Times*, the *New York Post*, and the *Los Angeles Times* supporting Senator Ted Kennedy's bill for stronger gun-control measures.

The Midas-team of Taylor and Burton could afford to indulge themselves. With their combined fortune of around $88 million dollars they invested in real estate, including homes in Switzerland and Mexico. Their possessions now included Rolls-Royces, a jet airliner, a yacht, a banana plantation in the Canaries, fine art (Elizabeth bought a Monet for $130,000), and the notorious jewelry.

Burton knew that the jewelry was an investment, and the diamonds have increased in value many times since then. To Elizabeth they were something to be worn and shown off: they were very beautiful, and who could be more suited to wear them? What would be the point in having them stuck away in a stuffy safe-deposit box. Hobnobbing with kings and queens and the professional royalty of the world, she need never feel underdressed. "I know it's vulgar," said Elizabeth one day, arching her hand with the Krupp Diamond glistening from her finger, "but would you have me any other way? —true to her fashion, having the first laugh on herself.

During the Burton era they spent a million a year on expenses. As Richard would point out, "—don't forget, we've got a staff of thirty to support." Anyone who had been lucky enough to work for them could never deny their generosity.

"The people around me, I need," Elizabeth confirmed. "We run a huge organization, a huge one. They are not playthings or hangers-on. As for the rest, it's only trimmings. Beautiful, but still trimmings." She was not as concerned with her trimmings as the public was. Her real treasures were love, her family, true friends, and the animals with which she surrounded herself—trite though it may sound. That was her true security. Or course, by most measurable standards she had everything else—except her health.

In London Elizabeth entered the Fitzroy Nuffield Nursing Home for surgery. She had gone to England for her next film, where she took a solo part for Universal in *Secret Ceremony*, with the then Mrs. Sinatra, Mia Farrow. (Elizabeth had expected Frank Sinatra to be in her next one, *The Only Game in Town*, but she got Warren Beatty instead.) Richard was with her, as his next film was to be made in England as well. Although the Burton charisma was losing some of its magnetism, Twentieth Century-Fox paid him $1.25 million to be Rex Harrison's aging homosexual lover in *Staircase*.

About the subject of the film and his part in it, Burton said, "I was a homosexual once, but not for long. But I tried it. It didn't work, so I gave it up. . . . Perhaps most actors are latent homosexuals. So you drink to overcome the shame." (That particular quotation was reputed to have been similar to something once said by Winston Churchill. Burton was fond of quoting Churchill, among other statesman. Because he is so eloquent and measures his words very precisely almost any quotation spoken by him would sound profound.)

Elizabeth underwent surgery twice at Fitzroy Nuffield Nursing Home. The first operation was exploratory and was reported as "minor female surgery;" the second, usually called "major female surgery," was for a partial hysterectomy. When someone commented that it was rather unusual for surgeons to operate on Sunday, a friend replied, "In her position they'd operate in Macy's window at midnight if she asked them to."

Burton was at her side during the operations which would

give her a fifty-fifty chance of having a baby. She was three hours in surgery. "A baby could be born," he said, "but Elizabeth could die. As far as I'm concerned that risk is out." Richard Hanley added, "Thank God there is no cancer involved."

On August 7, 1968, Elizabeth was released from the hospital, and a week later they embarked on a recuperative cruise on the Queen Elizabeth II.

An official for Cunard Line revealed that "they had a private dining room and their own waiter, what we would have offered the Queen."

Upon their return from the cruise they sailed on to France, where Elizabeth was to begin filming *The Only Game in Town*.

Her suite of dressing rooms at the old Boulogne studios in the suburbs of Paris was filled with flowers, mostly orchids. It was decorated in eighteenth-century French furniture, most of it inlaid in gold. There were handsome mirrors on the walls, and the massive bathroom had gold-plated taps and fittings. On the door, in gold, was her name, "Elizabeth Taylor Burton." Below in the courtyard her two Rolls-Royces stood in the sun: one for her, and one for her entourage of three secretaries, a press counselor, a hairdresser, a cook, and five small dogs—mainly Pekingese—that accompanied her each day to the studio. Walls had been knocked down to convert several rooms into a large contemporized eighteenth-century lounge for the dressing room. Outside the suite a burly bodyguard stood guard. On a settee sat Elizabeth, in blue chiffon, her eyes, which change from violet to midnight blue, a few shades darker than the dress, her hair flecked with gray strands that she didn't bother to hide.

"Oh, God, yes, I could give this all up without any trouble at all," she was saying. "Sometimes ... sometimes I long for obscurity. But it would always be relative obscurity, never total. My personal life sees to that. . . ."

To friends she confessed, "I'd like to be a hausfrau, and then I could eat as much as I want and drink as much as I want." In time she realized at least two of those ambitions, for as long as she would want them.

"I think I've lived life at every level," she said, and meant it.

She was talking without her husband's shadow over her. Burton was working elsewhere. She acknowledged, quite honestly, that if ever she wanted to forget she was a movie queen, she could now do so. "And yet," she would say, "I love acting. Both Richard and I want something more stable than our present existence. We're both at the mercy of schedules and scripts. We can't really plan our lives. Yet we're both gypsies. I just want to be alive. I don't want to be a puppet."

Her current picture was a love story set against the gambling grounds of Las Vegas. She was playing a woman who had given up hope, until she met Beatty, a rundown barpianist, who rekindled the fire. She was relieved to have a warm and sympathetic role for a change. "There'll be no climbing up the curtains, or tearing at the carpets." She laughed. "And I'm delighted with Warren—I think he's better suited to the role than Frank [Sinatra]."

As for choosing parts: "I'm not typecast. I don't always succeed, but I'm not playing to a particular kind of audience. This is one reason why I'm not worried about growing old—I was twenty-two when I played my first character role and aged from eighteen to fifty [in *Giant*]. And I don't think you have to be beautiful to keep your sex appeal; it's an inner thing. It's either there or it isn't. I rather love my gray hairs, you know."

On November 20, 1968, Elizabeth's father, Francis Taylor, died at his home in Bel Air at the age of sixty-eight. He had been under medical supervision since his stroke. The Burtons flew from Paris to Los Angeles for the funeral. Elizabeth was in heavy mink and Burton was in fur to his knees. *She* had given *him* a mink coat for his forty-third birthday. They returned to Paris on the twenty-seventh of that month to resume work.

Maria Burton, six, and Liza Todd, eleven, on holiday from their school in Switzerland, joined them in Paris for the Christmas holidays. It was a sad time for Elizabeth, still despondent over the recent death of her father, but she wanted to make things as pleasant as possible for the children.

The Only Game in Town lost $8 million and *Staircase* lost $5.8 million. Elizabeth did not work for two years after this, by choice. Richard came back strong with *Anne of the Thousand Days* and got another Academy Award nomination (his fifth) for his portrayal of Henry VIII. But it was his Anne Boleyn, Geneviève Bujold, who got the Oscar for best actress in that picture. He would try again with *Hammersmith Is Out*, *The Assassination of Trotsky*, and *Bluebeard*. *Time* magazine tolled the bell for Burton, ". . . once an actor, now performs mainly as a buffoon."

To start the New Year off auspiciously, on January 26, 1969,

Burton bought Elizabeth the La Peregrina Pearl, which King Philip of Spain had given to Mary Tudor in 1554. He paid $37,000 for it.

A few weeks later the doctors ordered a complete rest for the Burtons after their heavy film schedule, and on March 8 Elizabeth was reported to be in a hospital in Hollywood for gruelling tests on her ailing back. Richard hired a violinist to serenade her during her confinement. Her doctors said that a fused spinal disc was powdering. When it was rumored that she had cancer of the spine, Elizabeth spoke out, calling the rumor "absolute rubbish." She quietly left the hospital for their home in Puerto Vallarta at the end of April.

By mid-July they were back in London again. While there, Elizabeth read about twenty-one-year-old David Rider, a crippled polio victim who was planning to walk the length of Britain on crutches for charity but was disheartened by the lack of public interest in his venture. Elizabeth, whose daughter Maria was once crippled, immediately empathized with him. She would help. When it was revealed that he would be met by Elizabeth Taylor at the end of his walk on July 30, he got all the attention needed to make it a success.

The press always asked about her future plans. "I may never work again. Unless something comes along that absolutely captivates me. I think the life of pleasure—if you can call being married to Richard Burton, and mother of four children that—is the life for me." Of course she didn't believe it; her work was her life, had been for the last thirty-six years.

The life they continued to live was to eat and drink and travel in a style that some old-time royalty wished they could still afford; but they loved, laughed, and fought as only they could—with all the histrionics at their command. Richard, with his normally strong will, intense feelings, and deep convictions, weakened under the spell of *la dolce vita*. His drinking was no longer a sport; it became a weapon of escape, a necessity. For all his sexual suspicions about his wife, he was the one who made overtures to attract the attention of other women. In his imperturbable manner, Burton could be bitingly cruel, tearing into Elizabeth where she was most sensitive. He knew where and how to push the buttons.

One of the ladies charmed by him was Florinda Bolkan, thirty-two, introduced to him by a well-known woman about Italy, the Countess Cicogna. While Elizabeth watched from the table, Richard danced Miss Bolkan around the floor time and again. Whether or not it had anything to do with that episode, on October 25, 1969, he bought Elizabeth her next diamond, a 69.42-carat stone from Cartier, in New York. Thousands of people paraded through the main gallery of Cartier just for the chance of a glimpse of it. Robert Kenmore, chairman of the board of Kenmore Corporation, owner of Cartier, had bought the stone at auction for $1.05 million. Burton's agent was at the auction. When she received it, Elizabeth ordered a simulated copy for $4,000. She would alternate wearing the fake and the real diamond, to fool would-be thieves.

Before 1969 ended, Burton would have a hit, *Where Eagles Dare,* MGM's biggest money-maker for that year. But was it his box-office appeal or the film's strong all-star cast, story, and general appeal? It was probably a combination of all these things.

It has been said that Elizabeth Taylor hates interviews. Perhaps she is just simply beyond them after over thirty years of being consistently, microscopically analyzed—and too often misrepresented and misquoted. She will speak to members of the press cautiously and specifically, if it is not a trap or insulting to her intelligence. She is undoubtedly fully aware that any publicity for which you do not pay and over which you do not have control seldom turns out the way you hope.

Elizabeth is intelligent. She is honest, and she has an unfailing sense of humor. She just needed to be approached in the right manner. Burton would talk for hours over drinks with a journalist he deemed likable. However, the Burtons' publicity at the dawn of the seventies was mostly unfavorable, in spite of the fact that they gave a great deal to charities, most of it anonymously. Taylor received mixed press when she made her appearances for Israel and bought bonds in support of her pro-Jewish beliefs.

Close to home, Richard now visited his family in Wales often. On one such visit he agreed to appear in a highbrow film version of Welsh poet Dylan Thomas's play *Under Milk Wood,* with Elizabeth and his friend Peter O'Toole. It garnered flattering notices in the United Kingdom by the more "serious" critics, but lost out in the United States.

Burton felt slighted. Had he sacrificed his artistic integrity to the point where he wasn't being taken seriously or was he in competition with his award-winning wife?

Looking for someone to blame, he may have cast his eyes in the direction of his beautiful wife. Elizabeth had played

Rosie Probert, the village prostitute. Critic Stanley Kaufman, reviewing the film, wrote: "Cosmetized and fineried, she [Taylor] looks less like a smalltown Welsh whore than like part of the deal that included Burton." Respected critic Judith Crist wrote: "I have seen it three times! I shall see it three more times!" Kaufman seemed to be reviewing Taylor's appearance, while Crist her performance.

Burton might have been subconsciously tortured by both his failure to become the personification of the classic actor he felt he was and his repeatedly just missing the Academy Award. The recognition just kept slipping through his fingers.

How was it possible for Elizabeth to assuage these frustrations, which were conceivably at the depths of their discontent? She had been taken ill again and lingered so for many months, a malaise that was probably not helped by her emotional condition at this time.

Then in June she faced another operation and was flown from London to the home of Dorothy Allen in Palm Springs. Dr. Herman Swerdlow, a specialist in proctology, came in from Beverly Hills to operate. All that was disclosed regarding the surgery was that it was for an ailment of the lower intestine.

Burton, who was filming *Raid on Rommel* in England, remained silent. It wasn't until September that he broke through: "It's only in the past few weeks that Elizabeth has come up from under. It's not one of those women's things. It's one of those things that happens to all of us. I can't tell you more than that."

On Wednesday, October 7, Elizabeth, now thirty-eight years old, left her hospital bed for something she would make herself do, attend the wedding in London of her eighteen-year-old son Michael Wilding to Beth Clutter, nineteen, of Portland, England. Wearing a white wool trouser-suit, a maxi-length cardigan, and a pearl necklace, Elizabeth stole the show—she was a knockout.

A few days after the wedding Elizabeth began to receive mysterious telephone calls at the Dorchester Hotel from a man who threatened to kidnap her. Chief Inspector Dennis Burke of Scotland Yard's Criminal Investigation Division posted guards around the clock. The police were much more cautious than she. At that time Elizabeth was more concerned with endangered species of wildlife: she made a public statement pledging not to buy any fur that used the skin of wild animals.

239

*   *   *

In December 1970 she returned to films after an absence of
two years. The film industry was going through a difficult
time and, quite realistically, she said, "I'm taking a percentage and expenses. We all sink or swim together."

During the hiatus she had gained considerable weight.
While she was shooting *X,Y and ZEE*, Richard was making
Hammersmith Is Out, in Brighton, England. Five days before
Christmas, Richard gave $120,000 to Oxford University to
provide a center to further the interest of drama and its study
in the university.

The Burtons' marriage had survived another year. At the
start of 1971 Elizabeth found out that she was to become a
grandmother that coming August. "I am absolutely thrilled!"
she exclaimed. Then the petty quarrels that had kept the
Burtons' marriage simmering burst into an explosion that
erupted on the front pages. All she would say about the latest
celebrated brawl was "This time it's finished!" If Elizabeth
was indeed quite serious and wanted to end the marriage, to
the rest of the world it was just another tiff. They had had so
many.

On May 17 she was in Cedars of Lebanon Hospital in Los
Angeles for surgery. The media curtain dropped; no comment
was forthcoming. Dr. Rex Kennamer had nothing to say about
it to the press, and a few days later she checked out. Shortly
afterwards, perhaps as a reward for just pulling through
another physical ordeal and to patch things up again, Richard
gave her a $125,000 Kojah mink coat, the world's most
expensive mink. (Mink was not considered a wild animal.)

They went to their home in Switzerland for some privacy, a
rest, and some time alone together to sort things out. In
August of 1971 they received a personal invitation from
Yugoslav President Tito to visit him. Tito, an avid movie fan,
welcomed the suntanned pair at Brioni Island for the weekend. It was not surprising that before they left the northern
Adriatic port Burton had the idea to play Marshall Tito in his
film *Sut jeska*, depicting the partisan warfare of Communist
guerrillas of World War II. But nothing came of it in the end.

Richard Burton: An Intimate Biography, by authors John
Cottrell and Pergus Cashin, was published in London. According to them, Burton had really fallen in love with Elizabeth,
no matter how their liaison had originally started out. But
was it too late?

"I cannot see life without Elizabeth. She is my everything,

my breath, my blood, my mind, and my imagination," he said—spoken by a true thespian of the legitimate theater. Then, with all the drama of centuries of Welsh history and poetry: "If anything happened to her, I would wither and die."

Elizabeth responded, saying, "I need strength in a man more than any other quality. I rely on him totally now." It was in this vein that they closed another year on the highly public romance of the world's two leading screen personalities.

CHAPTER TWENTY-THREE

Elizabeth turned forty on February 27, 1972, and Richard planned to celebrate in Budapest, where he was filming *Bluebeard*. By now without too much originality, but with no less thought, he gave his wife a heart-shaped pendant first given as a present by Shah Jahan, builder of the Taj Mahal, to his wife, Mumtaz Mahal. Time does make changes—from Shah Jahan to Mumtaz Mahal, now Richard Jenkins from Wales was giving the pendant to his cinema goddess, three centuries later. The pendant is set in an 18-karat gold lattice-work and hangs from a gold chain studded with diamonds. When Burton was asked to reveal the diamond's worth he said he would do so in a year, when he would donate the equivalent to charity.

At the birthday party in the Hungarian capital, among such friends as Princess Grace and Ringo Starr, numerous movie people, and various other guests was British writer Alan Williams. Williams, author of a book on the 1956 Hungarian revolution, walked over to Elizabeth and demanded to know why she had not invited any Hungarians to the party. "Don't you know what happened here in 1956?" he remonstrated. Not the perfect opening to your hostess, whose birthday you were supposed to be celebrating, and who had been kind enough to invite you. He stared at her. "What does the Hungarian revolution mean to you?" Taken aback by such an attack Elizabeth started to cry.

Richard rushed over to her defense and angrily ordered Williams out. It was so uncalled for, as the Burtons, who anyway knew very few Hungarians, had in fact invited the few they did know to the party. They could hardly be expected to go out in the streets and pick up strangers. Elizabeth, who has been involved in so many causes, did not invite such behavior. What Williams did not know, though it in no way excused his behavior, was that Elizabeth intended to donate the equivalent of the cost of the party to UNICEF, and, as promised, she donated $45,000—the exact cost of the party—to the United Nation's Children's Fund.

Eventually all of the adverse publicity had its effect on her family. Elizabeth's son, Michael Wilding, said, in London, that he was going to reject the life into which he was born: "I just don't dig all those diamonds and things." He was planning to take his wife and baby, Leyla, to live in a commune in a nineteenth-century farmhouse in the desolate Cambrian mountains of Wales. He added wryly, "Mama has only Richard Burton on her mind, and he likes to live like a Roman emperor."

It could have been anything: Burton filming in Budapest, Elizabeth needing a break from the routine, but they had another fight. Elizabeth went to Rome and on a Thursday night in May she was seen with Aristotle Onassis, out for a late dinner at the plush Hostaria Dell Orso—without spouses, as they say, but with unnamed friends. In moments the *paparazzi*, rather amusingly titled "free-lance photographers," arrived.

Some stormed the front door, while others sneaked in through the kitchen. The waiters tried vainly to hold them back, as trays, drinks, and fists flew in all directions. It turned into a Mack Sennett comedy, Roman style. The jet-set dinner became a full-scale brawl between the waiters and a couple of dozen photographers. Onassis shouted and threw champagne at them, while Elizabeth did the sensible thing: she ducked under a table. The police finally did arrive and restored order. Taylor and the shipping magnate resumed their tête-à-tête, sipping champagne until the first light of dawn, after which they left the restaurant separately, each to return to their separate hotels.

The *paparazzi* get the biggest money for pictures that are unflattering and sensational. Elizabeth has tried to assert herself with the press, saying that much that has been printed about her is "actually a lot of bull." That may not be too ladylike, but it is a mild retort considering what she could have said. She has also said that she isn't interested in keeping up a running fight with the press to change her public image. Her comment, "Whether I have been fickle or not fickle—and nobody will ever know but those involved—

by God, it's none of their business. In living my private life, my responsibility is to the people who are directly involved with me," surely deserved a round of applause.

Oddly, the fiasco in Rome must have endeared the Burtons to the Italians even more. Elizabeth and Richard were presented with Italy's Rudolf Valentino Cinema Award in Valentino's hometown, Lecce. This award is given to stars most likely to become legendary. The award, however, did not stop the Burtons' fights, which continued unabated.

Elizabeth has always insisted that she doesn't believe in divorce. You can have a dozen divorces and still not believe in them. The best example for her was her own parents, who remained married to each other until the death of her father. Regarding any possible divorce between herself and Richard Burton, she said, "Richard, unless he wants to divorce me, will never be divorced by me. . . . Whatever will be called for to keep our marriage together—I think I will have the guts to do."

Whether it had anything to do with keeping a marriage together, or not, Elizabeth relied on Burton so much that if he didn't like a dress she wore she wouldn't wear it, even if it "came from Dior and cost two thousand bucks." And "Richard pays the bills," she said proudly. "That's only happened in my life once before—with Mike."

Could it be, though, that in foreseeing the inevitable, they tried to draw closer together? Somewhat prophetically, they would do a television play for Harlech TV in Wales, of which Burton was the largest individual shareholder, entitled—*Divorce His, Divorce Hers*.

Divorce His, Divorce Hers was the drama of a modern marriage that had been corroded by the pressure of a husband's work and the ache of separation for his wife. If it sounds like a soap opera, it was. The project, from beginning to end, was to be a disaster.

When it was aired on ABC TV on two successive nights in February, 1973, the audience ratings were poor and the reviews were scathing. This failure was said to have propelled Burton into further drinking and depression. Elizabeth was under pressure from all sides, as he continued his flirtations with younger actresses. In addition to this, her old friend and co-star from *Butterfield 8* Lawrence Harvey was dying of cancer, and there always seemed to be another movie to make. *Ash Wednesday,* her next, was to be filmed in Cortina, Italy. While in Cortina she broke out with measles and was quarantined in her hotel with her husband—for better or for worse.

Following this, they went their separate ways. Both she and Richard, drinking heavily, had had another argument. He shouted, "Get out!"—and she did.

She went to California. He went to New York and on to Long Island, to stay at the Quogue home of their lawyer and friend Aaron Frosch. Elizabeth stayed with her mother and visited many of her old friends, and she was seen out with Peter Lawford, whom she had known for years, from the early days at MGM. It may have been at this time that he introduced her to a Mr. Henry Wynberg.

At the beginning of July she checked into the Regency Hotel in New York, and on July 3 she issued a statement, on hotel stationery, in her own hand, announcing that she and Burton were separated. It was published in the newspapers, as follows:

> I am convinced it would be a good constructive idea if Richard and I are separated for a while. Maybe we have loved each other too much—not that I ever believed that such a thing was possible—but we have been in each other's pockets constantly, never being apart except for matters of life and death, and I believe with all my heart that this separation will ultimately bring us back to where we should be—and that is together.

Hopefully, she added, "wish us well, please, during this most difficult time."

The Burtons had always fought but, as Elizabeth would later admit, the fights became fiercer and fiercer. She added, probably in considerable understatement, "We several times hit each other."

Burton had been involved with several women, and Elizabeth's reaction was open and straightforward: "I am a jealous woman. Finally, the smallest glance or the smallest smile would cause me to come apart inside. I could no longer bear the fact of being deceived."

For all her screen portrayals and her reputation, she was known, by those who knew her well, to be a "mid-Victorian," "Miss Proper," "Miss Prude," never known to be untrue to either her husbands or her friends.

Adamantly she ignored the gossip that there was a "mystery man" in her life. "I can swear to you that I will never marry again," and when she said it she meant it, at the time.

245

Three days later, July 6, Elizabeth flew back to Los Angeles to see her mother, Sara, who was in very poor health. Reporters waited over half an hour before she got off the plane following the landing. Looking tired and shaken, with two silky terriers on red leashes running ahead of her, she stepped from the plane leaning on the arm of her adopted German daughter Maria, eleven. Elizabeth did not check into her usual retreat, the Beverly Hills Hotel. (Eddie Fisher was presently in residence there.) It was assumed that she would stay at the Holmby Hills mansion of Mrs. William Goetz. Edie Goetz had known Elizabeth since her early days in Hollywood, and it was to Edie that she had gone, just a few years ago, late one night, after a violent quarrel with Richard.

The Burtons made a date to meet in Rome around the middle of July. During the separation Burton told friends, "She worries about her figure, about her grandchildren, about her mother, about the color of her teeth, and expects that I drop everything to immediately devote myself to those problems." And in the next breath—"I can't live without her—this peace is driving me crazy."

Before going to Italy for the reunion, on July 12 Elizabeth visited the Motion Picture County Home. She and Roddy McDowall went to see her old co-star from *National Velvet* and *Lassie Come Home*, veteran actor Donald Crisp, on his ninety-fifth birthday. She never forgot old friends.

Elizabeth had a departure party at Disneyland with her children Maria, Chris, and Liza—and Mickey Mouse—before leaving on the sentimental journey to meet her husband in Rome, where they had first met during *Cleopatra*, seemingly a hundred years ago, but actually just nine years earlier. The seventeen-day separation was the longest they had ever had. Burton had been in and out of Italy, staying as a houseguest of producer Carlo Ponti and his wife Sophia Loren, in their villa near Rome. They had all been to the Moscow Film Festival together, where he happily told reporters he was going to meet his wife on the 20th of July in Rome.

When the day arrived, he went to the airport long before her private plane was to land at the Ciampino military airport. Burton, wearing a white polo-shirt and bright red sport jacket, was waiting inside a dark green Rolls-Royce limousine. He was pale and nervous as he peered out of the rear window at the plane, tapping his fingers on the leather upholstery for what seemed like an interminable wait before she finally got off.

First to appear down the plane's ramp were two large trunks, then two animal crates and her two small black-and-white dogs. Elizabeth followed, dressed in blue slacks, an orange blouse, and an embroidered denim jacket. A dozen assistants shielded her from a crowd of about one hundred newsmen as she moved quickly toward the car, where Richard swung the door open for her and she got in. They threw their arms around each other, kissing and hugging in the backseat. When he embraced her his hands were trembling, and her eyes were filled with tears. Then they laughed and broke into animated conversation. Seconds later they were driven away. Rome was working its magic again.

It wasn't until weeks later that they appeared in public. Obviously they had a lot of catching up to do. The inevitable, rather unnecessary question about divorce was asked. "What divorce? She's absolutely adorable," Richard said. "I love her."

Not only was she reconciled with her husband, but her estranged son, Michael, who had denounced his mother's riches and way of life now came back into the fold.

That fall Elizabeth collected $140,000 at a special fund-raising dinner to aid Israeli war victims. In retaliation Moslem youths petitioned the government to ban all Elizabeth Taylor movies.

Then suddenly she fled Rome—and Richard.

To use an old cliché, "Elizabeth went home to mother."

With her mother and the "mystery man" who had been whispered about around the time of the announcement of the separation, she attended a showing of her picture *Ash Wednesday* at the Directors' Guild of America headquarters. Wearing a short white mink coat and slacks, Elizabeth and her companion slipped in quietly and sat down next to Mrs. Taylor to watch the unfolding story of an aging woman who undergoes radical plastic surgery—upon completion of which she looked exactly like Elizabeth Taylor. The film was strictly run of the mill.

During this separation from Burton, Henry Wynberg became Elizabeth's escort. Henry Wynberg was a half-Jewish Hollander. He had been working as a bellhop in an Amsterdam Hotel when he quit to try his luck in New York in the mid fifties. Hating the cold winters in the East, he drove to

California, where, upon arrival in Los Angeles, he answered an ad for an automobile salesman in Santa Monica. Over the years he socialized with his celebrity clients and soon got himself invited to "insiders'" Hollywood parties. When Taylor met Wynberg, she was on the rebound.

Everybody, it seemed, wanted a piece of Elizabeth Taylor. In San Francisco, at the Fairmont Hotel, a glass collar she had worn in *Cleopatra* was sold at auction. It was for a benefit for the Fine Arts Program of the University of Montana. It sold for more than Frank Sinatra's monogrammed cigarette case, which was also included in the auction.

In November Elizabeth was back in the hospital. Once the prescribed routine physical was completed, she was scheduled to enter University of California Medical Center, where she went through two hours of exploratory abdominal surgery, necessitated by complications brought on by previous operations. She was forty-one years old and at the opening of her fifth decade she was very depressed.

From Scripps Clinic in La Jolla she wrote to twelve-year-old Ted Kennedy, Jr., who had just undergone major surgery. She said how much she admired and loved him for his bravery. In closing she wrote: "I am praying for you, and I hope when you have a few moments you will say a small prayer for me." Among other sadnesses, Lawrence Harvey had finally succumbed to stomach cancer a few days earlier.

Peter Lawford and Henry Wynberg were standing by for her discharge from the hospital, and Richard Burton was on his way over, encouraged by Sophia Loren, his co-star in *The Voyage*, being filmed in Sicily and at the studio in Rome.

Richard Burton walked to the door of his wife's hospital room, opened it, walked inside, and quietly closed it. Several hours later he left. When he returned, he brought with him a diamond necklace, and this time when he left, he was pushing his ailing wife in a wheelchair—on their way to an airliner that would fly them to Europe.

During a London stopover on their flight from Los Angeles, they held hands and smiled but said nothing to newsmen. Elizabeth looked tired but happy. Richard and a nurse hovered over her. During the flight the nurse administered pills prescribed by her surgeon, Dr. Herbert Machlader. Dr. Machlader discounted reports that the operation was anything more serious than the removal of an ovarian cyst.

At Heathrow Airport Richard shepherded Elizabeth through dozens of journalists. "I am a very happy man, but my wife is

248

very ill, and she does not want to answer any questions," he said in answer to their cross fire. Polite as the British newsmen usually were to them, Richard snapped when he was asked how the reconciliation came about: "Don't be stupid. I'm not going to tell you intimate details of that nature. We are flying now to Naples, where we will stay in a hotel, and then go to Venice and Rome, where we will spend Christmas with each other."

Elizabeth, in a very soft voice, thanked them for their concern about her health. "I'm heading for the sun and I intend to spend as much time as possible resting." Then they asked her to display the newest diamond that Richard had given her. She smiled. "It's lovely. It's heart-shaped, but I'm not going to strip off to show it to you."

No one even remembered Henry Wynberg. He had been all set to leave for an Hawaiian holiday with Elizabeth, and they were to have attended the Rose Bowl game together. But when she left with Burton, she didn't even say aloha! Elizabeth may have been so heavily sedated for the trip that she didn't even remember their date.

The Italian newspapermen were waiting for them when they arrived by private jet in a cold but sunny Naples on Tuesday, December 10, 1973. A limousine took them from the aircraft to a downtown Naples hotel. Elizabeth was wrapped in a chinchilla coat against the cold and was now displaying around her neck the heart-shaped diamond given to her as a get-together present two days earlier in Los Angeles. Christmas in Venice was one they both would never forget.

On January 5, 1974, Richard returned to Rome and to the studio with Elizabeth, who ran across the set to hug director Vittorio de Sica and Sophia Loren. They opened a bottle of Asti Spumanti, and Sophia toasted their marriage. As the crew surrounded her, inquiring after her health, she lifted her champagne glass. "I feel absolutely marvelous," she said joyously.

Elizabeth, worried about the lonely and ailing Peter Lawford, pleaded with Richard to put aside his bad feelings for the fifty-year-old actor. He resented Lawford for introducing Wynberg to Elizabeth, but he gave in to her, and they brought Lawford over to Gstaad for the remainder of the holidays.

Elizabeth was due to make an appearance at the Oscar ceremonies in April in Hollywood, and she expected Richard to join her on completion of filming *The Voyage*. When he didn't she was very distressed. She felt that if he had really cared for her, he would have been there with her at the ceremony to show the world that they were together again.

When he did return, he went directly to UCLA Medical Center to dry out. He was forty-eight years old. Elizabeth went to Hawaii—after all—for Easter with her mother, her children, and her brother Howard. When she returned she went into seclusion. Richard, meantime, was now registered at St. John's Hospital in Santa Monica. Elizabeth, unhappy over his condition, did not want to talk about the now open secret of his having become an alcoholic. There were so many others who would talk.

"What Richard probably needs," said a friend, "is a job, a good job—very quickly." Others commented, "We all go through periods of indecision in which we cannot channel ourselves." While still others said, "Richard doesn't know what he wants to do. He doesn't want to act; he just doesn't know."

Burton checked out of the hospital on May 25. Elizabeth was now back with Henry Wynberg, and on June 26, 1974, the Burton marriage was dissolved in Gstaad, Switzerland. Just like that! Elizabeth, wearing a pleated beige dress and heavy makeup behind dark glasses, walked out of the Swiss courtroom in a daze. Richard Burton was in New York at the Plaza Hotel, drinking heavily. It was a rather quiet and inauspicious ending to their life together, but it was disclosed that Elizabeth had told him that if he did not stop drinking, she would divorce him. He continued drinking, and she kept her word.

They divided everything equally, with Elizabeth keeping her jewelry and taking custody of their adopted daughter Maria. On Sunday, June 30, 1974, four days after the divorce, Elizabeth Taylor was sailing the Mediterranean in the Burtons' yacht, with Henry Wynberg. One of the world's best-known and most fortunate women now was one of the saddest and the loneliest.

Burton, in shock over the broken link to his life, said, "I wound up in the hospital because of booze. I was starting the day off with champagne with vodka chasers. By the time they poured me into the hospital I was a goddamned alcoholic," and, "I will love her for an eternity to come. It's a shame! It's sad. It's heartbreak. It's anything you want to say it is—but it's the dearest, sweetest memory I own."

250

Elizabeth's escape, this time with Wynberg as her passenger, was the pattern she had adopted. He was a man; she was at her most vulnerable and she needed a shoulder to cry on, someone who could take over and direct her. But why Wynberg? He had been called an operator, and she was normally too intelligent to have been taken in, but he was shrewd and knew her weaknesses. Again, in her own time of need she thought he needed her—to her an irresistible attraction. She was anxious to travel, to get away and work, so she accepted an offer from director George Cukor to do *The Blue Bird*, the first major coproduction of a feature film by the U.S. and the Soviet Union. She would play four parts in the picture, and it would keep them—the cast and company—in Leningrad four months over schedule. Preparing herself for the long, cold Soviet winter ahead, she took along a warm companion: Henry Wynberg.

Just before leaving for Russia she had another physical setback.

"They warned me I would always have trouble with this back," she said. "After keeping me in traction for weeks they took me to a hospital, stuck a needle into me, and probed and prodded it around. They have invented a new form of Chinese torture, but I'll go screaming into my grave before I'll give in to it." While she lay in Mt. Sinai Hospital to relieve the pain of her chronic back condition, Wynberg was never out of sight.

When she was released from the hospital shortly afterwards, she again proved her strong willpower over her physical disabilities.

On Saturday, January 25, 1975, filming began in Leningrad on *The Blue Bird*. Three months later Elizabeth was in Wellington Hospital, suffering from amoebic dysentery. She was sick from the food she had eaten in Leningrad. Now, after a meal of chili, sausage, salami, and champagne, she was feeling much better.

Richard telephoned her while she was there. With a tremor in her voice she said, "He's fighting a lost cause. . . . I feel sorry for him." She returned to Moscow to finish her various roles in the picture. Certainly not in love with Wynberg—she regained her senses—she also finished with him.

A divorced Richard Burton was haunted by the years they had had together. No other experience with anyone else could equal the love, the physical, emotional, and creative life they had shared. For him there could be no higher summit in their lives than that already climbed together. Perhaps the magic would still be there.

Elizabeth marries to stay married; she had never wanted it to end that way, and she began taking Burton's calls. The inestimable Burton persuasion was at work.

Like a will-o'-the-wisp she was here and then there. In Gstaad, Switzerland, one week. Jerusalem the next. Then Tel Aviv. There was a man beside her and another man was calling her. The man at her side was Richard Burton, and ringing the telephone off the hook was Henry Wynberg. "I would like to break both his legs," Richard said as his cure for the insistent ringing.

Next stop in September of 1975 was Johannesburg, South Africa. They visited Chobe and Kruger National Parks. The Chobe park, seven hundred miles from Johannesburg, is almost completely unspoiled and is renowned for its big game—elephant, rhino, hippo, and buffalo. They traveled over poor dirt roads to a lodge near the Chobe River, with its lazy, coiled crocodiles. From their veranda they watched the reptiles. To the west was a large pool where elephants came to drink.

The Burtons' ardent conservationist natures found a home in the atmosphere of the area. They fell in love with the place and with each other again and decided to get remarried in a mud hut in an African village on Friday, October 9, in Botswana, near the Kalahari Desert. As two rhinos and a hippo watched they celebrated with champagne. Ambrose Masalela, the local district commissioner, married them in the northern Botswana village of Kasane, five miles from the Chobe Game Park Lodge, where they were staying in the Rod McKuen suite, named for the poet and advocate of love.

Richard had bought a wedding ring made from ivory in a local African goods store. The bride wore a green dress with lace frills and guinea-fowl feathers, and the groom wore a red shirt, white trousers, red socks, and white shoes. After ten years of marriage and fourteen months of separation and divorce, Elizabeth and Richard were back together as husband and wife.

Richard might have believed that the simple ivory wedding ring he had given Elizabeth for their second marriage wasn't enough. Upon their return to London he purchased a 25-carat pink diamond, mounted with 16 carats of blue-white diamonds, valued at a million dollars. But Elizabeth said, "He doesn't have to spoil me anymore, just love me," she said, revealing a much changed woman. She wanted his love more than diamonds. He would have pleased her more by building a hospital in Botswana.

Languishing in the fishbowl of fame, Elizabeth and Richard celebrated his fiftieth birthday in November 1975, and just a few weeks later they were consulting their lawyers about a second divorce. Out of the jungles and back into civilization the retake on their romance paled when old habits came back to intrude. He would have been content to have just gone on living together. She cared too much, and the only way she could accept living together was to be married.

Richard just seemed to retreat, and Elizabeth went back to her sanctuary, her family. Why?—they were mostly compatible, yes, in spite of the fights. What was the whirlpool of conflict that constantly tore their life apart? Was it the hot words, regretted but unforgiven; a lack of awareness of each other's sensitivity? Too many people interfering, too many public parties, too much drinking? What of the deeply wounding flirtations? These were laughed off as too trivial to be taken seriously. But for all the escapes and forced laughter, the wounds did not heal.

Once again someone came along to save Elizabeth from the emotional gallows just at the crucial moment. In late March, she was invited to attend a dinner at the British embassy in Washington, D.C., in honor of Queen Elizabeth II's visit to the United States for the Bicentennial celebrations. Elizabeth needed an escort for this occasion and planned to arrive with her hairdresser. Instead she was talked into accepting a blind date with one John Warner, a tweedy, pipe-smoking, country squire from Virginia. Warner was urbane and handsome, with wide-ranging intellectual interests. He was from an old Virginia family. He was a member of a Washington law firm and, in 1969, at the age of forty-one, he had been appointed under secretary of the Navy. In 1972 he became secretary of the Navy. Divorced and with three children, he was a "man's man" and an idealist. He would have been a prize catch for any of the southern belles. Within minutes after they were introduced Elizabeth Taylor and John Warner were attracted to each other.

In fact, Elizabeth came, saw, and conquered Washington. It must have seemed like an extension of Hollywood, with its politics, back scratching, backbiting, and conspicuous consumption. She moved easily into this new phase of show business. Only the sets and the location had changed, and she probably found that the roles were a bit more stereotyped. At one gala party at the Iranian embassy, one hundred eighty guests were seated at fifteen tables, where mountains of caviar were being served. All eyes turned to Elizabeth when she made her entrance, wearing an orange and red dress (the colors of the Iranian flag) made by Halston for the occasion. Added to this was a generous serving of her emeralds and diamonds. She was a sublime enchantress, in the true Middle Eastern style, and she easily captivated Ambassador Zahedi.

Many of the city's officials and social movers—who would never pass up a party at the Iranian embassy at that time, and who were used to celebrities of all kinds—were somewhat unhinged by the presence of the cinema siren. The crush of photographers surrounded her, ignoring Henry Kissinger, Liza Minnelli, Baryshnikov, Eric Sevareid, congressmen, senators, and socialites, and perhaps another unpublicized guest— the Bicentennial administrator, Mr. John Warner.

Sitting in the oriental splendor of the embassy's Persian Room, she was bathed in a blaze of light from the camera flashes. An old pro with the press, even for her this was too much, so good-naturedly she simply said, "I can't take any more of this. My eyes are burning. I don't know how they all got in here." As the barrage continued she escaped to an empty courtyard as Ambassador Zahedi held back the photographers and followed her out. Later, poised and confident, she danced with almost anyone who broke in. Surely not to the amusement of many of the other ladies, who were given up for part of the evening.

"I've never seen anything like it," said Senator Charles Percy, commenting on Elizabeth's appearance at the Capital, where she caused a near riot. Elizabeth had been shown around the Capital by Senator Percy, with the blessings of his wife. He said later that she talked about the terrible health conditions she had found in Botswana.

"There are only twenty-eight doctors in the whole country. When Richard gave me this," she said, lifting a finger with a huge diamond on it, "I said, 'Richard, I don't need this. Let's give the money for a health center in Botswana.'" She now planned to give money on her own and raise money for the project.

In May she was the houseguest of the Iranian ambassador.

She was seen around town on the arm of Zahedi, and they seemed to be having a wonderful time when they were spotted together at the Rosecroft Raceway harness track in suburban Oxon Hill, Maryland. He may have been a very enchanting playboy-style ambassador to escort Elizabeth around, but there was someone she was much more interested in.

Probably provoked by the new headlines and the rumors and other publicity, on June 7, 1976, Richard Burton suddenly dashed over to Port-au-Prince, Haiti. He was intent on getting a speedy divorce, but Elizabeth refused to consent. Burton sighed, "I live on the edge of a volcano—an exciting volcano."

In August Elizabeth headed for Vienna to do *A Little Night Music*. John Warner also left for Europe with his fourteen-year-old son on a week's vacation. He said his son was fascinated by the Loch Ness monster and wanted to test his theory about it. Scotland for a monster, Vienna for a beauty; each had a reason.

Elizabeth took the role of Desiree Armfelt, a cynical actress, in the film of Stephen Sondheim's stage musical. She had not done a singing role since a 1948 trifle by MGM called *A Date With Judy*. "I was petrified at having to sing again," she said, "especially doing one of my favorite songs. Not just my favorite, but one that everybody in the world has recorded. And here comes Dumbbell to sing, 'Send in the Clowns.'

"We recorded the music in London, and they picked an orchestra with fifty-six musicians from the Philharmonic and elsewhere. Only the best. There I was in a big glass box with earphones on. I felt all of a sudden like a prisoner of war. It was me against the world. I had to try to hit the notes and make them, or fall on the floor. Fortunately, it's a very dramatic song, and you don't have to be a marvelous singer to do it.

"I decided not to half-sing and half-talk it, as in the case of other nonsingers in musicals. The most notable examples have been Rex Harrison and Richard Burton. I don't want to compete with that. So I thought I should try to sing it and just let it come out, along with my feelings about the theater—sort of sing-act it, rather than sing-talk it."

After recording the song, was she pleased with it?

"I'm never pleased with anything I do," she replied. "I don't like the sound of my voice. I don't like the way I look. I don't like to see myself act. I always say to myself, 'You should have done it some other way.' In *most* instances, I

255

want to crawl under my seat when I watch myself." No matter, she sang the song in a plaintive, poignant way that was vaguely haunting.

Now reporters focused their attention on John Warner and his recent meeting with Taylor. "It's a friendship and that's the only way to describe it," he said—spoken like a true politician. He admitted he found her "a fascinating individual" who lived a contributory life. Taylor's philosophy of helping people and her philanthropic contributions had obviously made an impression. Other than that, what could he really say? The subject of the questions was still married.

But not for long. In July, Elizabeth consented to Richard's request for a divorce. He and Susan Hunt were married immediately—so quickly that Elizabeth learned it from the press, which was a bit hurtful. However, on Sunday, October 3, Elizabeth flew into Dulles International Airport, Washington, from Europe. John Warner was there to meet her, and she was back on the set in Vienna within a few days. Soon afterwards, at a private party in Vienna, with Elizabeth's eldest son Michael and daughter Liza Todd and Warner's daughter Mary present, they announced their engagement.

The imposing John Warner had ambitions for the Senate. His reputation was that of a nice, decent, kind man. He wanted to take care of Elizabeth, now forty-four, as well as her eighty-year-old mother, who had spent weekends with them at the Warner farm in Middleburg. He was very understanding of Elizabeth's many illnesses. He felt that his children, who were all in their teens, would enjoy having Elizabeth as a stepmother. He dressed beautifully (he had closets full of clothes) and was independently wealthy. In addition to the farm in Middleburg, Virginia, he had a house in Georgetown, D.C. Until 1973 he had been married to Catherine Mellon, daughter of millionaire-philanthropist Paul Mellon. Their three children were in boarding school.

Warner, a conservative and an Episcopalian, was hardly what one would think of as husband material for the outspoken Taylor. But it was Warner's roots that attracted her most. During most of her marriage to Burton, Taylor had lived in hotels and other temporary residences around the world. Warner, with his much more stable background, would be an anchor for her. It was said he was keen to marry a movie star. He was reputedly insecure and needed a woman of some considerable style at his side to convince himself of his success, and the glamorous and widely known Elizabeth would certainly be an asset to him in his political career. At the very least, he would not go unnoticed in her company. Republican Senator William Scott's term would be up in 1978, and he planned to run for Scott's office. Warner, however, was not sophisticated or generous like Burton. And unlike Burton his nature was undemonstrative. Once, when a friend greeted Elizabeth with a peck on the cheek, she laughingly remarked, "That's about what I get from John."

Warner had yet to see Elizabeth's moody side or how she expected to be treated like a movie queen wherever she went. This shouldn't have been too surprising: she had been one for decades. Though she had undoubtedly been very lucky, she had also earned it, working hard at her career from an earlier age than most other professionals would ever be expected to. Any step away from those heights would not be done overnight. As for the political insiders and the old guard in Washington, they thought that the idea of Elizabeth Taylor campaigning with John Warner in the Virginia countryside was hilariously funny. (Shades of Auntie Mame.)

Of course, everybody had something to say about the movie star and the politician.

Just before the wedding Elizabeth, out riding, took a fall while taking her horse over a jump on the farm of her fiancé. She lost her balance and toppled over, suffering bumps and bruises. Considering the condition of her back, there probably wasn't a doctor in the world who would have prescribed horseback riding for Elizabeth, but, as usual, she defied the norms and still came up a winner.

8

CHAPTER TWENTY-FOUR

At sunset on Saturday, December 4, 1976, Elizabeth stood on a hilltop of Atoka Farms in Fauquier County. She wore a knee-length cashmere dress the color of heather and a tweed coat with a gray fox collar, and carried a bouquet of wild heather. She reflected all the colors of the late autumnal countryside. In the distance was the elegant mansion that was to be her new home, originally built in 1816. Nearby was a bright red barn, which housed a heated swimming pool. In front of her stood the Reverend Neal Morgan of Emmanuel Episcopal Church, and by her side was John Warner. There were about fifty people present, and with the sky ablaze with color in the setting winter sun, Elizabeth took her vows to love, honor, and obey. She gave her bridegroom a gold wedding band fashioned from gold melted down from an ornament she had given her father shortly before his death. He gave his bride a wedding ring that his father, John William, Sr., had given to his mother, Martha Stuart, fifty years before.

Warner was her sixth husband. No one could ever accuse her of not persisting in her aim to find the right mate. Elizabeth, forty-four, brought up in the Church of England, was a convert to Judaism; Warner was a trustee of the Protestant Episcopal Cathedral Foundation.

Elizabeth, who is not alive when she is not in love, now rejoined the living. Her need for a loving husband and marriage cuts through everything else in her life. That Saturday, at twilight, a little over a year after they had met and four months after her divorce from Richard Burton, Elizabeth prayed that this time she had found what she had been looking for all her life.

The next morning, looking around at the beautiful country-side, Elizabeth told her new husband, "It's as if I were a

258

child again, back in England. Really, it's just like then."
Elizabeth Warner rode over the spacious acreage (3,000) on
horseback, feeling completely at home for the first time in
years.

The next day they left for Israel, where she was to be guest
of honor at a hospital fund-raising dinner in Jerusalem.
Warner, as head of the U.S. Bicentennial Commission, would
dedicate a forest in behalf of the organization. From Israel
they went to visit her childhood home in Kent, England, and
then spent Christmas at her home in Gstaad, Switzerland.
Elizabeth's children joined them for the holidays. Michael
(26) came from London; Maria (17) from Germany; Liza (20)
from California; and Chris (23) from Washington. Elizabeth
always left the door open for them to come and go as they
pleased, wherever she happened to be.

The press, who for the last three decades had gained a lot
of mileage out of the life and loves of Elizabeth Taylor, now
had a new angle: Can Elizabeth Taylor Find Happiness as Mrs.
John Warner? The couple had been married for less than a
week, and reporters were already posing the questions, "Would
it last?" and, if so, "For how long?" Once again she was
compelled to live her private life in the public eye.

Given Elizabeth's desire for a home and husband, it seemed
ironic that for all her superstardom and the opportunities that
resulted from this, she had been fundamentally rootless. True
she had homes and apartments in different parts of the world,
yet she had no home base, no refuge. She had led her life on
the run, living lavishly in luxurious touchdown bases world-
wide, yet possessing no real focal point. Now she had one,
but the press was still determined to play its game of conjec-
ture and wondered openly—for how long?

Home for Elizabeth, beginning her married life with Warner,
was a townhouse in Georgetown and Atoka Farms, less than
forty miles west of the Capital. The Georgetown townhouse
(valued at close to a million dollars) is a large red brick
structure on S Street, a short, quiet lane that seems to have
been left over from the nineteenth century.

The social world of Washington now had a new curiosity, as
blasé hostesses fought to get the Warners into their soirees.
As soon as the New Year opened the race was on. The horsey
Virginians were at the gate. The Warners showed up at a
farewell ceremony for Secretary of Defense Donald Rumsfeld;
the Harvard University Hasty Pudding Club gave Elizabeth
their annual Woman of the Year Award; The American Heart

Association had a gala in Richmond for three hundred people and four hundred ninety showed up at $75 apiece to get a glimpse of the couple. And on and on. . . .

Elizabeth, with her healthy sense of humor, turned it around. "I think it's funny—people think I'm different," she mused. (Whatever she said was repeated around in the inner circle.) "I don't feel I'm a political wife—I think we're a team—I don't miss the jet-set life, happiness is the country life in Virginia." They stared as she petted horses, helped with the cattle, drove a pickup truck, climbed aboard a tractor, sipped sour-mash whiskey, and ate fried chicken. In her engaging manner she just shrugged it off: "I'm very much myself—life-style is in your head."

As for acting again? "The truth is my teeth don't ache to act again. I'm not climbing a wall, itching to be back on the screen. My life has passed into another phase, and I find it hard to think about acting. My energies are devoted to my marriage, to John. Not that he has asked me not to work. Quite the contrary. John is proud of what I've accomplished. It is I who do not wish to leave him to make a film. I guess I'm just not dying to do that 'Elizabeth Taylor thing' at the moment."

She told her oldest son, Michael, "I know you have always criticized me for not spending as much time as a mother should with her children. You have always said that my life was artificial and useless. I am not apologizing for what I did—or what I was. But I give you my solemn word that from now onward I intend taking a different path. I am going to devote all my energies to the political ambitions of John. And I will try to make up to you and the rest of the family for the time I spent away from you."

What might have brought about such a dramatic change was being married to a man of deep commitments. For the first time Elizabeth had someone who was not involved with the superficiality that surrounds so much of the world of filmmaking. Also, she was maturing. It had taken a long time—right into middle age. She may have often felt it, but now she must have fully realized that her life as a screen actress had no basic substance, it was mostly make-believe, like the films. Now she was reported to be boning up by reading dozens of books on politics and economics. She also decided to sell some of the diamonds she had accumulated over the past decade. The sale of the diamonds, once a symbol of her success as a star, would in turn be a symbol of her throwing off her old life and starting again.

However, this was not a liquidation sale. She still maintained her business shrewdness. She first put up her Cartier gem from Richard. It was expected to realize $2 million, either privately or at auction. Gone now was the retinue of hair-dressers, secretaries, press spokesman, and others, who once worked full-time to maintain the glamorous image of Elizabeth Taylor. Liza Todd, studying sculpture in Britain, was also pleased about her mother's outlook. Elizabeth had once tried to find a job in films for her daughter, but Liza refused, saying, "It is, as I see it, a very superficial, futile way of life."

Elizabeth would do what she set out to do. She demonstrated her perseverance again as she went full steam ahead with her determination to succeed in Washington. This would hold true for Warner's campaign to run for the U.S. Senate. She gave ample proof of it when she shook an estimated five thousand hands before suffering her first political injury—a broken blood vessel and a broken finger in her right hand. Always a trouper, she returned to the line after getting an ice pack and painkiller. When she made up her mind to do something, nothing in the world could make her change it—an indication of how she has survived all these years.

As much as she tried to start completely anew, the ghosts of the past would not let her forget. In June she read that the remains of her third husband, Mike Todd, were stolen from his grave in Chicago. Grave robbers dug four and one half feet to remove the glass top of his coffin and reach a rubber bag containing Todd's ashes. The vandals were never found, and the motive remains a mystery, as it was presumed there were no valuables interred in the grave. However, Eddie Fisher said, confidentially, that the only reason he could see for this ghoulish deed was the pair of gold cuff links he had given Todd that were buried along with the ashes.

Elizabeth Taylor, the very image of effortless high style, almost an American institution, now became a farm girl at heart, substituting corn on the cob for caviar, crashing through the gears of a tractor instead of lounging in the passenger seat of a limousine, and pouring over political scenarios as opposed to movie scripts. Soon, however, her old back problem emerged again, and no matter how she tried to hide the pain she eventually had to go to Georgetown University Hospital. Not one to stay down, she was soon on her feet again and, using a cane for support, was serving as honorary chairperson for the Eye Ball in September. That night, Elizabeth donated her eyes to the International Eye Foundation. The violet eyes, considered by some the most beautiful eyes in the world, would be deposited in the eye bank after her death. John Warner donated his eyes to the foundation at the same time.

In November of 1977 Elizabeth became a twenty-four-hour-a-day campaign wife. A typical week helping to raise money for Republicans started on a Sunday in Fort Lee, New Jersey at a $250-a-plate fund-raising dinner. The packed hall didn't exactly pay $250 for the prime rib dinner, baked potato, and peas, they paid to see the movie queen in a golden designer gown with matching turban. She took her place at the head of a long receiving line that never seemed to end—because many people were going through the line twice. Elizabeth, in pain from her back, asked for a chair to sit down. An overzealous photographer, who had gotten down on the floor to shoot her from different unflattering angles during all this time, became so unbearable that she shouted at him, "How would you like something flashing in your face like that?" After dinner and a speech by Warner the couple were whisked across the Hudson River to their suite at New York's Waldorf-Astoria Hotel.

The following night, again with Elizabeth the main attraction, she was with her husband at a televised celebrity bash, where there were more photographers. They never seemed to get enough pictures. Not even the ladies lounge was an escape; women would follow her in.

On Tuesday they flew back to Washington, D.C., where she was taken off the plane in a wheelchair. As though to apologize to the airline employees she said, "I'm sorry—but you see I have a bad knee and a bad back." Wednesday night in Manassas, Virginia, she had to sit on a chair to greet guests in a receiving line before joining her husband on stage. After he had made his speech, Elizabeth had a few words to say to the assembled audience: "Everyone here has to mentally get their finger out and go root for the Republicans." Some members of the audience were a bit startled by this, and one Republican wife almost fainted. "Frankly"—she sniffed—"that's not the kind of language we're used to having at our dinners." Maybe not, but it was something that they would all remember, and it cut through a lot of the usual rhetoric. It wasn't exactly Emily Post, but it was better than Western Union—gun point politics that reached its target.

Thursday, after the strain of grasping hands, smiling endlessly, being stared at, photographed from the ceiling and from the floor, she was forced to rest. On Friday she was back, beautiful and radiant, at a fund raiser for two local candidates in a private home in Waynesboro, Virginia. At $15 a couple, the admission fee was cheap enough, but unknown to Elizabeth an amateur photographer had made a deal with the guests: for an extra $5 dollars he would take a picture of them with the movie star. She caught on quickly and left the room. Her husband hastily went after her. She returned within minutes and allowed the pictures to be taken. It might be humiliating but it might also mean more votes for John. This was her job. At the end of that week she was hobbling on a cane.

Christmas, 1977, was spent in Switzerland. The whole of Elizabeth's family and some members of her husband's gathered in the chalet for the holidays. Warner, however, had to fly back to Washington ahead of Elizabeth, leaving her as the matriarch, a part which she thoroughly enjoyed. On New Year's Eve they went to a disco, where she really let herself go, dancing first with one son, then the other. The next morning she leaped out of bed with great joie de vivre, only to realize that she had injured her hip the night before.

The next few months were a repetitious carousel. In Washington John William Warner announced his candidacy for Republican nominee for the U.S. Senate. "This is the proudest day of my life," said Elizabeth. Now that she might become a senator's wife, Elizabeth planned to regain her U.S. citizenship and applied for naturalization papers. Since she was still a British subject, she was unable to vote for her husband. That didn't stop her. She covered over forty-five thousand miles during her travels, barnstorming around Virginia for him. As for switching to the Republican side after years of supporting Democratic causes from J.F.K. to Bella Abzug, she said, "I was always for the man, not the party. Besides how could I be a party person, when I never voted? I love my husband, I believe in him. He's a man who stands on issues, and he's one of the most honest men I've ever met." Smiling, she added, "There aren't too many like him in Hollywood.

"John and I have our differences on issues. But there's a great deal of similarity between politicians and actors. Both are in front of the public and have to be 'on' a lot. Both have rooters, fans, or backers. Both have people who'd like to see you fall. The only difference is that in acting you do Shakespeare and Tennessee Williams and rely on someone else's work. In politics, you're on your own."

Sitting in the living room of her home in Georgetown with her feet on the coffee table, Elizabeth was having a beer and thinking about all the people who had turned out to meet John Warner so that they could get a look at "that Elizabeth Taylor." The thought made her giggle. "This face has been around a lot of years. People want to see if my eyes are really violet or bloodshot, or both. Once they check me out they can go home and say, 'I saw Elizabeth Taylor and you know what? She ain't so hot!' And you know what? They're right." She laughed. "She ain't."

Some of the men who saw her now thought Taylor had gone from being a great beauty to being a great broad. That she has always been. She never thought of herself as a screen goddess or a sex symbol. Almost defiantly, it seemed, she gained weight. Elizabeth has often said, "I was never in love with the camera. I actually hate having my picture taken, and to be a sex goddess you must feel the camera is your lover, which is pretty damn dull lovemaking if you ask me." She laughed loudly. "Thank God I've always had a sense of humor."

Another protection she had was her ability to say "No!" to studio pressures. "Marilyn [Monroe] allowed herself to wear the very heavy burden of being a sex symbol. I watched Monty [Clift], born a free spirit, allow his wings to be clipped just because of studio pressures and the heaviness they bring. Not me.

"I lived—and still live—my life as I see fit. I live in an unpredictable fashion, and people have either damned or praised my nonconformity. In my time, I've been down, way down, with the public, and I've been up. Sometimes they've resented my freeness and other times they've applauded it. Right now," she added, "I'm up."

At forty-six, Elizabeth hadn't had a successful picture in years, including her last, A Little Night Music. She never read her reviews, though, and never knew how dreadful they were. She was still being referred to as a legend. . . . "The hell I am!" she snapped. "Legends have to be dead and I refuse to be that." She also refuses to be "that Elizabeth Taylor." "I'm me . . . just me," she insisted, adding, "And me today is Elizabeth Taylor Warner, Mrs. John Warner, if you please."

But when the ninety-second edition of the social register came out at the end of 1977, John Warner's name was dropped, presumably because of his marriage to Elizabeth Taylor.

On June 4 John Warner lost the GOP nomination to Richard Obenshain. But neither he nor Elizabeth Taylor Warner would be defeated. They went on. And when Dick Obenshain was killed in a tragic plane crash, his widow urged that John Warner take his place as the nominee. And so he did.

Warner found himself under a new strain. While in New York with his wife, who was celebrating her birthday at Studio 54 disco, he left the party to work on campaign speeches. The inevitable rumors began. Elizabeth was asked if it was difficult for a man to be married to Elizabeth Taylor. Laughing to herself at such an understatement, she replied, "Dearie, I'll give you a list of references who will attest to that fact!"

Disregarding the rumors, she explained, "John is a very caring man, not just of me but of people in general. He is really devoted to public service. It matters to him that he works toward making the world a better place." The Warner political polish had, it appeared, rubbed off on his wife.

There was another of Elizabeth's mishaps to occur before the day when her hard work and faith in her husband would pay off. Her nose for something good cooking in the kitchen put her in Lonesome Pine Hospital. What was cooking was some "good ole southern fried chicken," and what put her in the hospital was a chicken bone that got lodged in her throat. Nothing was going to discourage her healthy, vigorous appetite.

In November Elizabeth began her election vigil for her husband's race for senator. On November 29 she was rewarded. He made it. Soon after he was sworn in as senator, at fifty-two, she attended a morning coffee hour with the other wives in the old Senate chamber in the Capital. Now a museum, it still has the tiny old desks used by legislators of the early 1880s. Elizabeth sat at one of the desks, hands in her lap, as the "nineteen new people" were asked to stand and identify themselves. When her turn came she rose and, speaking barely above a whisper, said, "I'm Elizabeth Warner from Virginia." For the record, the metamorphosis was complete.

Elizabeth now made a new appearance. She had lost thirty pounds, and her legions of fans, who had been so dismayed in recent years by her corpulence, could breathe a sigh of relief. She herself was not all that concerned about a few extra pounds, particularly if it interfered with her enjoyment of a glass of beer. She couldn't understand why it was of so much concern to everyone else. More was written about her weight gains and losses than her fund-raising, her work for the Salvation Army, the Corcoran Gallery of Art, and the Wolf Trap music and arts festival. So the town was abuzz, wondering how she had achieved her new appearance.

"I do it by starving," she would tell them if provoked. She had used her secret for more than twenty-five years. When her weight began creeping up, between films, she'd begin her technique and lose several pounds in two weeks. She would have coffee for breakfast, scrambled eggs for lunch, and a small steak for dinner—"with pink grapefruit coming out of my ears," she'd wail. For her it was starving, having to give up the creamed foods in pastry shells and rich desserts she loved so much. For now, the calories were few and the protein high. At forty-seven she was beginning to look again as only Elizabeth Taylor could: the large and lustrous eyes, the raven dark hair—gone was the gray—the face narrow at the chin line.

While on trips with her husband, much of the time she would wear a white blouse and dark skirt or a pants suit. In her visits to the Senate gallery or at teas it would be a suit, set off by a lacy blouse. Elizabeth was definitely dressing down. If she always wore sufficient makeup, it was because she was fully aware that wherever she went there would be press and TV cameramen.

The first project she decided to undertake was Virginia's International Year of the Child celebration. As honorary chairperson she made speeches from the governor's office, she held news conferences in the state office building, and in the basement of a Roman Catholic church she taped two public service announcements—with all the poise and authority of Elizabeth Taylor Warner, the senator's wife. One time, when she repeatedly muffed her lines from an electronic prompter, the room went deadly silent. "AaaaaaaHHHHHhhhhhh!" she screamed in mock rage after the tenth blown line. Then, throwing up her hands, she laughed—much relieved—and so did everyone else.

Though usually smiling when she was with her husband in

public, she seemed terribly serious when he was not there. Actually it was really shyness, she was just plain shy when John Warner was not with her at public meetings. However, she was usually treated with the well-known southern hospitality by other political wives. Elizabeth could easily relax over lunch at the Governor's mansion, where Edie Dalton, the wife of Republican Governor John N. Dalton, would greet her with a "Hi, honey bunch!"

"They couldn't be nicer," Elizabeth said about the other senate wives. "I play a low profile, and they have accepted me. We're all in the same boat, with husbands busy and coming home at all hours."

At Washington socials partygoers looked over each other's shoulders to catch a glimpse of her famous jewels. Tired of being asked about them, she once said impatiently, "I haven't worn them in ages. That was kind of a phase in my life, a kind of camp and fun phase. Maybe my values have matured with my age." And there was always the talk of her having given up acting. "No, I'll do something about once a year—if something appetizing comes along."

Pressing her, they asked if she didn't miss the ultraglamorous movie star life. "No," she said, stubbing out a cigarette. "Otherwise, I'd take all of the jewels out of the bank and wear them, wouldn't I? Really, I live in the present, and I look forward to the future."

Elizabeth had new goals as a senator's wife. She wanted to make a contribution, too, in areas of special interest that she felt she understood: disturbed children, handicapped children, the elderly, and war veterans.

In early May Elizabeth spent several days in Washington Sibley Memorial Hospital, undergoing oral surgery, where she had five root canal operations.

Later that month a group of film stars, including Elizabeth, Katharine Hepburn, Frank Sinatra, Robert Mitchum, and Maureen O'Hara, urged Congress to create a special gold medal for the ailing actor John Wayne. Elizabeth appealed to a banking, finance, and urban affairs subcommittee: "Please Mr. Chairman, let us show him our appreciation and love," she pleaded. "He is a hero, and we have so few left." John Wayne was duly honored.

After two years of trying, gem dealer Henry L. Lambert persuaded Elizabeth to sell him the 69.42-carat diamond Burton had given her in 1969. Burton had purchased the flawless, white, 58-faceted diamond from Cartier in New

York, paying a million dollars for it. When it went up for resale on June 22, 1979, it was sold for $3 million to an Arab oil baron. A piece of the Taylor-Burton history went with it.

On Sunday, July 9, Elizabeth took a long distance call at her Virginia home from her son Michael in England. His father (her ex-husband), Michael Wilding, lay unconscious in a local hospital in Chichester, sixty-five miles south of London. The debonair British actor, an epileptic, had taken a fall at his home. Her first thought was to rush over to join her two sons, Michael, Jr. and Christopher, but she would never have made it in time, because soon after the phone call their father died of head injuries. Elizabeth, who had remained devoted to him, was deeply saddened. They had kept in touch over the years and always remained very friendly.

In Washington President Carter was coming to the close of his four-year term, and Elizabeth, who had liked Carter before he took office, now commented, "He's just turned out too wishy-washy about things. He's not strong enough to be president. I'm confident that he's a short-term president."

Nevertheless, it was Carter who had brought about the Camp David talks between Egypt and Israel, and in September, Elizabeth was in Cairo, where she had been invited to be the guest star at the opening of the fourth Cairo Film Festival. She had been denied entry to Egypt seventeen years earlier (to film *Cleopatra*), and her sequences had to be shot elsewhere. Also, her films had been banned in Arab countries for two decades because of her support and financial donations to Israel.

Elizabeth arrived in Egypt shortly before *Cleopatra* was shown for the first time (on September 15). The ban had been lifted a week earlier. On Sunday afternoon Elizabeth, wearing a simple polka-dot beige dress, was driven from the Sheraton Hotel to the Sadat residence on the Nile in suburban Giza, where she paid a courtesy call on Egypt's first lady, Jihan Sadat, and her three daughters. The next day she met with President Anwar Sadat and Prime Minister Mustafe Khalil in Ismalier. Dressed in an understated red and white dress, she chatted with Sadat at his villa near the Suez Canal. Cleopatra was never so decorous.

In Egypt the censorship board, having taken Taylor off the boycott list, gave approval to the Festival to screen her 1973 psychic suspense film *Night Watch*. She had hoped they would show *Who's Afraid of Virginia Woolf?* At the opening night festivities Elizabeth charmed everyone, including President Sadat and the Israeli producers, directors, and actors who had come as unofficial guests of some of Egypt's leading film critics and writers. The Festival was not a success, plagued as it was by politics, bureaucratic fumbling, and misunderstandings. Despite this, it worked for the Egyptian public, and crowds jammed the Kasr El Nil Cinema in downtown Cairo, where seats cost 50 to 75 cents.

Elizabeth had changed so considerably that her old Hollywood friends would scarcely have recognized her as the superstar they had once known. Gone was almost all trace of the tempestuous movie queen who had brawled in public with Richard Burton, and who had once poured a bottle of champagne over him because he flirted with other women at a restaurant. Gone were the dramatically sexy clothes, the blunt language sprinkled with four letter words, the willfulness. Gone too was the film star image.

In their place now was an almost sedate woman, who, after thirty-five years of pursuing her own career, was devoting her life to someone else's. While Elizabeth retained her individuality, she had consciously, deliberately placed John Warner first. She was working for him, not herself. To read her engagement calendar for 1979 would be to find a few typical entries such as: receptions, exhibitions at the Museum of African Art in Washington, a showing of *Roots 2* at the Kennedy Center for the Performing Arts, a dinner party at the home of Senator Barry Goldwater, a reception at Georgetown University, a gala at Kennedy Center for China's vice premier, Teng-Hsiao-ping, on his first visit to the United States, a reception for a labor union, a talk in Richmond, Virginia, about children in connection with International Year of the Child, acceptance of an award in New York from a Harlem youth center, attendance at a Shakespeare festival in Virginia High School, a luncheon for the first lady, Rosalynn Carter, not to mention everything from work with the Red Cross to the local fried chicken barbecue.

Not exactly a typecast for a middle-American TV housewife, but it was a far cry from the rock and roll and Riviera life of the sixties. For Elizabeth there were no choices—unfortunately for her no matter what she was involved in, or with whom, she always seemed to get most of the press coverage. She was never to be listed as the star attraction at any of these events, but whenever she arrived, flashbulbs popped, TV cameras whirred, and pens and pencils scratched hurriedly across note pads.

The locals in Virginia, mostly playing down their own considerable fortunes, prided themselves on shunning publicity and being unimpressed by fame, glamour, and riches; yet they talked of nothing else but Elizabeth at cocktail parties during her first several months there.

One day, Elizabeth and Warner drove to the plush Greenbrier resort in White Sulphur Springs, West Virginia, where the next day the senator was to address the American Textile Manufacturers Institute on the Strategic Arms Talks. During the meeting Elizabeth sat in the third row of the special gallery reserved for relatives and blew kisses down to her husband. Forty feet away Warner, very conservative as ever in a dark suit, tried to concentrate on the papers on his highly polished mahogany desk. Now and then he stole a glance at the gallery and wiggled his fingers in greeting. Each time he did so, Elizabeth leaned forward and blew more kisses.

Shortly thereafter, in November, Elizabeth kissed her husband good-bye, for a while. With James Mason she was to preside over the Golden Horse Awards—The Kinno prize (which means galloping forward to improve)—in Taiwan. She and Mason had been invited to co-host these "academy awards" of Taiwan. Two thousand people attended the televised ceremony in the Sun Yat-sen memorial hall. The master of ceremonies was Ching Kwan-chao (the equivalent of Bob Hope in Taiwan). Elizabeth, in a red chiffon dress, with gold threaded oriental calligraphy woven in, looked like an imperial Eastern empress. Before the awards James Mason, asked to define the difference between a star and an actor, said, "A star is a piece of merchandise. Elizabeth Taylor is a star" —then he caught himself—"She is also an actress who holds two Academy Awards." Actually no introduction was necessary. They all knew who she was.

After that, Elizabeth went to New York to attend the wedding of Liza Minnelli to Mark Gero at St. Bartholomew's Chapel in Manhattan. Elizabeth, who had been a friend and coworker of Judy Garland at MGM, had become a surrogate mother to Liza.

After the Christmas holidays the Warners had a rather interesting start to the New Year. They found themselves in sharp disagreement on the issues of draft registration for women and equal rights. The quarrel began in Easton, Maryland, at the Tidewater conference, an unofficial policy forum for elected GOP officials and their wives. Representative Margaret Heckler of Massachusetts said she opposed registration of women until the Equal Rights Amendment was in force. Mrs. Warner agreed. Representative Robert McClory challenged Heckler: "I don't see how you can support ERA without supporting equal registration."

John Warner interrupted the debate to read a resolution he had drafted opposing reimposition of the draft but supporting a renewal of registration, provided women were excluded. As he was chairman of the Abraham Lincoln table, he said he believed the Great Emancipator would have taken the same view.

"Abe Lincoln?" said Elizabeth. "How many years do you want to go back?" The senator observed that wives were part of the conference but did not have a vote. He said that testimony before the Armed Services Committee on which he was serving indicated that "women are volunteering for more jobs than the services have to give them."

"What kind of jobs are those?" his wife questioned.

"I'm proud to say that when I was secretary of the Navy," Warner told her, "I opened up many more jobs to women than they had ever had before."

"Rosie the Riveter jobs," Elizabeth said acidly.

Nervously Representative Bud Shuster of Pennsylvania observed that excluding women from the registration requirement would actually discriminate in their favor.

"It all depends on the way you look at it!" said Elizabeth undeterred.

"Now, Liz, hold on here," her husband warned her.

Then Representative William Dannemeyer of California spoke up saying that he thought the registration issue should not be confused with the problem of "alleged discrimination" against women.

"Alleged discrimination?" (she howled!) Then Senator Warner motioned his wife to be silent. Everyone at the meeting stared at them in hushed expectancy as Warner waved his hand at his wife in a gesture of impatience.

"Don't you steady me with that all-domineering hand of yours," she fumed.

"I'm sorry," he repeated, "but you don't have a vote on this issue." Exercising the greatest self-control she snapped back at him, "Well, you invited me here."

And turning away from him, she observed that her own reading of history was that "women have been in active combat since year one." She mentioned the role of women from Cleopatra to Margaret Thatcher. She saw no reason why

271

women should not be free to volunteer for combat duty. If anyone could prove that point, she was ready to do it right then. She won the floor even if she didn't gain any support at the table.

"Equal rights mean equal responsibilities," she said getting in a few more words.

The senator, who had gone to another table for a moment to confer on his resolution, came back and asked what she had been saying in his absence.

"That's for me to know and you to find out," she concluded.

By an overwhelming voice vote, the conferees rejected the inclusion of women in the draft registration. It appeared that the senator had had the last word. True to style, though, Elizabeth made her point even if she did stun the GOP convention. More importantly, it was probably at least partly as a result of this that she became soured on politics. Mrs. Warner, the Washington matron, dropped her pins and the gutsy Elizabeth Taylor picked up her cue. For whatever reason, she decided she was going back to work in her own industry.

On March 14, 1980, she signed to star in Agatha Christie's *The Mirror Crack'd*, an apt title for her departure from Washington. This was her first film in three years, since her cameo appearance in *Winter Kills*.

The Virginia representative legislators were further surprised, and some even outraged, when they saw ads that appeared on Sunday, March 16, 1980, for cartoonist G. B. Trudeau's book entitled, *A Tad Overweight, but Violet Eyes to Die For*, about the senator's wife. What next? From their view the whole dignity of the state capital, Washington, and the Senate might have been jeopardized by a pair of violet eyes. If they thought this was too much, they were in for another shock. For no sooner had they caught their breath than the following headlines exploded into print: LIZ TRADES SLAPS WITH POET.

At a celebrity studded gala at the Performing Arts Center at Wolf Trap in Virginia, Elizabeth was reputed to have slapped poet Rod McKuen, and he reputedly slapped her back.

"Slap Elizabeth Taylor," Rod McKuen told this writer at the Stanford Court Hotel in San Francisco, "I'd be afraid she would really punch me back.

"Elizabeth worked very hard to get us all there. We came from all over the world for this charity entertainment. It was

Elizabeth who got Burt Reynolds, number one male movie star, Liza Minnelli, the epitome of a Broadway personality, Johnny Cash, and other top people in their field. Elizabeth came all the way from England where she was doing *The Mirror Crack'd*.

The brouhaha started on stage during the show, according to the press, when Elizabeth, reading a poem, became furious with Johnny Cash, who was supposedly making much noise backstage. Burt Reynolds was allegedly making derogatory remarks, which caused Elizabeth to haul off and take a swing at him; missing, she hit McKuen. He retaliated by slapping her back.

"Why, Elizabeth and Johnny Cash read a poem together. Johnny had to leave during the second half of the show because his son was sick. And to say Burt made derogatory remarks—the only derogatory remarks he makes are about himself." McKuen went on, "To say I hauled off and hit Elizabeth while I was on stage, after she missed Burt and landed one on me, is absurd. There were over seven thousand people in the audience, and they would have witnessed it."

Rod McKuen, who had been invited to the Warner home for a nightcap after the show, had to decline because he was leaving for France in the morning to do a charity benefit in Monaco the next night. The press from all over the world telephoned about the "She Who Got Slapped" story. McKuen, denying it, offered a reward of $10,000 to anyone who could prove that it had happened. On the positive side the show earned $200,000 for the Performing Arts Center. McKuen and Taylor sued for libel. He demanded $50 million and Taylor $61 million. It would all be given to charity, including lawyers' fees. In the end the news story was retracted.

In an aside McKuen said, "Being a movie star, they [the social Virginians] had to resent her in the beginning. Elizabeth overcame that. She worked very hard." Jokingly, he said, "She blamed me for her second marriage to Burton. At the game preserve in Botswana they got remarried in the Rod McKuen suite. Elizabeth raised her children—there's been no scandal about them. One is a fashion model, one a photographer, and another a biochemist."

As things developed, Elizabeth Taylor Warner was to have a new neighbor. An actor friend from Hollywood, Ronald Reagan. With Elizabeth now more and more involved in politics in spite of herself, they would have more than old movies to discuss. Besides, his wife, Nancy Davis Reagan, was an MGM alumni. She and Elizabeth had both collected their pay envelopes from the same studio. The Reagans moved from their Santa Barbara ranch to Middleburg, Virginia, to be closer to the Arlington, Virginia, national headquarters of the Reagan-Bush campaign. Mr. Reagan was running for president.

To welcome the Reagans to the neighborhood Elizabeth and John threw a chicken barbecue in their honor. Four thousand people showed up at Atoka Farm to meet Mr. Reagan and to take a look at Liz while eating. As most of them were Republicans, no doubt a few votes could be picked up while passing the potato salad. Middleburg was quite content with its "our kind of people," and the "just-folks" southern Carters could never really feel at home there. The Virginians tended to be "fairly highbrow," particularly economically, and the ones living around Middleburg were perhaps the most exclusive of all. The equestrian set, who were tickled at Elizabeth Taylor's riding skills, remarked—not even trying to be complimentary—that Reagan, who wore Western and rode English, mixed up English and Western gear. No matter, they could not dispute his horsemanship, as he was equal to or better than most of them.

As for Elizabeth, when she had first moved to Virginia, she hunted with the senator on several occasions and also managed to fall off her horse a number of times—once seriously enough to be hospitalized. Evidently because she had ridden a horse at age twelve in *National Velvet*, she was expected still to ride like the winner in the Kentucky Derby.

Nancy Reagan rides but doesn't jump, and after talking to Elizabeth about it she was not encouraged to try.

One Wednesday, July 16, Elizabeth arrived in Detroit with her husband for the Republican National Convention. Nancy Reagan and she sat together in the Joe Louis Arena to watch the convention activity. Undoubtedly, the ladies had a lot to talk about and were very comfortable in each other's company.

At the National Theatre in Washington, in September, Elizabeth happened to—or so one is supposed to believe—sit next to producer Zev Bufman. Bufman is an entrepreneur. In the late sixties and early seventies, after several years in Hollywood, he ranked as an important and imaginative force. In the space of seven years he had built a chain of eight theaters in the South. His magic formula was to bring back the old hit shows. As there isn't all that much originality in the new shows of today, his idea was to revive classics of the American theater, so loved by those who had seen them and new to a generation who had not. Zev Bufman, a nice-looking, soft-spoken, mild-mannered man with a pleasant smile, is also a high-powered producer with a staff of one hundred, and homes in Miami, New York, and Aspen, Colorado.

The Israeli born Bufman was a commando in the Israeli War of Independence, which may have helped him in the theater, where guerillalike tactics sometimes are necessary. He revived an old chestnut, *Kismet*, which, revamped, became *Timbuktu*, with Eartha Kitt, and one night from the phone in a Florida cafe he bought the rights to *Peter Pan*, for Sandy Duncan. Then, at the National Theater in Wolf Trap, he brought *Brigadoon* back to life. His sitting next to Elizabeth Taylor on opening night was no accident and his intriguing question was a decided lure. He offhandedly suggested that she do a Broadway play sometime. "Why don't you call?" she answered.

In November Elizabeth went to New York alone. At the same time her daughter Maria arrived from London, determined to become a superstar model. They stayed at the Regency Hotel, Elizabeth's favorite in New York. Zev Bufman telephoned her in her suite as a reminder of their meeting in Washington and repeated his offer: "Would you like to do a play?" In no time at all it became Broadway's hottest rumor, there were even stories that she was going to repeat her role of Martha in *Who's Afraid of Virginia Woolf?* Elizabeth commented, "Martha is the most grueling part ever written. I wanted to do something meaty, but I didn't want it to kill me."

Bufman let it be her choice exclusively. She thought about reviving Noel Coward's *Hay Fever*, a comedy of manners about an aging actress and her wacky household. Still, she wasn't sure. Bufman invited some twenty working actors to read some plays aloud with her. Having the play audition for the actress was not the usual routine, but with Elizabeth neither would it be a usual performance. She met with Lillian Hellman to talk about her play *The Little Foxes*. When she chose to do it, she said, "For my first play I'd rather do drama. I'm more used to drama." There must have been sighs of relief that it wasn't to be another *Mame*, the hit musical so many movie stars got their feet wet with in front of the footlights.

The Little Foxes is a bitingly sinister play. It has one of the most cruelly realistic character studies ever written in its depiction of the pivotal antiheroine, Regina Giddens. Ruthless, greedy, blackmailing, murderous, vicious, Regina gets what she wants; she schemes and kills to get it. And at the final curtain she stands completely alone, unloved and unwanted by anyone.

Tallulah Bankhead, on stage, and Bette Davis, on the screen, gave splendid portrayals. Politically, Elizabeth was in the same ideological boat as the late Tallulah—the conservative wing of the Republican Party. Bankhead was a fierce anti-Communist, who didn't understand the play's political ramifications, as it was Hellman's indictment of late-blooming capitalists.

Anyway, this was the challenge Elizabeth wanted. She was ripe for the part.

"Regina is not just a total icicle, an avaricious bitch, as she is usually portrayed," Elizabeth said. "I've found so many facets in her. There is also a certain vulnerability in Regina." She felt that she had found new insights into the character that would enable her to offer fresh depths and shadings in the role.

She would be away from her home and her husband for a long period for the first time since they were married. "I've been wanting to do a play for a long time, and now that the election campaigning is over, this seems like a perfect time," said the forty-seven-year-old actress.

"It was my husband's idea that I do a play. I've campaigned so much in the last four years. He wanted me to do something on my own." He had urged her to go back into the spotlight of her career.

The Warners spent their Christmas holiday in Switzerland, before she had to report for rehearsal in New York.

Her rehearsal schedule was arranged so that she would be free to attend Ronald Reagan's inauguration on January 20, 1981. Rehearsals were to begin in New York on January 27, 1981.

There would be two out-of-town tryouts: at the Parker Playhouse in Ft. Lauderdale, Florida, on February 27 and at the Kennedy Center for the Performing Arts in Washington on March 18. Then she would open on Broadway on April 30 for a four-week run.

She took a break away from rehearsals to attend a private party at the White House for President Ronald Reagan's seventieth birthday. As she had in the past, when he was a private citizen, then as Governor, she kissed him now, the President of the United States.

A whole new chapter began for Elizabeth when, at forty-nine, with fifty-four movies behind her, she went on stage. Not this time for a one-night appearance or as the other half of a duo; this time she was to star in a play for an extended run, as a member of a company, or the "family" as she called them. The "family" included stalwarts Maureen Stapleton, Anthony Zerbe, Dennis Christopher, and other seasoned actors, plus the stage managers and crew, and director Austin Pendleton.

"Family is the closest you can describe it to outsiders," said Christopher, twenty-six, who played Regina's foolish nephew. "We're just a bunch of actors." Elizabeth speaking of her new schedule in the theater said, "I hang out with the family a lot. There's not much private or social life."

Elizabeth is about as fond of being interviewed as she is of being in the hospital. She sees the press only when she must and then says only what is absolutely necessary to promote whatever she is involved in. Once it is over she relaxes and gets back to her own earthy humor. She does it strictly as a duty, as in the case of *Foxes*, to sell the show. One of the press compared her to a child who has been told that if she doesn't eat her dinner she won't get dessert—with the added steel of a woman who, like Regina, is accustomed to getting exactly what she wants.

After decades of being simmered, poached, boiled, stuffed, roasted, fried, and fricasseed by the press of the world, she has every reason to be on her guard. The "ladies and gentlemen" of the press hover around waiting for her to make a self-revelation by which they could get a front-page by-line, at whatever cost to her, but she is too press-wise not to be wary after all these years. She would prove the wisdom of her caution again. No production of *Foxes* ever attracted so much publicity before. "I couldn't believe it," said director Austin Pendleton. "*The New York Times* actually ran a story that Lillian Hellman and I had a fight about the set. I've directed thirty shows, and in each and every one somebody has a row with somebody else about something. But it's never been worth a story before. I've never seen anything like this, never."

The cast list posted outside the Parker Playhouse in Ft. Lauderdale was in alphabetical order. Ninth on the list of eleven was the name Elizabeth Taylor. It seemed that the entire state of Florida wanted tickets. It goes without saying that if the sign outside the theater had read *Uncle Tom's Cabin*, starring Elizabeth Taylor as Little Eva, they would still have lined up from there to Tallahassee.

A local policeman was hired as Elizabeth's bodyguard. He drove her from the Yacht Club to the theater every night, in a Rolls-Royce Silver Shadow, and protected her from overzealous fans—whom Elizabeth faithfully obliged as much as she was able by signing autographs, sometimes from a stack of photos kept in the car trunk.

But at the bottom line, she—a movie superstar—was taking a big professional risk, and *Foxes'* "family" of actors admired her for it. Exposing yourself on stage is unlike making a film. On stage there are no retakes. In front of a live audience there can be no editing of mistakes.

"I always planned to do a play at some point in my career," said Elizabeth. "Did I think about the risk? For about half an hour. I don't expect to fail. People pay their money, and I have a responsibility to give them their money's worth."

The opening in Ft. Lauderdale happily coincided with Elizabeth's forty-ninth birthday. Senator John Warner was out front in an aisle seat. During intermission he went backstage to his wife's dressing room, and at the final curtain he went on stage to present her with a bouquet of lavender roses, for which she thanked him with a kiss.

On Sunday, their only day off during the run in Florida, Elizabeth chartered a yacht and treated the whole cast to a cruise. She always liked to say thanks in style.

As soon as it was announced that Elizabeth Warner was returning to Washington in a play, the southern gentry stampeded the box office. Her performances were no doubt sold out before she even left Florida for Washington, and it's a fair guess that there were many who were hoping to see her fall flat on her face. How will she look? Has she lost any weight? Can she really act? may have been questions uppermost in the thoughts of the opening night audience of her friends, her foes, and those waiting to decide.

Elizabeth, who had been the party prize of Washington since moving to Virginia, swept aside the entire "senator's wife" decorous image, and bit into her role of Regina. She was Regina: southern, captivating, and dangerous. As an actress, she had ripened into a fully-accomplished artist. She again became the toast and the talk of the Capital. On her own ground she had no peers, and some of the usual sang-froid of the social circles must have been a little unsettled by this demonstration of her skill.

During this run of the play, in March, Carol Burnett threw a victory dinner to celebrate her winning a libel action against *The National Enquirer,* and Elizabeth and her husband threatened their own lawsuit if the *Enquirer* did not retract an article that said their marriage was crumbling.

Then Elizabeth left Washington for New York to face the ultimate test. She was to open on Broadway on Thursday, May 7, 1981.

Producer Bufman spent $5,000 redecorating Elizabeth's dressing room in her favorite color, lavender. A $450 aquarium filled with lavender-colored tropical fish was part of the decor and there was a gold star six inches wide on her dressing room door. To finish off there was a 3/4 carat perfect diamond on her dressing room table on opening night. "What do you give a lady who owns the world's largest perfect diamond?" asked Bufman—and answered his own question. "The *smallest* perfect diamond." If this sounds a bit extravagant, it's only a sound. Any producer would have been happy to keep Elizabeth content, considering the way she was keeping the theater packed.

In her dressing room she had to go through the usual publicity mill before the opening. Wearing pink slacks, a knit top, and backless high heels that she kicked against the edge of the bed during the interrogation, she was asked the inevitable:

"I don't like questions about my weight because I don't think it's anybody's damn business," replied Elizabeth, who, four years earlier, had told a Richmond magazine, "I don't want to starve myself because my looks don't matter that much to me."

But she was noticeably thinner. "Just say I did it for the part, okay?" she snapped.

The woman whose looks set the ideal for a whole generation of women, whose adolescence paralleled her highly publicized transition from child star to teenage beauty, said, "Beautiful?" Pretty was more like it to her.

"I think I'm a nice person," she said. "Beautiful? Mrs. Sadat, Ava Gardner, Katharine Hepburn, and Lena Horne are beautiful!"

The Little Foxes had first opened in New York, in 1939, with Tallulah Bankhead, when Elizabeth Taylor was seven years old. Forty-two years later Elizabeth Taylor would make her own theatrical history at the Martin Beck Theatre. The ten-week engagement was sold out. There were some skeptics who were betting, and some who were probably hoping, that she wouldn't make it. She might even suddenly become ill. Bronchitis and fever had plagued her during her preview performances. Was she nervous? She certainly showed no nervousness about starting rehearsals and gave no indication whatever that would cause any of the cast to be intimidated by her presence. She did not feel that she had any past performance or reputation to overcome.

"I don't think anybody on any of the sets I've worked on would say that. From the day we started working on *Foxes* we were an ensemble. We were a team. If anything, I was the outsider, the interloper. So I was the one who could have been nervous about working with the pros."

As for its author—one would have to wait until the final curtain to get her reaction. In 1939 Miss Hellman said of Miss Bankhead, "Tallulah is a good actress, a very good actress, but she is also the biggest bore God ever created." Said Miss Bankhead of Miss Hellman, "Lillian is an excellent playwrite, but I despise her."

Opening night was Thursday, May 7, 1981. Elizabeth's dressing room was filled with flowers, which included dozens of lavender roses from her husband. Her mirror was festooned with telegrams, and the small refrigerator filled with champagne. Her three costumes for each act, with their elaborate underskirts, hung from racks. Made up as Regina, she looked almost too beautiful for the part. From a casting point of view one wondered how such a belle could have buried herself in a small southern town for so long. She was feeling a bit feverish, but she put it out of her mind.

Outside, in the theater, the black-tie audience that night included Rock Hudson, Joan Fontaine, Bill Blass, Lee Radziwill, and Liza Minnelli. Senator John William Warner sat on the aisle, so that he could jump up between acts and rush to her dressing room.

The Little Foxes is set in 1900, a time of elegant style. When the curtain went up on the drawing room of the Hubbard family, with the dining room stage-left, Elizabeth was waiting in the wings for her cue. She was not going to compete with the other Reginas before her. As she had said, "I want to give her a new aspect, a new dimension. She's a woman who's been pushed into a corner. She's a killer... but she's saying, 'sorry fellas, you put me in this position.'"...Then she heard her cue from her brother Oscar: "Sit down, Birdie, sit down, now!" Walking out through the dining room and into the drawing room, she spoke her opening line: "Mr. Marshall, I think you're tryin' to console me—" The audience reaction completely drowned out her line. A storm of applause broke out. It shook the theater.

She had made a visually stunning entrance, and just standing there she looked like a jewel in a velvet box, amidst the opulent Victorian furniture. She was simply spellbinding in her gown and upswept wig and the Elizabeth Taylor charisma. For the rest of the performance you could barely hear the audience breathing. Under the stage lights Elizabeth held their attention with all the skill and style of a Duse.

In the closing scene, as she approached the stairs, she said her final line to her daughter, Alexandra, "Would you like to sleep in my room?" Then the curtain came down and thunderous applause surged over the stage like a giant wave. Some of the audience, including critics who had come to laugh at the sight of a movie star trying the stage, stayed on to cheer her for a compelling performance in an alien medium. The curtain rose and fell as the cast took their bows. When Elizabeth stood alone, by now changed into a low-cut Halston gown, she got a standing ovation and tributes of roses and bravos. She quickly brought her "family" beside her, and author Lillian Hellman joined her for a final curtain call.

The audience, sensing that Hellman wanted to say something, quieted, and Hellman turned to Elizabeth and said, "Elizabeth, you were really quite good!" Elizabeth Taylor was in the theater at last.

There were two opening-night parties. The first stop was the traditional one at Sardi's. The second at Xenon, a discotheque on two floors, the A floor and the B floor. The A guests were seated beneath canopies of lavender ribbons and were waited on. The B's watched from the balcony, balancing plates on their laps.

Shirley MacLaine, Liza Minnelli, Halston, Sammy Davis, Jr., Jerome Robbins, Hermione Gingold, et al., were starting to arrive and were directed to the A floor. Jean Marsh, "Rose," the downstairs maid from *Upstairs/Downstairs*, got the A treatment. She was brought by her hairdresser. "I thought it would be a spectacle—very grand and old Hollywood," she said. "I came in a limousine. Normally I would come in a taxi. And the show and the curtain calls and

281

the flowers." She sighed. "Normally an actor eats spaghetti afterwards in a small room. I guess she's the only real star we have left."

Ann Miller, in an A corner on A level, greeted everyone with kisses. "I didn't see the show, honey, I was on stage in my show *Sugar Babies*. You know Mickey [Rooney, who was in *Sugar Babies* too] and I know her for thirty-five years. No, we couldn't make the show, honey, but we sent flowers."

The music of Sinatra and Ella Fitzgerald played in the background. At midnight Elizabeth arrived on the arm of her handsome husband, who was beaming with pride. In a room full of black sequined gowns, Elizabeth wore heavy white satin, her eyelids brushed dark Cleopatra purple, and diamonds and pearls around her neck and a large diamond ring. A black-sequined actress jerked her neck forward. "I think that's the famous stone, but I don't know which one," she said to her date. The rest of the gawkers tried to get close, but the half-dozen security guards surrounding them made it difficult.

Elizabeth could be heard saying, to friends here and there, "I thought they'd clobber me!" "If I can make it here, I'll make it anywhere." She was flushed, feverish, laughing, joking, saying over and over, "How kind of you." "Aren't you sweet." "—but, I'm shy"—and mostly—"I'm lucky." John Warner, still beaming, said, "I missed my first vote in the Senate tonight in two and a half years," and about his wife, "She was as cool and as calm as a general under fire. She said, 'We're a partnership. Come,' and I was there," but he concluded, "I'll be on the seven o'clock shuttle to Washington tomorrow."

Producer Zev Bufman made announcements and read reviews, but what more could anyone say after the biggest theatrical headline in twenty years, in *The New York Times* that day: WELCOME TO BROADWAY, LIZ!

Typically, the reviews were mixed. However she was nominated for a Tony. Zev Bufman was in Washington when he found out that Elizabeth had been nominated. He was first to know, and he told Nancy Reagan, who was second to know— before Elizabeth. The Tony Award nomination (named for Antoinette Perry, founder of the American Theatre Wing during World War II) meant that Elizabeth's performance would be voted on by 620 theater professionals and critics.

On Saturday, May 16, while staying at the Carlyle Hotel, Elizabeth tore a rib cartilage on her left side while coughing from a respiratory infection. Her doctor put her on medication and insisted that she rest. That evening the sold-out crowd of 1,350 at the Martin Beck Theatre, including standees, were told fifteen minutes before curtain time that Miss Taylor could not appear, and the performance was canceled.

The next morning Elizabeth suffered extreme chest pains, and her doctor, Michael Rosenbluth, put her in Lenox Hill Hospital—much against her will, as she wanted to get back to the theater. Hospital administrator Eric Mordhorst told inquirers that there was no change in her condition. They had quite a problem holding Elizabeth there, as she fought to recover and get back to work.

Nine days later, on May 25, fans gathered outside the Martin Beck Theatre stage-door entrance, many having waited for hours, as that afternoon, a weak and shaky Elizabeth Taylor arrived for rehearsal. Some scenes were revised to be less of a strain for her as, after missing eleven performances, she returned to the play. The packed house welcomed her return with the same enthusiasm as on opening night.

On a Sunday night, June 7, seven hundred of the Broadway clique gathered at the Mark Hellinger Theatre for the Tony Awards, which were to be televised across the nation. When Elizabeth presented one of the awards, reading the names from a teleprompter, she could not see the instrument very well because the surrounding lights were too bright and flubbed the pronunciations. Her giggle over the faux pas stole the show by taking all the hardened, scared pomposity out and putting some fun back in.

When the name for best actress was called, Glenda Jackson's was announced. And how did Elizabeth react? True to her fashion she gave a party for the losers the next evening at Sardi's. Her children Maria, Chris, and Michael were with her to celebrate, along with her husband John. Producer Bufman was there, as attentive as ever, looking after his star. (Elizabeth was a bit unhappy when one of the fish that he had given her died. "I never knew I could get attached to a fish," she said.)

Senator John Warner arrived back in town September 2, 1981, at the close of the play. When he went to call for his wife after the performance, there was a crowd of over two hundred fifty people in the alley that led to the stage door. This was not unusual, but on this particular night they broke through a barrier, crushing against Elizabeth, her husband, the bodyguard, and the family dog. The senator took charge of the situation. Seeing firemen across the street on a routine inspection of a restaurant, he signaled to them for help, and they formed a human barricade to get Elizabeth and her party down the alley and away from the surging crowd. Then they were lifted onto the fire truck and with lights flashing and sirens wailing the truck sped off to the Carlyle Hotel on East 76th Street.

It was reported that *Foxes* broke all box-office records for a Broadway play, grossing $286,000 a week. Now Elizabeth was about to make another debut. Zev Bufman guided her into making a special guest appearance as Mrs. Cassadine in *General Hospital,* a daytime soap opera. Elizabeth watched soap operas whenever she had time. "I'm wild about that show," she said.

She would play Helena Cassadine, the rich widow of a mad scientist who schemed, in a typical soap-opera manner, to "freeze General Hospital's Port Charles hometown." Taylor's character came on sweet but sinister. After leaving the audience waiting for nearly twenty-seven minutes she would suddenly appear. Fourteen million viewers would then get a flash of Elizabeth/Mrs. Cassadine, dressed to the teeth, dripping in diamonds and Hollywood glitter, looking into the camera with a glance loaded with hidden menace and meaning—a real cliff-hanger, just before the commercial break. She played her too few scenes with alternately a touch of Scarlett O'Hara, Regina Giddens, and a black-turbaned Evita Peron. She was so fascinating your attention was riveted to the TV screen for fear you might miss any quick shot of her. As the multitudes watched and the plot churned, Elizabeth/Helena, at a gilt-edged "blackmail" invitational party at her mansion, donated $10 million to General Hospital to atone for her husband's evildoings.

Elizabeth donated her $2,000 paycheck to two Virginia hospitals that had once treated her.

Said Elizabeth of the whole campy charade, "I had a ball."

In mid-September first lady Nancy Reagan agreed to serve as honorary chairman of a fund-raising tribute to one of the film world's longtime leading ladies, Miss Elizabeth Taylor.

On Saturday night, September 26, 1981, Elizabeth was named the third recipient of the Los Angeles International Film Exposition Trustees Award. The two previous award-winners were Alfred Hitchcock and Lawrence Olivier. After fifty-three films Elizabeth Taylor—companion to Lassie in 1943, an Academy Award winner as a trollop in *Butterfield 8* in 1960, and a second-time winner as a shrew in *Who's Afraid of Virginia Woolf?* in 1966—became the toast of Broadway in *The Little Foxes* in 1981. Gary Essert, founder and director of Filmex, said, "Just as Olivier was the actor's actor, she is the quintessential movie star. She's grown up on the screen. She's a phenomenon."

Elizabeth had led a life in the public eye and had done a great deal out of the public eye that was of public service. The world of Hollywood, where she grew up with the film industry, still meant a great deal to her, particularly MGM:

"Hollywood has spread all over the world, and acting is no longer confined to one place in California," she said, "but I can't help feeling sad about MGM. I know it sounds corny, but when I come here and have the time, I stop at MGM on my way in from the airport. I go in to say hello to the cops at the gate. They're the same ones.

"The first time I did that, it was depressing, because the concrete streets were cracked, and weeds were bursting through. I couldn't believe it, because when I was a child, it was like a fairyland. You would walk into the commissary, and there'd be maybe two thousand people. Mind you, I started when I was ten, and things probably looked bigger. But there were Roman senators, and cowboys and Indians, and so many people we remember. I used to watch them all, and drop my fork and just about faint. But when you walk in now, the commissary has shrunk. It looks tiny. And you know, nobody walks in anymore to make you drop your fork."

Elizabeth Taylor speaks optimistically about her future. A true survivor, she seems well prepared for whatever might come along. As she once said, "I've been through it all. I'm Mother Courage. I'll be dragging my sable coat behind me into old age."

EPILOGUE

The future.

There is an old Chinese expression that "the camera captures the spirit" and to act in motion pictures is to be captured in a mechanical world that boxes you in from all sides. You are governed by technical bodies you cannot escape.

From the time she was ten years old Elizabeth Taylor's steps were caged by chalk marks and focal distances, her voice was directed into microphones, and her image seen only as she moved within the cage on the thousands of images edited together in a pattern over which she had no control. Her acting school was MGM, and her teachers were directors. Her performances were recorded, stored, and placed in neatly labeled tins, projected through lenses and heard through speakers for audiences hundreds and thousands of miles away. Through many roles her physical appearance was established. The celluloid Elizabeth Taylor became real and intimate to countless people around the world, with its pleasing face, natural gifts, good mind, and graceful figure. Yet without great emotional capacity she could not possibly have reached the depths of these roles, and each new role brought its own problems—which were not just technical.

On the stage she found a different sense of awareness. Rehearsals from the beginning of the play to the end make for a more controlled performance. In acting for the screen there is not the same sense of continuity. For films you may do countless retakes until a satisfactory one is approved by your director. Scenes are not taken in order of the script, and the out-of-sequence acting is mainly reacting to someone else, and you have to mentally recreate a person who has qualities to which you can be sympathetic. Often the characters in the films are exhibitionists.

Elizabeth Taylor has lived some of her greatest performances off screen.

During the *Cleopatra* chapter some called for her banishment from Rome. She was spat upon, cursed, and reviled by people who were total strangers. They had never met her or even seen her before, but they felt they owned part of her, since they had bought her on film and paid more to read about her private and public life. Actually Elizabeth is a parody of a scarlet woman because of her naiveté. As a star she had a force that held her up, and at the same time a gravity that pulled her down.

Being naturally exuberant, she has attracted a good share of both phony and real friendships, but Elizabeth will choose relationships as long as they are exciting. Then she will stay with them. She has enormous depth of feelings, and friends are important to her, bringing a great source of support.

Elizabeth is always fascinated by people. Like a moth to a flame she chooses partners who are unique. Three of her ex-husbands are dead. Another one is hoping for a comeback, hoping that the spotlight will turn on to him again. He reopened his marriage to her in print, possibly to reawaken interest in himself: Eddie Fisher. Of him Elizabeth has said, "To Eddie I was ninety percent mother."

Another ex-husband, Richard Burton, has been ill. He had gone back to *Camelot*—the stage life he had led before he met Elizabeth Taylor—to be King Arthur again, and then had to abdicate to his replacement, actor Richard Harris. Because of illness he underwent surgery for a chronic back ailment and for a perforated ulcer. And Susan Hunt, his wife of five years, left him. Camelot, it seemed was gone—as are other "castles," like the Puerto Vallarta home (now rentable by the day, at half-price off-season).

Then in December 1981, Elizabeth announced that she and John Warner were separating. It was not very surprising, as the press had regularly been linking her romantically with *The Little Foxes* producer, Zev Bufman, with whom she has formed a repertory company, and with Tony Geary, the star of *General Hospital*. (How this will affect Warner's political career is not yet clear: before the split, it was predicted that he would be a power in Washington by 1984. Elizabeth loyally continues to praise his ability as a senator and his utter dedication to his work. In fact, "there didn't seem to be time for anything else." Including his wife.)

*   *   *

In late February all other speculation ceased and the eyes of Taylor watchers turned to London. Elizabeth was in town to do *The Little Foxes* and to celebrate her 50th birthday at a glittering disco party hosted by Bufman and attended by 120 guests, including such luminaries as Rudolf Nureyev, Ringo Starr... and Richard Burton!

He had been in Italy, filming a TV series on the composer, Wagner, and was scheduled to narrate a benefit performance of Dylan Thomas' *Under Milk Wood* in London. On the morning of Elizabeth's birthday, he phoned to ask if he would be welcome at her party. He was indeed. In fact, they arrived together—photos showed them holding hands in the limousine—and left together, returning to her hotel.

Will they remarry? "We are married," said Elizabeth, "to other people." But given her separation from Warner and his from Susan Hunt, this doesn't seem to be an insurmountable obstacle.

Burton also denied the possibility, but reaffirmed his love for her in terms that recalled the nostalgic, romantic days of old, and still left the question open.

What *does* seem certain is that Elizabeth will never relinquish her hope of finding a great and permanent love.

She saw something one day during a visit to the ruins of Pompeii that must have symbolized her ideal. In the now uncovered city she saw the fossilized remains of a young man and woman. She stood and stared at them for a long, long time.

"They are holding each other in an embrace of such love and affection. Their expressions are almost tranquil. They lay down and held each other and accepted death. They wanted to die together. To me, it's the most beautiful thing because it's real. It happened two thousand years ago, but they held on to each other at the moment of truth, the moment of death. And that's what life's all about—being able to hold on."

Her life is a drama. There have been and will be many co-stars and more supporting players, but she will always star. She has the one really good part, that of Elizabeth Taylor. Often when she makes the right decision, she will later have doubts, yet her strong mind and creativity will usually carry her through. She has also acquired an internal perspective of who she is. Her hair-trigger temper cools off quickly now, but she never forgets. She will continue to appear to have an icy exterior at times, which she wears to protect her emotional vulnerability; and, though it may be hàrd to believe, she will prefer to live simply but will continue to defy social standards.

"I've made it through nineteen major operations and what must seem, to some, to be as many marriages, and all because of my gut sense of survival." True, she is accident-prone but will come out of most crises in many ways stronger.

After all, as she said, "I haven't yet had tomorrow!"

FILMS OF
ELIZABETH TAYLOR

1. *There's One Born Every Minute* (Universal, 1942) with Hugh Herbert and Peggy Moran.

2. *Lassie Come Home* (MGM, 1943) with Roddy McDowall, Donald Crisp, Edmund Gwenn, Nigel Bruce and Elsa Lanchester.

3. *Jane Eyre* (20th Century-Fox, 1944) with Orson Welles, Joan Fontaine, Margaret O'Brien and Peggy Ann Garner.

4. *The White Cliffs of Dover* (MGM, 1944) with Irene Dunne, Alan Marshal, Roddy McDowall, Peter Lawford and Van Johnson.

5. *National Velvet* (MGM, 1944) with Mickey Rooney, Donald Crisp, Anne Revere and Angela Lansbury.

6. *Courage of Lassie* (MGM, 1946) with Frank Morgan and Tom Drake.

7. *Cynthia* (MGM, 1947) with George Murphy, Mary Astor and James Lydon.

8. *Life with Father* (Warner Bros., 1947) with William Powell and Irene Dunne.

9. *A Date with Judy* (MGM, 1948) with Wallace Beery, Jane Powell and Scotty Beckett.

10. *Julia Misbehaves* (MGM, 1948) with Greer Garson, Walter Pidgeon and Peter Lawford.

11. *Little Women* (MGM, 1949) with June Allyson, Peter Lawford, Margaret O'Brien and Janet Leigh.

12. *Conspirator* (MGM, 1950) with Robert Taylor.

13. *The Big Hangover* (MGM, 1950) with Van Johnson.

14. *Father of the Bride* (MGM, 1950) with Spencer Tracy, Joan Bennett and Don Taylor.

15. *Father's Little Dividend* (MGM, 1951) with Spencer Tracy, Joan Bennett and Don Taylor.

16. *A Place in the Sun* (Paramount, 1951) with Montgomery Clift and Shelley Winters.

17. *Callaway Went Thataway* (MGM, 1951) with Fred MacMurray, Dorothy McGuire, Howard Keel, June Allyson, Clark Gable, Dick Powell and Esther Williams.

18. *Love Is Better Than Ever* (MGM, 1952) with Larry Parks.

19. *Ivanhoe* (MGM, 1952) with Robert Taylor, Joan Fontaine and George Sanders.

20. *The Girl Who Had Everything* (MGM, 1953) with Fernando Lamas.

21. *Rhapsody* (MGM, 1954) with Vittorio Gassman and John Ericson.

22. *Elephant Walk* (Paramount, 1954) with Dana Andrews and Peter Finch.

23. *Beau Brummell* (MGM, 1954) with Stewart Granger and Peter Ustinov.

24. *The Last Time I Saw Paris* (MGM, 1954) with Van Johnson, Walter Pidgeon and Donna Reed.

25. *Giant* (Warner Bros., 1956) with Rock Hudson and James Dean.

26. *Raintree County* (MGM, 1957) with Montgomery Clift and Eva Marie Saint.

27. *Cat on a Hot Tin Roof* (MGM, 1958) with Paul Newman, Burl Ives and Judith Anderson.

28. *Suddenly Last Summer* (Columbia, 1959) with Katharine Hepburn and Montgomery Clift.

29. *Scent of Mystery* (Michael Todd, Jr., 1960) with Denholm Elliott.

30. *Butterfield 8* (MGM, 1960) with Laurence Harvey, Eddie Fisher and Dina Merrill.

31. *Cleopatra* (20th Century-Fox, 1963) with Richard Burton and Rex Harrison.

32. *The V.I.P.s* (MGM, 1963) with Richard Burton and Louis Jourdan.

33. *The Sandpiper* (MGM, 1965) with Richard Burton, Eva Marie Saint and Charles Bronson.

34. *Who's Afraid of Virginia Woolf?* (Warner Bros., 1966) with Richard Burton, George Segal and Sandy Dennis.

35. *The Taming of the Shrew* (Columbia, 1967) with Richard Burton.

36. *Doctor Faustus* (Columbia, 1967) with Richard Burton.

37. *Reflections in a Golden Eye* (Warner Bros.-Seven Arts, 1967) with Marlon Brando.

38. *The Comedians* (MGM, 1967) with Richard Burton, Alec Guinness and Peter Ustinov.

39. *Boom!* (Universal, 1968) with Richard Burton and Noel Coward.

40. *Secret Ceremony* (Universal, 1968) with Mia Farrow and Robert Mitchum.

41. *The Only Game in Town* (20th Century-Fox, 1970) with Warren Beatty.

42. *X, Y & Zee* (Columbia, 1972) with Michael Caine and Susannah York.

43. *Under Milk Wood* (Altura Films International, 1972) with Richard Burton and Peter O'Toole.

44. *Hammersmith Is Out* (J. Cornelius Crean Films, 1972) with Richard Burton and Peter Ustinov.

45. *Divorce, His; Divorce, Hers* (ABC-TV, 1973) with Richard Burton.

46. *Night Watch* (Avco Embassy, 1973) with Laurence Harvey.

47. *Ash Wednesday* (Paramount, 1973) with Henry Fonda.

48. *The Driver's Seat* (Avco Embassy, 1974) with Ian Bannen and Guido Mannari.

49. *The Blue Bird* (20th Century-Fox-Soviet Films, 1976) with Jane Fonda, Cicely Tyson and Ava Gardner.

50. *Victory at Entebbe* (Columbia-Warner, 1976) with Helmut Berger, Theodore Bikel, Kirk Douglas, Richard Dreyfuss, Helen Hayes and Burt Lancaster.

51. *A Little Night Music* (A New World Picture, 1977) with Diana Rigg and Len Cariou.

52. *Return Engagement* (NBC-TV, 1978) with Joseph Bottoms.

53. *Winter Kills* (Avco Embassy, 1979) with Jeff Bridges, John Huston, Anthony Perkins and Eli Wallach.

54. *The Mirror Crack'd* (EMI Films Ltd., 1980) with Angela Lansbury, Rock Hudson and Kim Novak.

ABOUT THE AUTHORS

RUTH WATERBURY was for many years editor of *Photoplay* magazine, and founder of *Silver Screen*. She has also contributed numerous articles to magazines such as *McCalls*, *Cosmopolitan*, and *Reader's Digest*.

Much of this book is based on her long acquaintance with Elizabeth Taylor, dating back to her film debut at age ten in *Lassie Come Home*. The result is an intimate, informed, yet always objective and fair portrait of a rare human being, revealing the basic underlying patterns of her controversial and unconventional life.

Ms. Waterbury lives in California.

GENE ARCERI was born and raised in Flushing, New York. After a brief spin in the theater (a career that began in a school play when he was cast as a "germ"), he joined the New York City Center on West 55th Street and assisted in creating the first subscription series for the New York City Opera and Ballet companies. He then moved to San Francisco, where he wrote for newspapers and magazines, eventually getting his own radio show on KQED (an affiliate of National Public Broadcasting), where he interviews famous guests in all areas of the arts.

In 1974, he won the award as most popular interviewer in the Bay Area. San Francisco is still his home.

THE PRIVATE LIVES
BEHIND PUBLIC FACES

These biographies tell the personal stories of these well-known figures recounting the triumphs and tragedies of their public and private lives.

☐	13592	CHANGING Liv Ullman	$2.75
☐	20563	END OF THE RAINBOW Mary Ann Crenshaw	$3.50
☐	14129	ALL ABOUT ELVIS Worth & Tamerius	$3.95
☐	20704	BURIED ALIVE: The Biography of Janis Joplin Myra Friedman	$3.95
☐	20416	HAYWIRE Brooke Hayward	$3.25
☐	22613	ELIZABETH TAYLOR: HER LIFE, HER LOVES, HER FUTURE R. Waterbury with G. Arceri	$3.50
☐	01334	'SCUSE ME WHILE I KISS THE SKY David Henderson	$8.95
☐	13824	ELVIS: PORTRAIT OF A FRIEND Lackers & Smith	$2.95
☐	14076	JOAN CRAWFORD: A Biography Bob Thomas	$3.50
☐	20756	MONTGOMERY CLIFT: A Biography Patricia Bosworth	$3.95
☐	01329	COMPLETE BEATLES— Deliah Communications	$39.95
☐	13030	SOPHIA: Living and Loving: Her Own Story A. E. Hotchner	$2.75
☐	20121	STRAWBERRY FIELDS FOREVER John Lennon Remembered Garbarine & Cullman	$2.95
☐	14038	RAGING BULL LaMotta with Carter	$2.50
☐	20857	AN UNFINISHED WOMAN Lillian Hellman	$3.50

Buy them at your local bookstore or use this handy coupon: